Refugee Women and Their Mental Health: Shattered Societies, Shattered Lives

Date Due

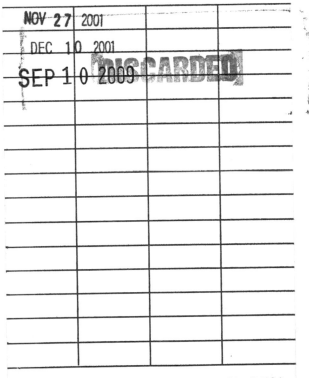

Refugee Women and Their Mental Health: Shattered Societies, Shattered Lives

Ellen Cole
Oliva M. Espin
Esther D. Rothblum
Editors

Refugee Women and Their Mental Health: Shattered Societies, Shattered Lives, edited by Ellen Cole, Oliva M. Espin, and Esther D. Rothblum, was simultaneously issued by The Haworth Press, Inc., under the same title, as special issues of the journal *Women & Therapy*, Volume 13, Numbers 1/2 and Volume 13, Number 3 1992, Ellen Cole, and Esther D. Rothblum, Editors.

Harrington Park Press
An Imprint of
The Haworth Press, Inc.
New York • London • Norwood (Australia)

ISBN 1-56023-030-4

Published by

Harrington Park Press, 10 Alice Street, Binghamton, NY 13904-1580

Harrington Park Press is an imprint of The Haworth Press, Inc., 10 Alice Street, Binghamton, NY 13904-1580 USA.

Refugee Women and Their Mental Health: Shattered Societies, Shattered Lives has also been published as *Women & Therapy*, Volume 13, Numbers 1/2 and Volume 13, Number 3, 1992.

Library of Congress Cataloging-in-Publication Data

Refugee women and their mental health : shattered societies, shattered lives / Ellen Cole, Oliva M. Espin, Esther D. Rothblum, editors.
    p. cm.
    Includes bibliographical references.
    ISBN 1-56024-372-4 (acid-free paper)–ISBN 1-56023-030-4 (pbk : acid-free paper)
    1. Women refugees–Mental health. 2. Women refugees–Counseling of. 3. Post-traumatic stress disorder–Treatment. I. Cole, Ellen. II. Espin, Oliva M. III. Rothblum, Esther D.
RC451.4.R43R455 1992
616.85′21–dc20
                                   92-24548
                                    CIP

CONTENTS

ABOUT THE EDITORS

Ellen Cole, PhD, was part of a team of mental health researchers in 1989 that visited three refugee camps on the border of Thailand and Cambodia. She describes it as a consciousness-raising trip that inspired the issue. She is Director of the Master of Arts Program of Prescott College in Arizona.

Oliva M. Espin, PhD, specialized in therapy, research, and training on cross-cultural issues in psychology, and the psychology of Latina women. A fellow of five divisions of the American Psychological Association, she is the co-recipient of the 1991 APA Award for Distinguished Professional Contribution to Public Service. Currently, Dr. Espin is Professor of Women's Studies at San Diego State University.

Esther D. Rothblum, PhD, the daughter of a Jewish refugee father, grew up in Austria, Yugoslavia, Spain, Brazil, and Nigeria before becoming a U.S. citizen while an adolescent. A clinical psychologist, Dr. Rothblum is Associate Professor in the Department of Psychology at the University of Vermont. She recently completed a Kellogg National Fellowship that focused on women's mental health in Africa.

Refugee Women and Their Mental Health: Shattered Societies, Shattered Lives

Foreword

Theanvy Kuoch
Sima Wali
Mary F. Scully

A Nation is not conquered until the hearts of its women
are on the ground.

Then it is finished.
No matter how brave the warriors
or how powerful the weapons.

–Cheyenne Indian proverb

We are writing this foreword at a convening of refugee women in San
Francisco in April of 1991. While we write, over one million refugees are
massed along the borders of Iraq. Pictures of children standing barefoot
in the snow fill our television screens and mothers around the world can't
sleep at night thinking ''what if that were my child.'' Officially we are
told that over 500 people a day are dying, mostly the children.

But, we know too well that soon the images will fade from our televi-
sions, and the human faces of refugees will become numbers and political
issues. The profound trauma that creates refugees numbs our minds and
threatens our sense of humanity. In fear of such raw human suffering, we
turn away and attempt to readjust our reality.

We have watched before as refugees become the problem, not the
victims of the problem. Too many times we have seen survivors of geno-

---

Theanvy Kuoch, MA, is a survivor of the Cambodian Holocaust. She is the
executive director of Khmer Health Advocates Inc., and a family therapist.

Sima Wali, MA, is an Afghan refugee and the executive director of Refugee
Women in Development.

Mary F. Scully, RN, MA, is the associate director of Khmer Health Advocates
Inc., a family therapist and a former refugee camp worker.

xi

cide, victims of persecution and casualties of war become economic migrants, displaced persons and illegal aliens. As they are re-labelled, we also begin to forget their trauma.

The human face of refugees is female. Over 80% of the adult refugee population are women who are attempting to protect and provide for their children. Unlike their husbands, brothers and fathers who are in the military, they are not protected by a Geneva Convention. As a people with no country, they have no human rights. When a sovereign nation decides it no longer wishes to host refugees, their label is changed to displaced person and they lose even the limited protection provided by the United Nations High Commission for Refugees (UNHCR).

The number of refugees in the world has doubled in the past decade and until the conditions that create refugees are changed, we can only expect that the numbers will increase. What has remained the same are the conditions which refugees face in their search for survival.

Torture, rape, abduction, forced prostitution, and domestic violence are common with all refugee women from all economic, racial, and ethnic groups. We know from a study conducted by Refugee Women in Development and Harvard University that violence follows refugee women even after they are resettled in a new country. Women who are raped during their journey to freedom are more likely to be victims of domestic violence in their new homes.

The price that refugee women pay for their freedom is extremely high. The women of the San Francisco convening have identified physical and mental health as priority issues for refugee women from all ethnic groups. They clearly articulate the concern for mental health providers to deal with the issues of trauma and not revictimize this population with diagnoses and treatment that ignore the trauma and are used only to maintain the status quo.

Refugee women are the caregivers of the family and the keepers of vital traditions, traditions that ground the family in its culture. Unless the needs of these women are addressed, the stability of a generation of children will be lost and indeed, nations will be lost.

We are pleased to be able to write the foreword for a volume which deals with the mental health and treatment of refugees. We know that therapists who work with refugee women are privileged to testimonies which will never be heard in a court of law. While governments, courts, and historians can manipulate facts and events, the therapist will continuously look into the human face of the refugee story. As a witness, the therapist must deal with the task of helping to give voice to the suffering and strength of refugee women and to act as an advocate during these crucial years.

SECTION I:
INTRODUCTION

Refugee Women
and Their Mental Health:
Shattered Societies, Shattered Lives

Ellen Cole

In the summer of 1981, I was walking past the Goddard College Admissions Office when a staff member beckoned to me to step in. She whispered that there was a caller on the line with an unrecognizable accent who seemed to have some questions about our M.A. program in Counseling. Would I please, please talk to her. Here's a synopsis, from memory, of what I heard:

> My name is Theanvy Kuoch (which she pronounced, to my ear, Tienvy Kwee). I was a French professor at the university in Phnom Penh, in Cambodia. I have been living in the camps in Thailand for four years, and I just arrived in the United States one week ago. I

Ellen Cole, PhD, is a Psychologist and Director of the Graduate Program at Prescott College. In 1989 she spent three weeks on the border of Thailand and Cambodia, visiting Cambodian refugee camps with a team of mental health researchers, practitioners, and former refugees. This collection was conceived in Thailand and three years later is born in the United States, with hopes for disseminating information and engendering compassion and solutions.

1

have no papers, no transcripts, and I will never have them. My country was destroyed by Pol Pot. I want to come to Goddard college to get a Master's degree in Counseling so I can help my people. May I come?

With only limited authority, my immediate reply was "yes." I knew nothing about this woman, about her academic record, her character, her financial status. But her story jolted and touched me. And I continue to be jolted and touched by the stories of refugee, for by now I have heard dozens, perhaps hundreds of them.

Since 1981, with "Vy's" help, I have learned a great deal about the plight of refugees in the U.S. and throughout the world. The internationally accepted definition of refugee is a person who has left her or his country due to a "well-founded fear of persecution" (Suhrke, 1983). Many countries have extended this definition to include persons not necessarily persecuted, but those who have escaped from intolerable political and social disruptions and violence in their homelands. One might consider those from the U.S. who left during the McCarthy era or the war in Vietnam as exiles if not refugees. It is believed there are substantial numbers of people throughout the world who have crossed international borders for fear of persecution but who remain undocumented, unregistered, and uncounted, and substantial numbers who have been displaced within their own homelands as a result of human conflict. For all of these reasons numbers are inexact, but some things are known: Unlike immigrants who leave their homes or their countries by choice, refugees cannot go home. Many have been maimed and tortured; nearly all have lost family members through war or political upheaval; all have seen violence of terrible dimensions.

Current reports estimate there are over 15 million legally designated refugees throughout the world, with another 15 million who have fled their homes but not their homelands (U.S. Committee for Refugees, 1990; Vernez, 1991). The *N.Y. Times* (Miller, 1991) estimates an additional five million refugees and displaced persons created by the recent Gulf War. Refugees come from Afghanistan, Palestine, Mozambique, Iraq, Iran, Kuwait, Vietnam, Cambodia, Laos, the Soviet Union, Nicaragua, El Salvador, Guatemala, Bangladesh, Ethiopia, Albania, Argentina, Chile, Yugoslavia, Spain, and more. They are resettled in more than 85 countries, primarily in Sweden, Australia, Canada, the U.S., France, and Germany, but also in developing countries, themselves in need of assistance (U.S. Committee for Refugees, 1990). Between 1975 and 1990 there were one and a half million refugees admitted to the United States. They came from

Africa, Asia, Eastern Europe, the Soviet Union, and Central America (U.S. Department of State, 1990), and the majority settled (in descending order) in California, New York, Texas, Illinois, Massachusetts, Florida, Washington, Pennsylvania, and Minnesota (U.S. Department of Health and Human Services, 1990). At the same time, millions of refugees are ineligible for resettlement and ineligible for repatriation; many of them have lived in refugee camps for ten years or more. The picture is one of unbearable sadness and suffering, of shattered societies and shattered lives. Every single report about refugees published in the late 1980's and early 1990's describes mounting numbers of refugees and displaced persons, decreasing funding, and a future that looks "increasingly grim, even deadly" (Winter, 1990).

Some studies report that 50-60% of the world's refugees are children (United Nations High Commission for Refugees, 1990; U.S. Committee for Refugees, 1990). It is well documented that 75% of those refugees awaiting resettlement in camps are women and that 80% of the refugees from Cambodia and Afghanistan are women (Refugee Women in Development, 1990). In 1980, the United Nations High Commissioner for Refugees designated women as a particularly vulnerable segment of the refugee population, citing a variety of hazards including rape and sexual violence (Refugee Women in Development, 1990). It is to these courageous refugee women that this volume is dedicated, with hopes it will tell their stories and continue the work many of them have begun: the work of changing the world.

The editors have made three perhaps controversial decisions in assembling this collection. First, we have decided to organize the articles by topic rather than culture. Thus, in one section, you will find articles about refugees in Sweden and refugees from Palestine, the Soviet Union, and Vietnam. Another article about Vietnamese refugees appears in a different section. It seems to us that this division underscores the universality of the refugee crisis, while at the same time not ignoring cultural differences. Second, you will find some repetition from article to article. Several authors, for instance, define "refugee" and delineate the effects of escape and resettlement on individuals and families. We have decided to retain some of the repetitiveness because some things need to be said and heard more than once, and because it is our wish that each article stand alone as well as combine to form an integrated unit. Third, there are several authors in this collection for whom English is not a first language. Although we have done some editing and the authors themselves have done a great deal of editing to make their articles as clearly articulated as possible, there are a few instances in which we have decided to keep non-standard English intact. There is an integrity, we feel, to this decision, and we think you will agree that many of the voices are alive with feeling, much stronger for being true to those who speak them.

As with all projects, many hands and eyes and minds combined to complete this one. Thank you to our editorial assistants, Janice S. Berman and Angela L. Curtes, and to Jean Lathrop, Mary Scully, Richard Miller, and Linchy Nuon, who have dedicated their lives to helping refugees from Central America and Southeast Asia, and who provided much of the inspiration for this collection. A special thank you to Kay Walraven, a wonderfully wise "soundingboard," and to my dear friend Theanvy Kuoch (Vy), for daring to make that improbable telephone call.

REFERENCES

Miller, J. (1991, June 16). Displaced in the Gulf war: 5 million refugees. *N.Y. Times*, p. 5E.

Refugee Women in Development (1990). *What is a refugee?* (Available from RefWID, Washington, D.C.)

Suhrke, A. (1983). Global refugee movements and strategies and responses. In M.M. Kritz, *U.S. immigration and refugee policy* (pp. 158-162). Lexington, MA: Lexington Books.

United Nations High Commission for Refugees (1990, September). Suffering in silence. *Refugees*, 36-38.

U.S. Committee for Refugees (1990). *World refugee survey: 1989 in review.* Washington, D.C.: U.S. Committee for Refugees.

U.S. Department of Health and Human Services (1990, December 21). *Refugee reports.* Washington, D.C.: U.S. Department of Health and Human Services, Office of Refugee Resettlement.

U.S. Department of State (1990, December 21). *Refugee reports.* Washington, D.C.: U.S. Department of State, Bureau for Refugee Programs.

Vernez, G. (1991, June). Current global refugee situation and international public policy. *American Psychologist*, 46(6), 627-631.

Winter, R.P. (1990). The year in review. In U.S. Committee for Refugees, *World refugee survey: 1989 in review* (pp. 2-6). Washington, D.C.: U.S. Committee for Refugees.

A Personal Introduction

Esther D. Rothblum

In attempting to pinpoint my own interest in co-editing, with Oliva Espin and Ellen Cole, a volume on refugee women's mental health, I was struck with the history of my own family of origin. My family has always moved, sometimes voluntarily, sometimes due to political circumstances, and this has influenced my life in multiple ways. As I summarize some relevant events, I recognize how much knowledge I have about male relatives in comparison to the very little I know about the women in my family, even those in my mother's family. Also, I am aware of the role that economic privilege has played in my family, even to the point of saving our lives. This is very different from most of the accounts in the chapters that follow.

In describing my family of origin, I realize that I need to describe each generation separately, although their own lives, and mine, are intertwined, and so are the events that affected their lives. My great-grandfather Marcus Greif, born in 1865, became the mayor of Putila, a community in the Bukowina of what is now Rumania. I am named after his wife, Frieda Esther Greif, born in 1868. My great-grandparents eventually moved to Vienna, Austria. During World War II, they were deported to the Nazi concentration camp Theresienstadt, where my great-grandfather died on June 19, 1943. My great-grandmother died on May 17, 1944 in the train on the way to the Ravensbrueck concentration camp.

Their daughter Pessel married David Rothblum, who was born in Crakow, Poland, and came to the University of Vienna to study law. My grandfather has assumed legendary proportions in my family, and many of us are named after him (my middle name is Davida). In addition to his

Esther D. Rothblum, PhD, is a Clinical Psychologist and faculty member at the University of Vermont. The daughter of a Jewish refugee father, she grew up in Austria, Yugoslavia, Spain, Brazil, and Nigeria before becoming a U.S. citizen in adolescence. Her research has focused on women's mental health, and she has recently completed a Kellogg National Fellowship that focused on women's mental health in Africa.

practice of law, he was a Hebrew scholar, a writer of short stories, and a life-long advocate of forming a Jewish state.

March 1938 was the "Anschluss" of Austria and the Nazi regime. A few days later, Nazis required my grandmother to wash the sidewalks outside her sons' school. One week after the Anschluss, the S.S. troops searched my grandparents' house for the children of Jewish neighbors, and made it clear that they would send my grandparents to Dachau if the friends weren't found. My grandfather knew that Hitler's former attorney was in Vienna that week, and they had been acquaintances during law school. With the help of a passer-by (the family barber), he sent a note to this attorney, who phoned the house and told the S.S. to leave. Years later, this attorney was hanged by the Nazis as a traitor.

My father and uncle left Vienna for Switzerland immediately after that incident. My grandparents no longer felt safe in their home and moved into the Rothschild Hospital, an all-Jewish institution, from where my grandfather continued to practice law. At that time, my grandfather won a suit that included reimbursement for costs incurred during previous trials. In a moment of inspiration, he asked the Third Reich to allow him to travel to Belgium to collect part of this sum, and to take my grandmother along as a caretaker for his failing health. He received passports and exit visas, and in Belgium applied for a visitor's visa for Palestine (along with my uncle), where my grandparents remained for the rest of their lives. After he arrived in Palestine, my grandfather continued to practice law and also headed a publishing house. He wrote regularly for the *Haboker,* a daily newspaper, under the pseudonym Dadar Hapilith (for Dr. David Rothblum and the Hebrew word for "refugee"). He died in 1947, one year before Israel became a nation.

From Switzerland, my father worked for several months in Greece before emigrating to the U.S. in 1939 and becoming a U.S. citizen in 1943. He joined the U.S. army and was stationed in Algeria and Italy. When the war ended, my father returned to Austria with the U.S. armed forces. He has often described the Kafkaesque atmosphere that existed in post-war Austria in which he, as a Jew and former Austrian, was working for the U.S. Marshall Plan on reconstructing Austria's industry.

My father worked for the Marshall Plan in Vienna until he met my mother, who was Austrian and thus an "alien" in the eyes of the U.S. Foreign Service. He was advised to take a post in another country if he planned to marry her. Eight days after my parents were married, they drove to Yugoslavia, where my father began a foreign service job. He kept a packed knapsack handy in order to be able to escape in the event of a Soviet takeover of Yugoslavia, which was considered imminent.

When I was born, the U.S. Foreign Service did not permit its staff to use the local hospitals, so the embassy's air attache flew my pregnant mother to Vienna without official approval to cross the airspace of Soviet-occupied Austria. She was required to wear a parachute, but the straps did not fit over her at that stage of her pregnancy.

My brother and I were issued "Nansen" passports–travel documents for people whose nationality was in doubt or who have "no nationality." At the time, U.S. law stipulated that children born abroad could be U.S. citizens only if at least one parent was a U.S. citizen who had spent at least five years in the U.S. Neither of my parents met that requirement. Many years later, that law was changed to include a parent who had served in the U.S. military, and so my brother and I were "naturalized" and our documents allow us to consider ourselves "citizens at birth."

My first languages were German, Serbo-Croatian, and French. At age four, we spent a year in the U.S., where I learned English. We went on to live in Spain, Brazil, and Nigeria. Our stay in Nigeria coincided with a number of coups and ultimately with the Biafra war. My family bought a small motorboat in the event that we would have to leave the country quickly. We lived on an island across from downtown Lagos, the capital of Nigeria, and the small nation of Benin was only several hundred miles away by sea. We kept provisions in our small motorboat and practiced leaving the island once in uncharted and very shallow waters. By the summer of 1967 the Biafra War had escalated even to the capital, and my family took advantage of vacation plans to Austria to take as many valuable belongings with us as luggage and carry-on bags. While we were away, the U.S. Embassy decreed that women and children could not return to Nigeria. My father returned to Nigeria while the rest of us stayed in Austria. To this day, I have no idea which of my former classmates survived the civil war.

How has my own life been affected by these experiences? I yearn to travel, and feel most at peace when I am in an airplane and no one knows my whereabouts. I write articles while driving my car, using a small notepad by the steering wheel. There are many places I call home, and none in which I would want to live forever. I was reluctant to become a homeowner, and if my place were on fire, would know exactly where to find my passport. I believe very strongly in the published word as a means of keeping records and memories in times of political changes, and spend much of my time convincing women to put their ideas and knowledge into writing.

As I prepare this foreword on May 26, 1991, there are refugees all over the world struggling to cross closed borders. Today's newspaper carried four front-page stories about refugees. Ethiopian president Mengistu Haile Mariam has just resigned, and Ethiopia is cut off from food and fuel. Israel has airlifted nearly 15,000 Ethiopian Jews. The U.S. government decided to continue its policy of barring immigrants who are HIV positive. And Kurdish refugees are entering northern Iraq into "safe" areas.

In the accounts by and about women refugees that follow, the emphasis is on women from different cultures who fled for safety from persecution or danger. This is the first volume that focuses on mental health issues facing refugee women. What does it mean to leave a place of origin or birth? What inspires women to take the risk of leaving a familiar culture for the unknown? How do women survive the physical and psychological dangers of the journey to refuge? Adaptation can also mean staying and facing adversity at home, as in the case of Palestinian women in the article that follows. What is the process of adaptation to the new environment, and what are the costs and benefits of survival? This volume contains articles about these experiences facing women in a number of nations and cultures. Each author's experiences is unique, but also reflects the commonalities of survival and courage, a process that is not complete even years after arrival in the new country or adaptation to the new culture.

Roots Uprooted:
The Psychological Impact
of Historical/Political Dislocation

Oliva M. Espin

Elie Wiesel has written that once you have been in a situation of constant danger, you never feel fully safe again (1984-5). His description, referring to the horror of the Holocaust, fits the experience of many of the women described on these pages even though the historical events that have disrupted these women's lives are different. Holmes and Rahe (1967), and Rahe (1972), who have done research on the effects of stressful events on illness and health, tell us that events such as getting a new job, moving to a new place or losing a partner, create stress that can lead to the development of physical illness. Needless to say, the stress created by living under the fear of bombs, government persecution or other similar life-endangering situations, as well as the dislocation created by leaving one's country under uncertain conditions, are greater and capable of producing even more dramatic effects (Espin, 1987). The life experiences of the women described on these pages evoke in me the memories of experiences that had a powerful impact on my life.

On the basis of my own personal experiences, I believe that there is much to be learned from the individual narrative. I have found that sharing my own experiences produces a cathartic and self-exploratory effect

Oliva M. Espin, PhD, is Professor of Women's Studies at San Diego State University. She has trained psychotherapists in the Boston area for 15 years before coming to San Diego. She specializes in therapy, research and training on cross-cultural issues in psychology, and the psychology of Latina women. She is a Fellow of 5 divisions of the APA and co-recipient of the 1991 APA Award for Distinguished Professional Contribution to Public Service.

Other versions of this paper have been published in *Sojourner* and *The Americas Review* and presented at the *Women's Theological Center* in Boston and the *Minority Pre-Forum on Ethnography and Education*, University of Pennsylvania.

in the audience as well as one that helps clinicians empathize with clients who have undergone similar experiences.

For the last few years I have been engaged in the experiential analysis of my own migration story as a research project following a method denominated "experiential analysis" by Shulamit Reinharz (1979, 1983). In her formulation, the personal experience of the researcher is not only valid but essential in the development of studies that would be contextual and relevant. For Reinharz, a relevant research project should provide "an opportunity for catharsis or self-discovery" (1983, p.176) for both researcher and subjects and a "research product likely to provide resources or answers to pressing problems in living" (p.176). "The record of the researcher's feelings and ideas is also data" (p.175) because "all knowledge is contingent on the situation under which it is formed" (p.177) and, for all researchers, "one's own race, class, religion and gender predispose us to consider some settings more interesting and important than others" (p.179).

The work of many authors who have either used life narratives or discussed their value (see, for example: Allport, 1942; Bertaux, 1981; Denzin, 1986, 1989; Espin, 1984; Mercer, Nichols, and Doyle, 1989; Ortiz, 1985; Plummer, 1983; Rabin, Zucker, Emmons and Frank, 1990; Runyan, 1984; Vaillant, 1977) for sociological and psychological research has demonstrated the value of studying life histories and biography for the social sciences. They have demonstrated that the data provided by life narratives produces a richness that could not be obtained through the use of other methods. That is why I would like to share with the readers (who I assume to be social scientists and/or clinicians) the results of my experiential analysis of my own experiences of uprootedness and the life narrative on which it is based. My intention is to provide the immediacy of a first person narrative, together with a long-term account of the effects of historical dislocation and uprootedness.

In 1984 I returned to Cuba for a two-week visit for the first time after an absence of 23 years. I left Cuba when I was 22 years old, so at the time of this visit I had lived, roughly, half of my life in Cuba and half of my life away from Cuba. This coincidence made the time and timing of the visit particularly significant. The visit provoked in me innumerable reflections on the experience of uprootedness in my life and on the significance of having lived half of my life away from my country of birth.

The purpose of this paper is to share some of those reflections and some of the experiences that led to them. The experiences I want to share refer to the uprootedness of the second half of my life as well as to the intense experiences involved in that two-week trip to Cuba. I believe that

these reflections can shed light on the experiences of exile and uprootedness in the lives of others.

I do *not* intend to discuss Cuban politics, to take positions pro or
against the Cuban revolution, or even argue the soundness of my decision
to leave Cuba in 1961. Obviously, my life experiences, like anybody
else's, are deeply connected to a specific time, place, and historical event.
However, any discussion of the specifics of this historical event (i.e., the
Cuban revolution), would distract from the subject of this paper, namely,
*some psychological consequences of uprootedness and historical disloca-
tion.*

Even though my experience of uprootedness is in one sense absolutely
mine, individual and unique, it is in another sense generalizable to any
person who has ever undergone the effects of massive political dislocation. Because I am a psychologist, and I see the meaning of my experiences mostly in psychological terms, I will describe the psychological
impact of historical dislocation on me in the hope of generalizing my
experiences to those of other people, particularly women, who have experienced or are presently experiencing similar events.

After this preamble, let me describe briefly the experiences of historical
dislocation and uprootedness as I have felt them in my life and as they
became intensely obvious to me as a consequence of my visit to Cuba in
1984.

I was barely 20 years old when Fidel Castro came to power in January
1959. By then, I had already experienced a number of events that had
created in me the sense of instability that usually precedes actual uprootedness. For example, Batista's first takeover and his dismissal from the
Armed Forces of my father and all others who were not his sympathizers
just two years after my birth; Batista's defeat in the presidential elections
of 1944; his second takeover in 1952, after the suicide of one of Cuba's
most honest political leaders; the terror and tension of the Batista years
and, finally, the entrance in Havana of Castro's Rebel Army in January
1959, a joyful event also characterized by suddenness and intense emotions. The Bay of Pigs invasion in 1961 culminated a series of unexpected
changes and surprising turning points. Through all those years, historical
events beyond my control had transformed the course of my life. Although I had previously been aware of the dangerousness of other historical events such as the Second World War, Roosevelt's death, the atomic
bombs in Hiroshima and Nagasaki, these events were happening far away
and their impact in my life was not the same as that of the political events
happening in Cuba.

I–like other Cubans of my generation, like thousands of young people in Europe before and during World War II, like thousands of young people yesterday and today in Central America, the Middle East, Southeast Asia, throughout the world–had learned to live immersed in a situation of constant danger, *without being consciously aware of that fact.* I first recognized that I had been living in daily subliminal terror while watching a film in a theater in Madrid, Spain, when I left Cuba. I was suddenly overcome by the realization that I could enjoy the movie without needing to keep a part of me on the alert, worrying about the possibility that a bomb might go off, that the police might raid the theater or that something similarly dangerous might occur. Mind you, in my 22 years in Cuba I was never hurt by a bomb, nor was I ever arrested. Yet bombs had killed and maimed many young people, some of my adolescent friends had been executed or imprisoned and I *knew* it could happen to me too. The most amazing aspect of this experience was the realization that, I had *learned to always be alert without even knowing that I had learned it.*

Studies involving children and adults who have been exposed to situations incredibly more dangerous than anything I have ever experienced shed some light on how psychological survival, development and growth are achieved in spite of the negative effects produced by violent events created by disruptive political situations (see, for example: Coles, 1986; Dimsdale, 1980; Loomis, 1962; Reinharz, 1971; Williams & Westermeyer, 1986).

The most immediate feeling experienced after leaving such a situation of constant danger is relief . . . together with sadness and grief for those left behind. Confusion and frustration about all the new places and people and customs encountered soon add further burdens. But then, slowly, the unfamiliar starts becoming familiar, daily events start blurring the intense feelings of the first few weeks and years, and life settles into a new routine. Years go by and life goes on.

I lived in several countries after leaving Cuba, earned several higher education degrees, developed important relationships and friendships along with a sense of better self-understanding, worked hard and enjoyed life. Cuba was not constantly in my mind. For the most part, I remembered the events of my 22 years in Cuba as *intrapsychic events of my individual life.* Here and there I was confronted with my uprootedness, but it was not a constant or acute pain.

Perhaps I was lucky: if I lived away from Cuba, at least I was living in other Latin American countries. The sense of being "different" was not as vivid there as it later became in the United States. But in spite of similarities in language, customs and values, I always had a *sense of not fully belonging*. There was the sound of popular folk music that was familiar to everyone but me. And there was my memory of another popular folk music that only I knew. There was the unfamiliar taste of food that was a daily staple for others. And there were tastes that I longed for which were unknown or inaccessible in that particular country. Even though we were all conversing in Spanish, there were words and expressions that seemed unusual or even offensive to me. And there were expressions I used which did not have any meaning for my closest friends.

So I learned to speak my Spanish with a Costa Rican accent while my Cuban one receded, and I learned to enjoy Costa Rican food and to love Costa Rican music. My friends, co-workers, and classmates forgot to include me in their lists of foreigners. And yet, once in a while, the subject of my nationality would come up when someone was angry with me or when I could not remember events in Costa Rican history. To this day, those years in Costa Rica are very close to my heart, my Costa Rican friends continue to be central in my life. But they know, as I know, that I am not really Costa Rican.

There were things I shared with them, however, that I cannot share now with my close friends in the United States. No matter how fluent I am in English, *my innermost feelings are in Spanish*, and my poetry is in Spanish. This deepest part of myself remains hidden from people who are extremely important for me, no matter how hard we all try. I can translate, but translated feelings like translated poetry are just not the same. If there was a difference between me and my friends in Costa Rica, there is an even greater difference between me and my friends in the United States. It is amazing how much hamburger and Coke versus black beans and coffee remind an uprooted person of that difference!

Indeed, the loss experienced by an uprooted person encompasses not only the big and obvious losses of country, a way of life, and family. The pain of uprootedness is also activated in subtle forms by the everyday absence of familiar smells, familiar foods, familiar routines for doing the small tasks of daily life. It is the lack of what has been termed "the average expectable environment" (Hartmann, 1964) which can become a constant reminder of what is not there anymore. It is the loss of this "average expectable environment" that can be most disorienting and most disruptive of the person's previously established identity. In some cases, this disruption of the "average expectable environment" and its impact on the individual's identity (Garza-Guerrero, 1974) can be at the core of profound psychological disturbance. Although the lack of my "average expectable environment" was not destructive for me in this way, I have experienced its loss, more or less keenly, throughout the second part of my life. My return to Cuba in 1984 brought into focus what this loss had entailed for me.

After twenty-three years away from there, I realized that I *needed to go to Cuba*. As if I did not trust my own decision to go, I planned for my trip hastily. But, the more I had to wait for my permit from the Cuban government, the more I knew I needed to go. I was not sure how it would feel to be there, but I knew that I had to do it and I knew that I had to do it alone. Without friends. Without people who had never been to Cuba before. Without people who had also been born in Cuba and thus had their own feelings about being there. This was my own emotional journey.

My journey back to Cuba did not start with the actual trip. For weeks before it I had sudden flashbacks of familiar scenes, places, events that I had forgotten or at least not remembered for the last 23 years. During the year after the trip I also had flashbacks of the events and places of my trip and of my previous life in Cuba. These flashbacks were so vivid and powerful that they absorbed me and distracted me from the activity of the moment. They made me think of the flashbacks, of almost hallucinatory quality, that are sometimes experienced by people suffering from Post-Traumatic Stress Disorder (Figley, 1985) or involved in mourning and bereavement (Parkes, 1972). In fact, it seems that I have been involved in a grieving process, no matter how unaware of it I may have been, and it is possible that I will continue to be involved in it for the rest of my life whenever these feelings are reactivated.

After a 45 minute flight from Miami, I arrived in Havana around 5 a.m. The transition was quick and dramatically abrupt. You have to understand that for me there had been not 90 miles between Cuba and the United States, but almost a quarter of a century and a dense wall of memory. The lights of Havana brought tears to my eyes. They had been so close and so out of my touch for so many years. . . ! By 7 a.m. I had checked in at the hotel, taken a shower, had breakfast . . . and cried, because for the first time in 23 years I had had Cuban sugar in my morning coffee. . . . The moment I stepped out of the hotel I knew exactly where I was, what corners to turn, what buildings would be waiting for me on the next block, and which one of the buses going by would take me to which place in the city. In a few hours I had visited my old neighborhoods, I had gone by my school, I had walked familiar streets and had come back to the hotel without ever having the slightest confusion about were I was or getting lost.

Cuba had been like a forbidden paradise for half of my life. Suddenly, this forbidden paradise was all around me. For years Cuba had been a dark and painful memory. Suddenly *it was present, and clear, and the sky was blue, and everything was as it always was and as it was always sup-posed to be.* And, *everyone spoke with a Cuban accent!* This deep sense of familiarity, of everything being right, of all things being as they are supposed to be was something I had never experienced since 1961.

The experience of total familiarity was, of course, facilitated by the fact that there has been minimal construction in most Cuban cities during the last 30 years. But, aside from the familiarity of the physical environment, there was something more to my experience than just the same buildings and the same bus routes, probably best illustrated by my intense reaction to Cuban sugar and the Cuban accent. Strangers almost always assumed that I was not a visitor, only on a few occasions did some of my clothes give me away. I was even told at one of the dollar stores in Santiago that they could not sell me the t-shirt I wanted to buy; didn't I know that these stores were only for foreign visitors?

But the joy in this sense of belonging was made painful by the realiza-tion that it will never again be part of my life on a continuous basis. I believe that, in the deepest sense, this is what uprootedness is all about: *that you do not fully fit or feel comfortable in your new environment and that most of the time you do not even know that you don't.* It takes an experience like my going back to Cuba to realize that what you have mistaken for comfort does not compare with what the feeling of belonging really means.

On my first morning in Havana I went to the school I attended from first grade to senior year in high school. The main door to the school was closed, but the door of what had been the chapel was open. The statues of the Virgin Mary, the Sacred Heart of Jesus, Saint Joseph and the Cruci-fix were not there. Neither were the pews or the confessional boxes. The floor was covered with mattresses, the room was full of gymnastics equip-ment and a small group of girls about 5 to 8 years old were graciously exercising to the rhythm set by music and a teacher's voice. I had visions of myself and other little girls receiving our First Communion in that same space, and I could not stop thinking about what my life would have looked like if I had done gymnastics rather than Communion in that place. And I wondered what the lives of these little girls would look like in the future . . .

As part of my emotional pilgrimage, I also wanted to visit the homes where I had lived. In spite of all the previous experiences, nothing had prepared me for what I would encounter in the apartment where we lived last before leaving Cuba. I went there for the first time on the evening of my second day in Havana. As I walked to the door, a shadow on the side attracted my attention. It was too dark to see, but I knew what it was. I touched it and my fingers confirmed what I had realized in a fraction of a second: my father's nameplate was still affixed to the column at the entrance. Nobody was home that evening, so I returned the next day. And here, in the daylight, was my father's name on a bronze plate. It had not been removed after 23 years! This time a young man opened the door, and I told him the purpose of my visit and asked for his permission to come in. If the sight of my father's name on that bronze plate had sent chills through my spine, the insides of that apartment provided me with an even stranger experience. *All of the furniture was the furniture we had left,* the same furniture that had been part of the first 22 years of my life. In fact, the man who opened the door had been taking a nap on my parents' bed, the bed on which I was conceived!

I am sure some of you own pieces of old family furniture. I am sure some of you have gone back to old family houses. But I do not know if you have ever experienced the impact of a physical space where nothing has been moved an inch, in a quarter of a century, since you were last there, yet where other people and their lives are now occupants.

A daughter of the poet Carl Sandburg had shared a cab with me from the Havana airport to the hotel. When I had told her that this was my first visit to Cuba in 23 years, she had told me that the house of her childhood, now a museum of her father's life, was both a familiar and strange place for her. At that moment, I had not fully understood her. Two days later, standing in the middle of the apartment that had been my home for several years, I knew what she had meant.

In addition to what I have described, my trip to Cuba made me realize that for years I had felt as if *my memories had had no geography.* But that, in fact, what I remembered had actually happened in a *definite physical space that continues to exist in reality and not only in my memory.* That Cuba exists beyond what I think or feel or remember about her. This realization, which may seem all too obvious, was the more powerful because *before my return I never knew that I felt as if Cuba did not have a real existence beyond my memory.*

My trip evoked other strong feelings, as well. It may not come as a surprise to know that in spite of the intense and powerful sense of belonging that I experienced in Cuba, I was always alert and vigilant. Among everything that Cuba triggers in me, the need for being vigilant and alert is always included.

Beyond this powerfully intense experience of familiarity and strangeness, my trip put me in touch with childhood friends and made me reflect about the differences in our lives, about the choices to stay or leave that have dramatically influenced our life projects. None of us has any way of knowing what our lives would have looked like without the historical dislocations that have marked them. The only known fact is that powerful historical events have transformed the life course of those of us who left and those of us who stayed in Cuba. Those who stayed, if not uprooted, have also been under the effects of dramatic historical transformations. It is impossible to know if our decisions have resulted in a better life project for any of us, although we each hope and believe to have made the best decision. Bandura's (1982) discussion on the importance of chance encounters for the course of human development addresses the impact that chance may have as a determinant of life paths. For some people, chance encounters and other life events are additionally influenced by historical and political events far beyond their control. It is true that all human beings experience life transitions, but for people who have been subjected to historical dislocations life crossroads feel, intrapsychically, as more drastic and dramatic.

It seems rather obvious that the impact of sociocultural and historical change on psychological development should be incorporated in any discussion of human development (Elder, 1981). As Bandura (1982) asserts "a comprehensive developmental theory must specify factors that set and alter particular life courses if it is to provide an adequate explanation of human behavior" (p.747). This is particularly important if we want to understand the experiences of individuals whose lives have been dramatically influenced by traumatic historical and political events because "the danger of any period of large-scale uprooting and transmigration is that exterior crises will, in too many individuals and generations, upset the hierarchy of developmental crises and their built-in correctives; and [. . . make us] lose those roots that must be planted firmly in meaningful life cycles." (Erikson, 1964 p.96). It seems that the use of a methodology that includes life history narratives and an experiential analysis of those experiences could provide social scientists with a tool to understand what the experiences of historical dislocation and uprootedness entails for psychological development. Considering that these experiences are part of so many lives in the world in which we live, the importance of such endeavor for the social sciences seems quite obvious.

In my case, what I learned once again from this trip is that *who I am is inextricably intertwined with the experience of uprootedness*. And what this uprootedness entails, particularly after this return trip, is an awareness that there is another place where I feel at home in profound ways that I did not even know or remember. That place, however, is not fully home anymore. And this reality is, precisely, the most powerful reminder of my uprootedness.

After this initial return, I have visited Cuba again. Now I know that I will continue to return periodically for short visits. Each visit renews my love for my country of birth and gives me back another small piece of the puzzle of my life. I would love to have the possibility of being back in Cuba for a longer period of time, but I know that most probably Cuba will never be my permanent home again. Like all long-term immigrants who return home, I missed my daily life here while I was in Cuba.

Let me also say that I do not believe I have "a corner on uprootedness." In fact, I do not believe that my experience has been particularly difficult. During the past 30 years I have been lucky enough to secure reasonable good jobs, I have developed meaningful friendships that I deeply treasure, I have learned new things about myself and the world that I might not have learned had I stayed in Cuba, and I have evolved valuable adaptive skills as a result of coping with so many changes. It is precisely because my adaptation has been relatively successful and yet so painful at times that I am convinced of the profound psychological impact that uprootedness can have. If I, who have been able to survive and make sense of my experiences in a productive way, have felt and experienced what I have just described for you, it is reasonable to assume that the pain and confusion experienced by other women less fortunate than I will be more extreme and difficult to survive.

The obvious next step for me as a researcher is to collect life narratives from other people who have undergone similar experiences, particularly from individuals who may have returned to their countries of birth after many years of absence, and compare those experiences. I believe there is invaluable data to be gathered through this process and powerful generalizations to be made that would further our understanding of human development in general and of the impact of the experience of uprootedness in psychological development in particular.

It seems evident to me that the details of my own narrative, as well as other life narratives may provide invaluable information toward understanding the experiences of other immigrants and possibly be useful in structuring programs of psychological assistance and mutual support.

My own "success story" also can provide a sense of hope about the possibility of recovery from the trauma of uprootedness and the hope that the suffering of the women refugees of today can be a source of insight and understanding for others in the future. But above all, I hope that all the stories in this volume will contribute to strengthening our resolve to alleviate the pain created by political dislocations all over the world. And, most important, let us resolve to do everything we can, as individuals and citizens, to avoid the occurrence of these events in the world.

REFERENCES

Allport, G. (1942). *The use of personal documents in psychological science.* New York: Social Science Research Council.

Bandura, A. (1982). The psychology of chance encounters and life paths. *American Psychologist, 37* (7) 747-755.

Bertaux, D. (1981). *Biography and society: The life history approach in the social sciences.* Beverly Hills, CA: Sage.

Coles, R. (1986). *The political life of children.* New York: Atlantic Monthly.

Denzin, N.K. (1986). Interpretive interactionism and the use of life histories. *Revista Internacional de Sociologia, 44,* 321-337.

Denzin, N.K. (1989). *Interpretive interactionism.* Newbury Park, CA: Sage.

Dimsdale, J. (1980). *Survivors, victims and perpetrators.* Washington, D.C.: Hemisphere.

Elder, G.H. (1981). History and the life course. In D. Bertaux, *Biography and society: The life history approach in the social sciences.* Beverly Hills, CA: Sage.

Erikson, E.H. (1964). *Insight and responsibility.* New York: Norton.

Espin, O.M. (1984, August). *Hispanic female healers: Implications of their life histories.* American Psychological Association, Toronto, Canada.

Espin, O.M. (1987). Psychological impact of migration on Latinas: Implications for psychotherapeutic practice. *Psychology of Women Quarterly, 11,* 489-503.

Figley, C.R. (Ed.). (1985). *Trauma and its wake: The study and treatment of Post-Traumatic Stress Disorder.* New York: Brunner/Mazel.

Garza-Guerrero, C.A. (1974). Culture shock: Its mourning and the vicissitudes of identity. *Journal of the American Psychoanalytic Association, 22* (408-429).

Hartmann, H. (1964). *Essays on ego psychology.* New York: International Universities Press.

Holmes, T.H. & Rahe, R.H. (1967). The Social Readjustment Rating Scale. *Journal of Psychosomatic Research, 11* (213-218).

Loomis, C. (1962). Toward systematic analysis of disaster, disruption, stress and recovery-Suggested areas of investigation. In G. Baker and L. Cottrell, Jr. (Eds.), *Behavioral science and child defense.* Publication #997. National Academy of Science-National Research Council.

Mercer, R.T., Nichols, E.G., & Doyle, G.C. (1989). *Transitions in a woman's life.* N.Y. Springer.

Ortiz, K.R. (1985). Mental health consequences of the life history method: Implications from a refugee case. *Ethos, 13,* 99-120.

Parkes, C.M. (1972). *Bereavement: Studies of grief in adult life.* New York: International University Press.

Plummer, K. (1983). *Documents of life.* London, England: George, Allen, and Unwin.

Rabin, A.I., Zucker, R.A., Emmons, R.A., & Frank, S. (1990). (Eds.), *Studying persons and lives.* New York: Springer.

Rahe, R.H. (1972). Subjects recent changes and their near-future illness suscepti-
bility. *Advances in Psychosomatic Medicine, 8* (2-19).
Reinharz, S. (1971). Coping with Disaster. Unpublished manuscript. Department
of Psychology, University of Michigan.
Reinharz, S. (1979). *On becoming a social scientist.* San Francisco: Jossey-Bass.
Reinharz, S. (1983). Experiential analysis: A contribution to feminist research. In
G. Bowles and R.D. Klein (Eds.), *Theories of women's studies.* Routledge &
Kegan Paul.
Runyan, W. (1984). *Life histories and psychobiography.* New York: Oxford Uni-
versity Press.
Vaillant, G. (1977). *Adaptation to life.* Boston: Little, Brown & Company.
Wiesel, E. (1984-5). The refugee. *Cross-Currents, 34*(4) 385-390.
Williams, C. & Westermeyer, J. (1986). *Refugee mental health in resettlement
countries.* Washington, D.C.: Hemisphere.

SECTION II:
UNDERSTANDING REFUGEES:
FROM THE INSIDE OUT

Coping with Stress:
A Refugee's Story

Delia H. Saldaña

SUMMARY. Le is a married 35 year old South Vietnamese refugee who works two jobs to support her three children and elderly relatives. The family of eight was one of many boat people whose journey to freedom involved prolonged stress as they left their home secretly and withstood the deprivation of a refugee camp for more than a year before being chosen by a sponsor to relocate in the U.S. Ten years later, Le proudly recites the new responsibilities she has acquired through this transition which have profoundly affected her roles as an employee, mother, and wife. Her story reveals several key elements which hold theoretical significance for the study of successful coping. She refers often to the salience of family values learned early in her life, and the importance of adhering to these during the most stressful periods. She lists several attitudes that helped her maintain hope and focus on her goals during the most

Delia H. Saldaña, PhD, is Director of Research and Program Evaluation for Community Services at the San Antonio State Hospital. A native Chicana from San Antonio, her research focuses on stress and coping in minority populations and cross-cultural service delivery models.

21

difficult times. And, she describes a variety of supportive networks that were developed at different stages of the refugee experience that contributed to a successful transition. These elements clarify the interwoven effects of predisposing factors, coping, and social support on psychological functioning, and imply parameters that clinicians may find helpful in working with a refugee population.

When you cross a river, you use a piece of wood. Upon reaching the other side, don't forget that wood.

–Old Chinese Proverb

CASE STUDY

Le is a 35 year old refugee from South Vietnam who has been in the United States for ten years. Together with her husband, Minh, she works two jobs to support their three children, as well as Minh's grandmother, mother, and aunt in a modest three bedroom home with one bath.

Le is one of the many thousands of Vietnamese "boat people" who found their way to the United States and other countries in the early 1980's. Sponsored by a Presbyterian church, she and her family fled an oppressive Communist government who usurped private property and threatened citizens in its struggle to garner supplies for the war effort with Cambodia. Her voice still filled with outrage, she describes midnight raids in which neighbors' personal possessions, money, even food supplies were confiscated and they were thrown into the street to find another place to live. Although the marauders provided vouchers for "purchase" of the materials obtained, actual payment was never made and people lost savings accumulated over several generations without warning. Fabricated stories of consorting with the enemy or other wrongdoing were often offered as justifications for the government's actions, and the peaceful life that had characterized Le's village prior to the war was shattered.

However, leaving this chaos wasn't easy. Le remembers that at first many left. Those working with the U.S. government, or who had money or connections abroad, left by plane. But for Le's family, who like others feared for their lives and resented the daily indoctrination of their children into Communist ideology, leaving meant arranging secret liaisons with boats for hire who offered a gamble for safety. This required amassing a hefty price for every person who was to board the boat, and not letting word leak that an escape was being planned. It meant resolving to leave behind family and friends, home, and any possessions that could not be carried on board in a small parcel. It meant realizing that once out the door, there was no turning back; for once payment was offered for flight, more than just the money spent for travel was gone. Homes evacuated were immediately fair game for government occupation, and spoiled attempts at escape meant danger for those who risked returning to the neighborhood.

In part, this may be why the entire family made plans for their flight. In fact, Minh refused the offer of a friend to leave separately, with plans to later send for the others. Aside from an elderly uncle, Minh was the only male in the family. His protection was needed at home, and he had inherited a strong commitment to take care of older family members.

Four years into the war, a contact was made: "My uncle-in-law has a friend who owns a fishing boat." Payment had to be secured: in gold bullion, since currency was not accepted. And the price was steep, for it was necessary to help encourage shore patrols to "cover their eyes" and allow passengers to board the vessel. Upon arriving at the dock, however, Le's family was surprised to find that the greedy boat owner had arranged for far too many others, desperate like themselves, to leave. As family upon family got on board, the boat began to capsize. Finally, the owner's family agreed to stay, leaving 198 people to begin their uncertain journey toward freedom.

The first of many setbacks began as soon as they left the dock. Barely out of the harbor, mechanical problems forced the old wooden boat to stop and send back to shore for repairs. Meanwhile, everyone waited, fearful of imminent discovery. The next four days and three nights at sea were long but mostly uneventful. Luckily, Le says that the waters were calm and storms minimal, and at night everyone would be very quiet to keep from tantalizing the sharks swimming all around.

As the boat approached Bidong Island, a small patch of land near Malaysia that served as a refugee camp, several fishing boats were spotted nearby. The large wooden boat once again developed problems, and one of the boats offered to help guide it to the island. A line was cast between the boats, and the smaller one began tugging the large boat along. However, as the island grew closer, it appeared that the little fishing boat was in fact leading the larger boat away from the land, and the passengers became frightened. Stories had circulated about pirates at sea who raped and pillaged unsuspecting victims. Quickly the line was cut and the larger boat was left stranded in the water, hundreds of yards from the shore.

As dark fell, a large storm approached and the fragile boat began to creak apart in the strong winds. Surely the old wood could not withstand this menace. The passengers began to scream, and then to jump, reasoning that an attempt to swim to shore was better odds than staying in the old boat. Le could not swim, but Minh placed her along with her 9 month and 3 year old daughters on his back and carried them to land. He then went back to bring his grandmother, mother and aunt. Minh's uncle, a strong swimmer, also jumped in but suffered a stroke while in the water and became completely paralyzed. Others helped drag him to shore.

The next morning, only the skeleton of the boat's hull and mast remained. The exhausted group of passengers was left on the island, alive but without food, water, or shelter. "For ten days we lived like that," says Le, "until the Red Cross arrived."

But even the Red Cross could not compensate for the miserable conditions in which the refugee camp itself was maintained. Le's family found out that they were Boat #190 to arrive at the camp, and already more than 40,000 people were in the camp when they got there. Health care was the worst aspect of camp living: much of Bidong Island was nothing but jungle. There were no shelters: people pieced together what they could from the nearby woods, using rice bags to cover the sparse frames and hang in the doorways. Illness from drinking the water thrived despite attempts to boil everything, and many died, including Minh's grandmother. Children faced daily hunger, existing on meager rations that consisted mostly of rice and water, and many suffered with ongoing skin diseases that reflected their poor nutrition and sanitation.

Few formal supports were available. Toward the end of the year and a half that Le's family was on Bidong, a clinic was established and staffed by one of the refugees who was a physician. A Red Cross nurse provided acupuncture for Minh's uncle, who slowly recovered from his stroke. But most social support was obtained through the chance encounter of old friends and relatives from Vietnam. The poverty, crowding, and disease led to irritability and suspiciousness among camp residents: food supplies were guarded zealously. But violent crime was virtually nil. Despite the fights that broke out periodically, robbery and assaults were not generally a problem, and people slept with only rice bags separating them from their neighbors.

When asked what the biggest source of stress during this period was, Le states that it was the fear that she and her family might stay at the refugee camp interminably. People could leave the camp only if they were selected by "sponsors" elsewhere, who would pay for their passage to another country. Of course, those who were young, educated, or had transferable work skills were the most desirable candidates. Working against Le's family was its size: once again, neither Le nor Minh would consider leaving if their elderly relatives could not also come along. The resolve to keep the family together was strong despite fears of sickness and death, especially of the small children. An offer from Australia was spurned since it included only Le, Minh, and their children. It was not until more than a year later that they received an invitation from a sponsor church in the U.S. to move the entire family of eight.

Upon arriving in the U.S., Le was overcome with the relative sumptuousness of the home they encountered. The sponsor church had paid rent on a small house for two months, and provided modest furnishings, linens, and a stocked refrigerator to greet the family. Within five weeks, the pastor's wife helped Le find a job as a short-order cook in a restaurant, where she helped prepare food she had never before tasted and learned English by constantly referring to her pocket dictionary. Established Vietnamese friends who lived nearby were helpful in getting a job for Minh. Reinvigorated with the promise of a new life, Le worked hard, putting in 60 to 70 hours at her job despite being paid for only 40. She viewed the arrangement as fair: "They liked me, they taught me English, and sometimes gave me fruit to take home to my family. I always did my best." Unfortunately, she left after a year, distraught over a stolen wallet that her manager refused to help her report to the police. "It had my social security card, my green card. I had only been here a little while: I didn't know what might happen without my papers. He said that only rich people came to this restaurant. Nobody would have stolen my wallet. But it was gone." A second job working in the kitchen of a nursing home was soon replaced by her current employment as a computer repair technician. She was hired without particular skills in this area, but luckily entered the market at a time when training was provided and staffing needs were high. Within three years she was promoted over others with more seniority to serve as a line leader, a position she still holds today. Did she encounter discrimination or resentment? "A little. But here, there is so much equal opportunity. I saw it, and took it, and with time those people came to accept me."

When asked what she lost by leaving her native country, Le looks slightly puzzled. "Of course, my family," she says, "but no real property. We had just married and had very little." She emphasizes, "I didn't really lose. I gained. Most of what I gained is that I feel really good about myself. There, I didn't know what I could do. The woman is brainwashed: you are told that you are stupid and so you feel stupid. There is not so much respect over there: I was just a daughter-in-law. That's nothing. I would never go back: my house is no longer there, and there is no future for my daughters. I want them to have opportunities. Like my oldest one–

she likes music and that costs money. But I try my best to make them enjoy what they think they can do.''

The change still presents a challenge. Le is concerned about the U.S. custom that insists that parents listen to their children. "Not like home," she says, "where children did the listening." And she fears that her daughters may not retain the same commitment to family that helped guide her through the roughest times. She works so hard in part because she sees her role as being a provider for three generations. She must provide for her children, provide for the elderly women still living with her, and provide for her own future in case her children should not feel willing to do so. But there is no resentment in this woman's perspective as she talks about current responsibilities. "I have more freedoms, *and* more responsibilities," she states with pride. "Here, much more than in my old country." And what are her dreams for the future? "I want to work in an office," she says. "I want to dress nice. I worry about my job now. My age is growing, and parts of my body may not work so good any more. Maybe I will get a little more education, and then I can get in an office. So that way I can work longer."

Le continues to maintain an optimistic assessment of her life. She is able to contrast the opportunities and responsibilities she currently faces with a much harsher existence, which helps reframe any current difficulties she may encounter. Her concerns about her children's greater voice in family matters are similarly mediated: "I try to learn from that. In one way, its good. The children can explore their talents, what they do and how they think about it." She feels positive about her increased status within her marriage: "Now we're equal. I always go by what my husband says. But I talk to him. I tell him what I think." And her willingness to work hard and maintain a perspective devoid of bitterness or resentment are important contributions to her psychological well-being. "I don't feel bad at all to work hard," she states simply. "All I need is happiness." Does she feel she has attained that? "Oh, yes," she exclaims. "I feel good about myself." Listening to this woman talk, it's hard to disagree.

ANALYSIS

This woman's indomitable spirit has seen her through all the change, and implied stress, of her life. And she seems to have weathered it with grace. She quotes the proverb at the beginning of this piece, using it to explain why she must continue to respect and care for her elderly family. But these words also refer to how she has used her longstanding traits of insight, determination, optimism and perseverance to adjust to what life has brought her. And the words refer as well to the values and goals that she wants to retain for her children, of holding onto their cultural roots.

Literature on individuals who cope successfully with stress implies that pre-existing factors such as personality traits and prior functioning must be linked to more current information about the types of stress encountered, supports used, and behavioral or attitudinal approaches adopted to deal with stresses (Burks & Martin, 1985; Gottlieb, 1981; Lazarus & Launier, 1978; Pearlin & Schooler, 1978; Riger, 1984).

Le's case certainly documents the importance of early correlates of later attitudes. Her resiliency toward the overwhelming stresses she has encountered appears related to values learned in her younger years. She recites examples of her life before marriage where she learned to value independence and self-reliance, as well as a strong commitment and loyalty to family. These attitudes served her well in her later experiences, and continue to be salient markers of her approach to life.

Equally important, however, are the types and qualities of supports that were available and utilized during times of highest stress. This woman's history alludes to overwhelming chronic stresses, many of which are similar to other immigrants' experiences. Anticipation of the war's devastation on one's way of life and threat to family's safety, the secrecy and tension associated with planning an escape, and the careful monitoring of assets to buy passage but avoid discovery are all elements of chronic stress that pre-date the tangible change of actually leaving one's country. Moreover, the uncertainty that accompanies flight, and real or imagined dangers en route can contribute substantially to distress. Although Le minimizes the difficulty of her transition once on American soil, language barriers, overt discrimination, and economic limitations are frequent markers of the immigrant experience. These types of chronic stresses have been noted to far exceed the adverse effects of acute life event stresses with more controllable elements (Belle, 1982; Pearlin, Lieberman, Menaghan & Mullan, 1981).

It may seem paradoxical that one of the key elements that initially exacerbated the stress associated with leaving Le's native country–her persistent emphasis on maintaining the cohesiveness of her extended family–might be related to her later resilience in coping effectively with the traumas experienced down the road. Le's ability to maintain a measure of personal integrity by continuing valued traditions might have afforded important solace by reinforcing her own self esteem. Minh's endorsement of these same values helped share the burden in more than purely emotional terms. House (1981) described various complementary aspects of support (instrumental, informational, appraisal) that accompany emotional support in more tangible ways. Others have elaborated on the manner in which increased self esteem (Wills, 1985), meaningful social contact, and available confidants (Brown, Bhrolchain & Harris, 1975; Miller & Ingham, 1976) help impede the negative effects of high stress by impacting the individual's *perception* of the effectiveness of available supports.

Another element which contributes substantially to Le's ability to withstand the many transitions she has endured is her appraisal process. Recent studies (Cronkite & Moos, 1984; Fleishman, 1984; Folkman, Lazarus, Gruen & Delongis, 1986; Pearlin et al., 1981) have attempted to understand the relationship between coping resources (longstanding attitudinal, personality, and cognitive factors) and coping responses (behaviors). In general, it appears that what people *are* determines what they *do*. Le does not elaborate on the multiple behaviors in which she engaged during the ten years of stress reflected by her story. However, she alludes to a variety of attitudes and perceptions that continue to help her maintain a positive outlook and approach new challenges in an energized, competent manner. New marital roles and responsibilities are construed as opportunities for development previously denied in her native country, work-related stresses are viewed as expected adjustments on the part of coworkers that will eventually be overcome, freedoms faced by her daughters outweigh the restrictions their lives would have had otherwise. Pearlin and Schooler (1978) have argued that a varied repertoire of coping responses is superior to emphasizing a single approach to dealing with stress. Furthermore, they suggest that women's documented tendencies to report greater levels of psychological disturbance might be related to socialization patterns that encourage less adaptive coping styles (e.g., selective ignoring to cope with marital or parental stresses). Helping individuals improve the efficacy of their own coping involves becoming more aware of the differential impact of coping behaviors for varied situations, as well as encouraging greater congruency between adaptive attitudes and concordant behaviors.

Clinicians interested in helping women deal more effectively with the varied and often chronic stresses faced by immigrants might appreciate the structure and clarity of a stress and coping conceptual model. This approach can help distinguish between several classes of variables that undeniably influence each other. By clarifying the boundaries between categories of variables, a stress and coping framework allows the clinician a theoretical guide which can help emphasize relative strengths and weaknesses in coping effectively with stress. While others (Aroian, 1990; Dunk, 1989; Harel, Kahana & Kahana, 1988; Lee & Lu, 1989; Lin,

Masuda & Tazuma, 1984; Rack, 1988; Salgado de Snyder, 1987; Salvendy, 1983) have used the notion that stressful transitions of immigration are related to mental health, little systematic study has clarified the direct and indirect roles of demographic variables, acute and chronic stresses, coping resources, and coping behaviors on psychological functioning. (See Figure 1.)

For example, it is important to separate the differential effects of demographic variables. Studies on various groups of immigrants have noted that age, gender, level of education, language accommodation, socioeconomic status, and factors in the native country have significant impact on psychological functioning (Aroian, 1990; Dunk, 1989; Rack, 1988; Salgado de Snyder, Cervantes & Padilla, 1990; Zambrana & Silva-Palacios, 1989). The weights assigned to each of these demographic variables reflect their different links to the incorporation of socially appropriate attitudes and coping behaviors that impact mental well-being. Some researchers have drawn these types of connections. For example, Salgado de Snyder and colleagues (1990) compared country of origin and vulnerability to family conflicts, while others have noted an association between generation level and report of acculturative stress (Mena, Padilla & Maldonado, 1987), or between age, gender and effectiveness of supports in reducing demoralization (Flaherty, 1986; Yu and Harburg, 1981).

It is also important to understand the way in which coping resources such as appraisal help mitigate or exacerbate the negative consequences of stressful situations. Some investigators have concentrated on generalized approach styles. Seipel (1988) noted that locus of control was significantly correlated with positive self evaluations, while Scott and Stumpf (1984) noted that subjective satisfaction with role performance overrode social evaluations when assessing general adaptation. Others have focused more on cultural values that may help shape adaptation to the new country (Ho, 1990; Padilla, 1985; Punetha, Giles & Young, 1987; Salgado de Snyder, 1987).

It is not only what one thinks, but also what one does to enhance coping resources. Lyman (1985) suggested that immigrant women followed specific pathways in developing support networks. The diversity of supports created may in part reflect immigration policies and economic factors of the host country (Wong, 1985). Several studies have nevertheless noted the often beneficial aspects of self-created supports for immigrants (Christensen, 1987; Die and Seelbach, 1988; Hartman and Hartman, 1986; Kibria, 1990; Padilla, Cervantes, Maldonado & Garcia, 1988). It has also been noted that support networks sometimes create stress by increasing

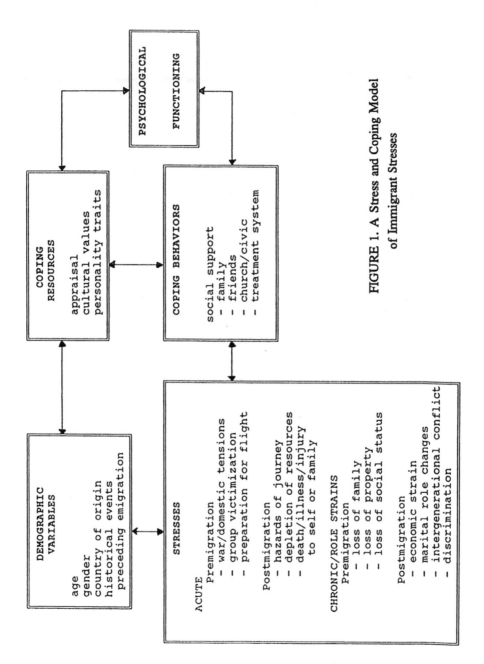

FIGURE 1. A Stress and Coping Model of Immigrant Stresses

intergenerational conflicts (Baptiste, 1990; Osako & Liu, 1986) or inhibiting acculturation (Wong-Rieger & Quintana, 1987).

Attention to categories of variables such as those described above (demographic factors, appraisal, supports) can enhance the understanding of an individual's adaptation to various levels of stress encountered in the immigration process. Although several investigators have addressed the nature of stress for immigrant populations, few have addressed the relationship of these experiences to particular aspects of the migration process (Creed, 1987). Vargas-Willis and Cervantes (1987) emphasize that it is important to clarify whether stresses reflect primarily premigration experiences (including loss of family and familiar surroundings) or postmigration stresses associated with culture change (economic standing, language, group subordination). A more systematic approach can include standardized assessment of stresses (e.g., Cervantes, Padilla & Saldago de Snyder, 1990; Padilla et al., 1988), and help define treatment by reinterpreting the underreport of symptoms in light of group norms (Ho, 1990; Kuo, 1984), noting extreme stresses related to the immigrant's past (Lee & Lu, 1989), and tailoring traditional approaches to the client's current context (Baptiste, 1990; Edleson & Roskin, 1985; Skodra, 1989).

It is important to realize that an objective assessment of stresses, attitudes and coping behaviors does not preclude a sensitive and caring clinical relationship. On the contrary, a careful delineation of the multiple challenges and adjustments that Le and her family have undergone can help clarify what types of adaptive reactions were most successful. This information can combine with clinical insights to guide the practitioner in appreciating a client's strengths as well as areas of needed support. Repeated application of a conceptual model will help the therapist to formulate a system by which to understand similar material presented by other clients. And the empathy and compassion requisite to any successful therapeutic relationship will help communicate information gained from objective analysis.

Le and her family are doing well. Of course they continue to undergo stress. But Le's boundless energy, enthusiasm, and optimism transform even the most difficult experiences into opportunities for growth. Her daughters have gained a rich inheritance through the "river" their mother crossed, and the "other side" that she has helped them reach. With her support, they will be able to gaze toward even more distant banks. With her example, they can strive to overcome the inevitable stresses they will encounter. And with her love, they, too, may remember not to forget the "wood" that opened new ways in which to grow.

REFERENCES

Aroian, K. (1990) A model of psychological adaptation to migration and resettlement. *Nursing Research, 39* (1), 5-10.

Baptiste, D. (1990). The treatment of adolescents and their families in cultural transition: Issues and recommendations. *Contemporary Family Therapy: An International Journal, 12* (1), 3-22.

Belle, D. (1982) *Lives in Stress: Women and Depression.* Beverly Hills: Sage Publications.

Brown, G.W., Bhrolchain, M., & Harris, T. (1975). Social class and psychiatric disturbance among women in an urban population. *Sociology, 9,* 225-254.

Burks, N. & Martin, B. (1985). Everyday problems and life change events: Ongoing versus acute sources of stress. *Journal of Human Stress, 11,* 27-35.

Cervantes, R.C., Padilla, A.M., & Salgado de Snyder, N. (1990). Reliability and validity of the Hispanic Stress Inventory. *Hispanic Journal of Behavioral Sciences, 12* (1), 76-82.

Christensen, C.P. (1987). The perceived problems and help-seeking preferences of Chinese immigrants in Montreal. *Canadian Journal of Counselling, 21* (4), 189-199.

Creed, F. (1987). Immigrant stress. *Stress Medicine, 3* (3), 185-192.

Cronkite, R.C., & Moos, R.H. (1984). The role of predisposing and moderating factors in the stress-illness relationship. *Journal of Health and Social Behavior, 25,* 372-393.

Die, A.H., & Seelbach, W.C. (1988). Problems, sources of assistance, and knowledge of services among elderly Vietnamese immigrants. *Gerontologist, 28* (4), 448-452.

Dunk, P. (1989). Greek women and broken nerves in Montreal. *Medical Anthropology, 11* (1), 29-45.

Edleson, J.L., & Roskin, M. (1985). Prevention groups: A model for improving immigrant adjustment. *Journal for Specialists in Group Work, 10* (4), 217-224.

Flaherty, J.A. (1986). Demoralization and social support in Soviet Jewish immigrants to the United States. *Comprehensive Psychiatry, 27* (2), 149-158.

Fleishman, J.A. (1984). Personality characteristics and coping patterns. *Journal of Health and Social Behavior, 25,* 229-244.

Folkman, S., Lazarus, R.S., Gruen, R.J., & Delongis, A. (1986). Appraisal, coping, health status, and psychological symptoms. *Journal of Personality and Social Psychology, 50,* 571-579.

Gottlieb, B. (1981). *Social networks and social support in community mental health.* Beverly Hills: California: Sage Publications.

Harel, Z., Kahana, B., & Kahana, E. (1988). Psychological well-being among Holocaust survivors and immigrants in Israel. *Journal of Traumatic Stress, 1* (4), 413-429.

Hartman, M., & Hartman, H. (1986). International migration and household conflict. *Journal of Comparative Family Studies, 17* (1), 131-138.

Ho, C. (1990). An analysis of domestic violence in Asian American communities: A multicultural approach to counseling. *Women & Therapy, 9* (1-2), 129-150.

House, J.S. (1981). *Work stress and social support.* Reading: Mass.: Addison-Wesley.

Kibria, N. (1990). Power, patriarchy, and gender conflict in the Vietnamese immigrant community. *Gender and Society, 4* (1), 9-24.

Kuo, W.H. (1984). Prevalence of depression among Asian Americans. *Journal of Nervous and Mental Disease, 172* (8), 449-457.

Lazarus, R.S., & Launier, R. (1978). Stress-related transactions between person and environment. In L.A. Pervin & M. Lewis (Eds.), *Perspectives in Interactional Psychology.* New York: Plenum.

Lee, E., & Lu, F. (1989). Assessment and treatment of Asian-American survivors of mass violence. *Journal of Traumatic Stress, 2* (1), 93-120.

Lin, K., Masuda, M., & Tazuma, L. (1984). Problems of Eastern refugees and immigrants: Adaptational problems of Vietnamese refugees. *Psychiatric Journal of the University of Ottawa, 9* (2), 79-84.

Lyman, J.M. (1985). Support networks developed by immigrant women. *Social Science and Medicine, 21* (3), 327-333.

Mena, F.J., Padilla, A.M., & Maldonado, M. (1987). Acculturative stress and specific coping strategies among immigrant and later generation college students. *Hispanic Journal of Behavioral Sciences, 9* (2), 207-225.

Miller, P., & Ingham, J. (1976). Friends, confidants and symptoms. *Social Psychiatry, 11*, 51-57.

Osako, M. M., Liu, W. T. (1986). Intergenerational relations and the aged among Japanese Americans. *Research on Aging, 8* (1), 128-155.

Padilla, A.M. (1985). Acculturation and stress among immigrants and later generation individuals. *Spanish Speaking Mental Health Research Center Occasional Papers,* Report No. 20, 41-60.

Padilla, A.M., Cervantes, R.C., Maldonado, M., & Garcia, R. (1988). Coping responses to psychosocial stressors among Mexican and Central American immigrants. *Journal of Community Psychology, 16* (4), 418-427.

Pearlin, L.I., Lieberman, M.A., Menaghan, E.G., & Mullan, J.T. (1981). The stress process. *Journal of Health and Social Behavior, 22*, 337-356.

Pearlin, L.I., & Schooler, C. (1978). The structure of coping. *Journal of Health and Social Behavior, 19*, 2-21.

Punetha, D., Giles, H., & Young, L. (1987). Ethnicity and immigrant values: Religion and language choice. *Journal of Language and Social Psychology, 6* (3-4), 229-241.

Rack, P. (1988). Psychiatric and social problems among immigrants. *Acta Psychiatraica Scandinavica, 78* (344, Suppl), 167-173.

Riger, S. (1984). Coping with stressful environments and events. In K. Heller, R. H. Price, S. Reinharz et al. (Eds.), *Psychology and community change.* Pacific Grove, California: Brooks/Cole Publishing Co.

Salgado de Snyder, N. (1987). Factors associated with acculturative stress and depressive symptomatology among married Mexican immigrant women. *Psychology of Women Quarterly, 11* (4), 475-488.

Salgado de Snyder, N., Cervantes, R.C., & Padilla, A.M. (1990). Gender and ethnic differences in psychosocial stress and generalized distress among Hispanics. *Sex Roles, 22* (7-8), 441-453.

Salvendy, J.T. (1983). The mental health of immigrants: A reassessment of concepts. *Canada's Mental Health, 31* (l), 9-12.

Scott, W.A., & Stumpf, J. (1984). Personal satisfaction and role performance: Subjective and social aspects of adaptation. *Journal of Personality and Social Psychology, 47* (4), 812-827.

Seipel, M. M. (1988). Locus of control as related to life experiences of Korean immigrants. *International Journal of Intercultural Relations, 12* (l), 61-71.

Skodra, E. (1989). Counselling immigrant women: A feminist critique of traditional therapeutic approaches and reevaluation of the role of therapist. *Counselling Psychology Quarterly, 2* (2), 186-204.

Vargas-Willis, G. & Cervantes, R.C. (1987). Consideration of psychosocial stress in the treatment of the Latina immigrant. *Hispanic Journal of Behavioral Sciences, 9* (3), 315-329.

Wills, T.A. (1985). Supportive functions of interpersonal relationships. In S. Cohen & S.L. Syme (Eds.), *Social support and health.* Orlando, Florida: Academic Press.

Wong, B. (1985). Family, kinship, and ethnic identity of the Chinese in New York City, with comparative remarks on the Chinese in Lima, Peru and Manila, Philippines. *Journal of Comparative Family Studies, 16* (2), 231-254.

Wong-Rieger, D. & Quintana, D. (1987). Comparative acculturation of Southeast Asian and Hispanic immigrants and sojourners. *Journal of Cross Cultural Psychology, 18* (3), 345-362.

Yu, L.C., & Harburg, E. (1981). Filial responsibility to aged parents: Stress of Chinese Americans. *International Journal of Group Tensions, 11* (1-4), 47-58.

Zambrana, R. & Silva-Palacios, V. (1989). Gender differences in stress among Mexican immigrant adolescents in Los Angeles, California. *Journal of Adolescent Research, 4* (4), 426-442.

Birth, Transformation, and Death of Refugee Identity: Women and Girls of the *Intifada*

Mary K. Roberson

SUMMARY. One of the most complex and seemingly intractable political controversies at this time is the Arab-Israeli conflict. At the center of this conflict lies the Palestinian question. Although relevant history stretches back more than a thousand years, this article begins with a brief sketch of the specific events that forced Palestinians to leave their homeland and become refugees in 1948, as well as pertinent history to the present. One woman refugee's story focuses on the transformation of her refugee identity over time: the initial coming to awareness as stigmatized refugee, accepting the refugee identity, developing refugee pride, and finally the death of her refugee identity as replaced by a growth of identity as a Palestinian woman with a right to and determination for statehood. Last, current refugee (and non-refugee) life under Israeli occupation is described. Women and girls of the Occupied Territories have been empowered by participation in the *intifada*, the Palestinian uprising, which has also served to transform their identities from victim to survivor.

A BRIEF HISTORY

The United Nations Partition Plan of 1947 (UN Resolution 181) recommended that historical Palestine be divided with 55% of the land being

Mary K. Roberson received her PhD in Clinical Psychology from Michigan State University. Dr. Roberson is currently Assistant Professor and Associate of the Center for International Studies at the University of Dayton. Academic and clinical interests include women's studies, psychology of women, women's spirituality, and psychotherapy with the culturally different.

allotted to form a Jewish state and the remaining 45% to constitute an Arab state. During the Arab-Israeli War of 1948-49 following the Israeli declaration of statehood, Zionist Jews (predominantly recent immigrants) forced over 700,000 Arabs from their homes in what is now Israel proper (Regan, 1990). Said (1989) states, "Far from being . . . a case of Jews arriving into a land without people, as a people without land, the Zionists in fact came to Palestine, found another people already there, and dispossessed and alienated that people, the Palestinians, with the moral approval and support of the West . . . " (p. 171). Almost 400 Arab villages were destroyed at that time (Said, 1989).

By the end of the 1948 war, Israel had increased its land holdings so that it occupied 77% of historical Palestine. Most of the Palestinian refugees were not allowed to reenter the land of their birth and thus eventually scattered, creating a new diaspora which today is comprised of approximately 3.8 million Palestinians predominantly in Arab and Western countries throughout the world (Maksoud, 1991). Many refugees, however, settled on the remaining 23% of historical Palestine–only a portion of the land designated for Arab Palestinians by UN Resolution 181. These areas are now called Gaza Strip and the West Bank. Palestinians, refusing to give up claims to their property and the right of return, still today remain uncompensated for their losses.

In 1967 during the Six Day War, the Israeli military invaded and occupied Gaza Strip (previously under Egyptian control), the West Bank (previously under Jordanian control), the Golan Heights of Syria, and Sinai of Egypt.[1] Since October of 1967 the refugees of the 1948 War, combined with the indigenous people of the West Bank and Gaza Strip, have lived under Israeli occupation.

In November of 1967 the UN Security Council passed Resolution 242 which condemned the acquisition of territory by war and called for

1. (i)   Withdrawal of Israel armed forces from territories occupied in the recent conflict;
   (ii) Termination of all claims or states of belligerency and respect for and acknowledgement of the sovereignty, territorial integrity and political independence of every State in their area and their rights to live in peace within secure and recognized boundaries free from threats or acts of force.
2. (i)   Achieving a just settlement of the refugee problem (reprinted in Harkabi, 1988, p. 227).

Provision (ii) guaranteed the security of Israel. Another very central document is UN Resolution 338 (October, 1973), calling for the cessation of military activity, implementation of UN Resolution 242, and the negotiation of just and durable peace in the Middle East,. thus recognizing the political rights of the Palestinian people.

Israel has refused to implement these UN resolutions.[2] Moreover, the government of Israel has stated that it intends to implement expansionist Zionism policies designed to further displace the Palestinian population by driving them out of the Territories. They plan to achieve this by various forms of taxation, school closings, collective punishment, as well as by "transfers" or expulsion, and more. All of these actions are violations of the 4th Geneva Convention regarding treatment of civilians under occupation. (Some of these policies are described and documented below in the section, Life Under Occupation in the Territories of Palestine.) Approximately half of the Christian Palestinian population has emigrated since the occupation began (K.L. Nasir, personal communication, May, 1990), and the emigration continues. Christians are particularly vulnerable because they have more ties to the West and therefore have more connections to make emigration attractive.

Since the occupation began, Israelis have been constructing settlements for Jews in the Occupied Territories, another violation of international law, further displacing Palestinians and confining those that remain.[3] Large quantities of the best land have been confiscated by the Israeli government for these settlements, depriving the Palestinians of living space and scarce water resources. The confiscations and settlement construction are rapidly increasing at the time of this writing. For example, statistics indicate that in the months immediately following the Persian Gulf War, approximately 300 acres of land per day were confiscated in the OPT (Payson, 1991b) and that 40% of Israel's water is supplied by aquifers under the West Bank (Payson, 1991a). "A[n Israeli] Housing Ministry document . . . says authorities are planning to build close to 30,000 units" (Rodan, 1991, p. 14). Peace Now estimates "the apartments will increase by ten-fold the Jewish population" in the Territories, a population which now stands at about 100,000 (Rodan, 1991, p. 14).

BIRTH, TRANSFORMATION, AND DEATH
OF REFUGEE IDENTITY

I conducted a 6-hour interview (personal communication, September 25, 1991) with Muna, a Christian Palestinian, who at age 10 was forced from her home in Lydda at gunpoint during the 1948 war. She and her family were given only a few minutes to gather what belongings they could carry in their arms. In shock, they were unable to prepare for the journey ahead. Muna recalled with vivid detail the terror her family experienced, along with approximately 60,000 other Palestinian Arabs (Palumbo, 1987) in their forced flight from Lydda and surrounding towns and villages. This was the beginning of Muna's experience as a refugee. As I listened to her story, four different expressions and transformations of her identity as refugee emerged.

Coming to awareness of refugee identity: "We became this label." Almost dying of thirst during their walk from Lydda to what is now called the West Bank, Muna nursed from her mother who had given birth to her brother days earlier. A desperate search for water occurred after her mother's collapse. Although they found some, they had no container. Muna's cousin dipped his shirt into the water and returned to her mother to squeeze the moisture into her mouth. Thankfully, Muna's mother survived. Many didn't (Rahib-Petry, 1991).

Muna's family arrived in Ramallah and managed to find a one-room apartment to rent for their family of eight. It was during this initial stage when United Nations and Red Cross relief efforts began for the hundreds of thousands of displaced Palestinians that Muna gradually became aware of her new status as refugee. "We were upset. Being a refugee, you're stigmatized; you're poor; you're nothing. Even though these [refugees] had come from very good homes. Nobody would trust you; nobody would lend you money." Refugees were stereotyped as potentially dishonest in their requests for aid or loans by both the indigenous middle class people and the relief agency workers. People expressed surprise when visiting their crowded apartment because they found it to be very clean.

Unlike Muna's family, most refugees lived in the open under the trees and in the schools during the summer months after their arrival. When the school year began, tents began to arrive. The refugees lived in these tents for about two years before some cement block dwellings were built to form the current camps. Monetary relief was given equally to refugees living in tents and people in rooms, even though the latter were paying rent. In some other forms of aid, the people living in tents were actually favored. Muna recalled with humiliation the time she went to the Red Cross worker and said, "'We need some help. We need clothing.' It was cold, my feet were swollen from chilblains. I had frostbite in one finger. Jaffa and Lydda were warm, and in Ramallah it was in the mid-30s. We didn't have clothing or money to buy any. The Red Cross worker looked at me and said, 'We don't have any; you go home.' And I said, 'You don't have anything for us, but you do have for those in the tents?' And he was very rude. And I went home and never went back again. That was very, very humiliating. To go and beg for these things and to be told no."

Muna explained, "They started labeling us as refugees. . . . And we became this label. . . . But I thought, 'the fact that we are refugees and we are poor, that doesn't mean that we are poor in mind, that we cannot make things, that we cannot do things.'" After her father, a shoemaker, was rudely turned down by a former business associate for a loan to begin a business, the family began to work very hard day and night making and selling various products, just to scrape by.

Self acceptance: "I refused to be ashamed." Through the hard work of each family member, they gradually built a very modest, small home for themselves. Being a refugee became more normal and accepted, "and we lived with it. It's a reality. It's a fact." Muna received a scholarship to a private boarding school, attended predominantly by middle and upper class children. Muna tells of some refugee girls who would not go to other girls' parties, because they would then have to invite the girls to their homes. "But I would not say I don't want to go. My mom, she always welcomed our friends to come to our home. . . . And even though it meant we were not going to eat that day, she made us cookies and cakes to give to our friends. I opened my house. It was neat; they came; and we had fun. It didn't bother us. I refused to be ashamed."

Refugee pride: "We started to look at it positively." Muna's 7th grade Arabic teacher was very political, and convinced the few refugees in this private school that they should be proud of their status; they were Palestinian. Referring to the identity card which registered them as refugees, Muna recalls the teacher's statement: "She said, 'You should never give that up, because this is your passport that you are from Jaffa or Lydda or Ramleh or wherever. Your roots.' I had nothing else to tell me where I was from. My birth certificate was lost. Our deeds to our lands were lost. They were left there in the municipality in our homes. We couldn't carry anything with us. We had no way to say our identification."

This affirming validation of refugee identity plus their family's relative financial success over time transformed Muna's sense of refugee identity from stigma to pride. "We were improving ourselves. . . . The refugees were working very hard–much harder than some of the Ramallah people. We were more than half the population. We started selling and working and controlling the whole business there. So, we started to look at it positively. If people wanted to say something negative, we told them, 'Look at what we've done.'" After completing high school, Muna was offered a relatively high paying job. Because she would have been required to give up her refugee status and along with it her refugee identity card, she refused the job.

Death of the refugee identity: "We are Palestinians." For Muna, a refugee in the diaspora, the turning point from refugee victim to Palestinian survivor came earlier than the *intifada*. For her, it was when the PLO was formed that her Palestinian identity began to supplant her identity as refugee. "It was inside always. We always knew we were Palestinians, that we wanted our homeland. But we were always waiting and hoping–the United Nations, Jordan, Egypt, the Arab countries–waiting, waiting, waiting. But then we realized, you have to do your own work for yourself. And then we started to say, 'Forget this refugee thing. We are Palestinians.'"

Muna now feels she is no longer a refugee for another reason, this time in identification with Palestinians in the Occupied Territories. She paraphrased a letter to the editor which stated,

> *Webster's Dictionary* defines *refugee* as "one who flees, or has fled, to a foreign country to escape danger and persecution in their native land and country." Palestinians in America, Jordan or other countries can be called refugees because they have escaped the dangers of their native land. This word, however, cannot be applied to Palestinians still in [the Occupied Territories].
>
> *Webster's Dictionary* defines another word, *concentration camp*, as "a camp where persons (prisoners of war or political prisoners) are detained or confined. . . . The moment the West Bank and Gaza became occupied by Israel in 1967, the camps became "concentration camps," not "refugee camps," because the people became political prisoners under the same government from which they had earlier escaped. (Wagner, 1990, p. 4)

Muna said, "I had it in the back of my mind. I could not explain it. I couldn't dare say it. People would start screaming at me and telling me not to make the comparison. But it is very similar. Yes, there are no ovens to put people in, but these people in the territories–every day something in them dies."

Lasting influence of the refugee identity. Muna explained examples of the many ways her experience of being a refugee still influences her life. For one, she appreciates food–she cannot bear to throw food away. But also she characterizes her family as follows: "We wanted education, we worked hard, we never played or fooled around like everybody else. We were always serious. We lost our sense of humor."

Muna recalls her years in an American university in the late 1960s, demonstrating with other students against the Viet Nam War. "I walked in the march with the students. And the second day I didn't feel well. I was in bed over the weekend. But I heard the radio saying that the students got into the ROTC building, and there was going to be trouble. The army was going to come. I was in bed at home, yet I started shaking. I was really upset. I said to myself, 'Oh my God, they are going to come here.' And it's still with us now. At least it is still with me.'' Muna was referring to post traumatic stress anxiety symptoms that emerge in the context of conflicts that involve the military–no matter how distant (e.g., Lebanon War, Persian Gulf War) (personal communication, April 12, 1991). Muna is now 53.

TODAY'S LIFE UNDER OCCUPATION IN THE TERRITORIES OF PALESTINE

Current estimates indicate more than 1.7 million Palestinians live in the Occupied Territories (e.g., Sabbagh, 1991). In Gaza, over 70% of the 860,000 inhabitants are refugees. In the West Bank approximately 25% of refugees live in camps; in Gaza Strip over 50% live in camps–creating one of the most densely populated areas on earth (McDowall, 1989). The camps are where many refugee Palestinians have been living for more than 40 years in 'permanently temporary' conditions. Because they are lacking in civic services, infrastructure, and employment opportunity, the camps "are places where people exist rather than live" (McDowall, 1989, p. 20).

Swann (1989a) concluded from the statements of Palestinians from the Occupied Territories: "The refugees and non-refugees were not . . . essentially different, but represented two aspects of the Palestinian people" (p. 4). Thus a special issue of the *Journal of Refugee Studies* (Swann, 1989b) speaks of the entire Palestinian population as more unitive since the oppressive experience of an unjust occupation overwhelms the potential social class barriers and differences that these two groups might experience. In support of this observation, psychological research evidence described later in this paper (Hein, 1990) suggests that, in fact, there are no significant differences in the levels of anxiety between camp and non-camp children.

Since the occupation in 1967, Palestinians–refugees and non-refugees alike–have been experiencing violations of their human rights as defined by international law. As a cumulative effect of these violations and as a specific response to an incident in Gaza in December of 1987 during which four Palestinian workers were struck and killed by a truck driven by Israeli soldiers, the uprising of the Palestinian people, the *intifada*, began.

Friedman (1989) states that according to the *Dictionary of Modern Written Arabic*, *intifada* means "tremor, a shudder or a shiver." It is derived from the Arabic root *nafada* which means "to shake, to shake off, shake out, dust off, to shake off one's laziness, to have reached the end of, be finished with, to rid oneself of something, to refuse to have anything to do with something, to break with someone" (p. 375). This word was chosen to convey the notion of aggressive nonviolent resistance (Martin, in press). Previous leadership laid some groundwork toward developing the Unified National Leadership, both in a governmental and community sense. Thus, when the "shaking off" began, the *intifada* almost organized itself.

Though abuses by the occupying Israeli forces were occurring prior to the *intifada*, the Palestinians living in the territories had to a certain extent been integrated with or co-opted by Israel. Many were trying to live with the occupation, resisting in non-productive ways, and/or waiting for their Arab neighbors and the international community to intervene on their behalf. The *intifada* marked the beginning of the Palestinian people's full recognition that they must take primary responsibility for gaining their own self determination and statehood. This was a turning point from the shock and denial of victimization as refugees toward the development of a survivor identity as Palestinians.

In November of 1988, the Palestinian Liberation Organization (PLO) declared Palestine's independence, began to function as a government in exile, and publicly recognized Israel's right to exist. The PLO has the popular support of the Palestinian people, both in and outside of the Occupied Territories. For the refugees, the PLO gives them an identity as a people instead of an identity as a refugee problem. The PLO is the embodiment of the Palestinian people (Maksoud, 1991). There is no formalized PLO membership system, especially in the Occupied Territories where Israel has outlawed the PLO which it regards as a terrorist organization. But in an unpublished Gaza Strip opinion poll conducted in the spring of 1991, approximately 75-85% of those surveyed wish the *intifada* to continue and still view the PLO as representing them. The PLO has the support of Palestinians throughout the world (Aruri, 1991).

With regard to women's participation in the Palestinian political leadership prior to the *intifada*, Haddad (1980) stated that "female participation in the PLO structure verges on little more than tokenism" (p. 120). However, women's political leadership in the territories has increased over time due to the constant loss of male leaders through imprisonment or deportation, especially since the *intifada*. (Baumman and Hammami [1989] have compiled an annotated bibliography on Palestinian women.)

THE INTIFADA *AS EMPOWERMENT IN OCCUPIED PALESTINE*

The occupation abuses have been documented by many human rights and humanitarian organizations (e.g., World Health Organization, Amnesty International, Save Our Children, United Nations Relief Works Agency, Middle East Watch, Al-Haq). For example, the United Nations Economic and Social Council's Commission on the Status of Women (1990, p. 7) lists *some* of these violations as experienced by women, most of which also affect men and children:

> collective punishment such as detentions or searches of houses, curfews, cutting off of electricity and water supply, . . . land confiscation, demolition of trees and crops, employing cultural taboos, . . . shooting, [detainment and] imprisonment of women [without charge], deportation of husband or wife, closing down of women's organizations and women's production centers, destruction of hospital equipment, destruction of property in the home, and destruction of family homes, . . . beatings, verbal insults, forced cleaning of slogans from walls and, above all, school closings.

A concrete example occurred during and after the Persian Gulf War. The Occupied Territories were under a 24-hour curfew for 45 days, surpassing the previous record of 42 days. Curfew is house arrest, since individuals may be detained without trial for up to five years and/or fined heavily for curfew violations. In addition, the territories were declared a military zone, giving soldiers permission to shoot to kill (White, 1991). In part, this confinement meant the people could not work outside the home and therefore had no money to purchase food and other necessities; children could not attend school; often people could not receive proper medical care; farm crops and businesses failed; and more. Subsequent to the War, new restrictions on trade and travel outside of their immediate territories led to a complete collapse of the already weakened economy and an estimated 40 to 50% unemployment (Collins, 1991).

Nongovernmental agencies report increased malnutrition and physical illness in the territories (Palestine Human Rights Information Center

[PHRIC], 1991). The psychological stress of living in this high density (average 5 people/room in the camps), enclosed situation has been enormous, especially for women (Sabbagh, 1991). However, such a collective punishment of 1.7 million people also serves to further increase their anger and determination to be a people with a state. (It is necessary to mention these and other harsh facts and statistics because the United States' press rarely prints such information.[5])

The Occupation and its response, the *intifada*, pervades the entire existence of all Palestinian lives creating tremendous individual, family and community stress. Provision of quality mental health services is virtually nonexistent in contrast with the actual needs of the people, predominantly for political and economic reasons (Dubrow, Fernando, Brauer, & Mellor, 1991; Roberson, 1990).

Two research studies of 250 families and 840 children (ages 6 to 14) were conducted over a period of seven years by Hein (1990). Specifically, Hein used detailed interviews, the TAT, and standardized measures of anxiety with the children from both camp and city. He found in his longitudinal study that levels of anxiety in the children decreased significantly over time as measured before and just after the onset of the *intifada*. In addition, there were no significant differences between the camp children and the more advantaged children in the city, supporting the conclusion that the stress was due to occupation rather than social conditions of poverty and overcrowding. Last, he found that girls were significantly more anxious than boys were, presumably because more boys continue to play an instrumental role while more girls tend to be expressive in their *intifada* activities, remaining in the home more of the time.

Hein's study provides evidence that the activities of protest have some beneficial effect on children in terms of empowerment. It is reasonable to hypothesize that the positive effect of regaining some sense of identity and standing up for one's rights might generalize to adults as well. More and more, girls and women are moving into the empowering leadership and confrontational activities of the uprising. In addition, the *intifada* provides a sense of hope and collective identity for all the people of Palestine. It is a well organized resistance with many dimensions, all with the goal of achieving self reliance—"refusing to pay taxes, organizing and reinforcing neighborhood committee structures for health, agriculture, education, and other avenues of life, all aimed at breaking the ties with the Israeli infrastructure and developing independent Palestinian institutions instead" (Giacaman, 1989, p. 143).

WOMEN AND GIRLS OF THE INTIFADA

During a fact finding trip for mental health professionals to the West Bank and Gaza Strip, I interviewed several women and girls about their roles in or experience of the *intifada*. Identifying information in this article will be withheld in order to safeguard the individuals' from repercussions or retaliation.

Some women have become leaders in their communities. The importance of the *intifada* far outweighs the necessity for strict maintenance of the gendered division of labor. However, many of the women in the instrumental leadership roles find themselves in the same position as women in this country. That is, they must now have two jobs–outside and inside the home. But most of the women community leaders with the necessary freedom of movement are older, middle class and well-educated–well beyond the tasks of child bearing, child rearing and maintaining a large, extended family household. In short, they achieve the freedom of movement to become leaders at a time of life when they are seen in their own culture as somewhat asexual (Salman, 1987).

I asked one woman community leader (personal communication, May, 1990) what she would like to tell the American people. She replied,

> Just tell them to think of the Palestinians as human beings. And as people like any other people in the world who are under occupation, who are oppressed. And all that we are looking for is our identity and homes for our families and schools for our children, like all of the people of the world. . . . And if they hear of any attacks [on Israelis], it is because that person was annoyed. They have to understand that his brother might have been killed or paralyzed or his mother. They are human beings; sometimes they can't control themselves. And when they hear that the Israelis are bombarding camps, they have to understand that *this* is terror. And all that we want from the world is justice.

In addition to their expressive roles, traditional Palestinian women play a confrontational role by placing themselves between the Israeli soldiers and their sons who are being beaten or detained. Our delegation saw one such family in Gaza who had just been admitted into the hospital. The emotion was still very high from the incident, as they told their story full of terror and rage. Israeli soldiers entered their family home and began beating the teenage boy while the father was held and forced to watch.

The mother then placed herself in front of her son to shield him from the soldiers' blows. The mother and son showed us fresh billy club shaped welts on their backs and shoulders. Using their bodies, their quick wit and sharp tongues, often women do save their sons and others from being arrested and detained.

Other women have lost their children and husbands. I interviewed one camp widow from Gaza (personal communication, May, 1990). The eldest of her two sons was in prison–one of approximately 12,500 (PHRIC, 1991) political prisoners detained without charge or trial with legal representation (including some women [e.g., Hamdani, 1987]). Her youngest son had recently died from a poison gas attack on the camp. The residents were under curfew and thus forced to remain in their homes. The crowded arrangement of houses–each built with openings for ventilation purposes, combined with the military's indiscriminate use of gas, led to her son's death. She sadly showed us the certificate which listed gas as the cause of death. Her son was not the only one, a refrain we heard from several mothers we spoke to.

The World Health Organization (1990) reports that there were 7810 tear gas casualties in the first two years of the *intifada* (1987-1989); 1448 of these were children under the age of 6. Forty-nine of the casualties died from their injuries; almost half of the deaths were children. The total number of casualties in two years from all forms of violence (beatings, gunshot wounds, etc.) in the same report was 43,706 in two years (15,078 were children under age 16). As of April, 1991, PHRIC estimates total casualties figures at 112,000. Statistics indicate that 10% of the fatalities and 23% of the injured were women (United Nations Economic and Social Council, 1990). Sosebee (1991) found that anywhere from 4% to 26% of the population of 11 Gaza Strip communities and camps have been injured or killed.

The numbers are numbing, but as Rahib-Petry (1991) points out, we must remember that each one represents a human being with a name. This large number of injuries and deaths in a small population in a small geographical area in a very community-oriented culture has the effect of creating an entire population in continual mourning. I am haunted by the image of a poster that hung on the wall of an office in Jerusalem. It depicted a crying, grieving woman clutching her son. The caption stated, "How much could you take?"

Later, our delegation asked if we might make a monetary contribution to the widow from the camp. We were told that no one starves in the *intifada* and that the Women's Committee would attend to her needs. These committees organize help for families in need of financial support or other assistance. Binson and Ameri (1990) have documented the role of women's organizations in providing structure for women's participation in both the activities of the struggle for liberation and also increasing socioeconomic equity with men within the society itself. Unfortunately, "even these organized efforts are thwarted under curfew" (Sabbagh, 1991, p. 16).

Women have made some gains toward equity, although in a way that still segregates them from men for most part. However, Kazi (1987) warns that "when these movements successfully gain their national independence, women are [usually] conveniently pushed back into the domestic sphere" (p. 36). For this reason and also because of the need to have maximum freedom to mobilize for liberation, many women who are active in the national struggle also recognize the need to address simultaneously the social and economic issues of women. Thus, especially in Gaza Strip where the fundamentalist Hamas group continues to force a campaign of *hijab* (veiling), these women are battling oppression on two fronts (Abdo, 1991).

Our delegation was invited by a young woman in late adolescence to a meeting in the West Bank, during which a demonstration was to be planned. She showed us the posters that girls and young women carry in their marches. The three posters depicted different women in traditional Palestinian dress in direct confrontation with Israelis: riding a galloping horse and throwing stones (an artistic vision), holding onto the arm of a boy who was being arrested by a soldier, holding the base of a sling shot for a younger boy, and spreading her hawk-like wings as a protector of the children and the mosque in the background. These are the freedom fighter images with which this young woman identified.

While our delegation was at a different West Bank home, a ten year old girl entered the room to ask her parents if she could participate in the children's march scheduled for that afternoon. Reluctantly (because of fears for her safety), they acquiesced since most all of the children participate in demonstrations. The girl wore a cardboard poster strung over her shoulders which stated in Arabic, "We want our state and identity." She carried two small triangular flags, one green and the other white. The Palestinian flag is illegal, so the children each carry one or two of the four flag colors (black, green, red and white). (Such creative civil disobedience has also been demonstrated by village women hanging out their laundry in the pattern and colors of the flag.)

Together with many other children carrying similarly colored balloons, the girl later marched by the house singing and chanting, "Let us live. We have the right to live as human beings. Give us our childhood." After the march, she returned to the house to tell us her experience: "The army saw us, but they decided to be kind. They went away and came back. Finally, they told us to stop. We ignored them. We said, 'P-L-O!! Israel no!!' They shot a sound bomb, but we stayed. Then they shot tear gas and started shooting live ammunition into the sky, so we ran away" (personal communication, June, 1990). Children can distinguish the different types of ammunition by their sound.

These are the stories of just of few of the *intifada's* brave female soldiers. Palestinian women in the Occupied Territories labor day and night for their liberation, both inside and outside the home, as do their families. Whether the domain of work is either nontraditional or traditional in terms of female gender role, Palestinian women serve as the bearers of the culture, nurturers of the children and less able adults, and–especially through the Women's Committees–the caretakers and leaders of the communities. Women and children living in the territories are central to the *intifada*. Many Palestinian women living in the diaspora also work with the same level of commitment for the establishment of a Palestinian state.

A FINAL NOTE

As I write this article, I reflect on the April, 1991 television footage which flashed before me daily of hundreds of thousands of Iraqi Kurds fleeing their homeland in the aftermath of the Persian Gulf War. I now have a visual image of what 1948 must have been like for the Palestinian refugees arriving in what is now the Occupied Territories–no tents, no food, no water, only terror and despair. I also reflect on the mood of the people in the Territories after a month long visit there in June of 1991. Despite the courageous efforts of the Palestinian women, children and men participating in the *intifada*, increasingly the backs and spirits of the people are breaking under the International Law and human rights violations of an oppressive Israeli occupation. The fate of the Palestinians, as did that of the Kurdish refugees, rests on the response of the International Community.[6]

NOTES

1. In addition, the Israeli government annexed Jerusalem in violation of UN Resolution 181. The Israeli government still maintains that they need the Occupied Palestinian Territories to ensure their national security, a claim which is against international law and now has been largely refuted even by some Israeli and

American Jewish experts on the Arab-Israeli conflict (e.g., Harkabi, 1988; Friedman, 1989). In 1979 the Sinai was returned to Egypt.

2. The United States has consistently vetoed UN Security Council resolutions which would have brought pressure to bear on Israel. However, at the time of this writing during a "window of opportunity" following the Persian Gulf War, the current position of the United States is for Israel to "give land for peace," calling for a process which will end with Israel's withdrawal from the territories. Secretary of State James Baker stated to the press on his 4/9/91 trip to Jerusalem that all parties should work now toward the implementation of UN Resolutions 242 and 338.

3. Sharon (1991) stated that it is the decision and policy of the Israeli government to accelerate housing construction for Jewish settlers in the Occupied Territories. In addition, Friedman (1991b) reported that "Shamir, the Israeli Prime Minister, has declared that Israel no longer interprets Resolutions 242 and 338 as requiring it to give up any more land. . . . Since Israel returned the Sinai to Egypt it has fulfilled the resolutions' territorial requirements" (p. 3).

4. Muna is not the only one making comparisons between what Palestinians under occupation experience and what Jews have experienced during their long history in the diaspora. Some Israeli and American Jews discuss this topic as well (e.g., Ellis, 1991). "Camp is a memory, a reality and a symbol the Israeli's live by. They cannot remain indifferent to this word" (Linn, 1991, p. 40). Recognizing the harm that comes to a people who are oppressing another people, many Jewish peace organizations in the United States and Israel also work to end the unjust occupation (e.g., Jewish Women's Committee to End the Occupation of the West Bank and Gaza, Women in Black, Jewish Committee on the Middle East, Israeli Mental Health Professionals for Peace, New Jewish Agenda).

5. Reports of media distortion and Israeli misrepresentations of events are plentiful (e.g., Emery, 1990, regarding the al Aqsa Mosque incident). Nixon (1990) states in her human rights report on the status of Palestinian children,

> Although there was remarkably little correspondence between this report's findings and [Israeli] official statements, there was agreement with much of the soldier testimony carried mainly in the Hebrew-language press. The soldiers' published accounts of official and unofficial military orders, compliance with orders, and common troop practices are an important corroborating source for this report's findings. (p. 2)

6. Without some pressure from the international community, the situation for resolution of this longstanding conflict between Israel and the Arab world appears bleak. Israel's leaders have both historically and in the present set many preconditions for negotiation. For example, the criteria set for *the Israeli choice* of the Palestinian negotiating delegation effectively eliminates the possibility of many of the recognized Palestinian leadership and thus, also conveniently eliminates the

possibility of moving away from the status quo situation (Aruri, 1991). Never in history has any country been allowed to choose who represents the opposing side in negotiations, resulting in the ultimate denial of self determination of the Palestinian people–the ability to choose who speaks for them.

REFERENCES

Abdo, N. (1991). Women of the *intifada*: Gender, class and national liberation. *Race & Class*, *32*(4), 19-34.

Aruri, N. (1991, April). *Will Palestinians be in the new world order*? Paper presented at the conference, Linkages in the Middle East: Opportunities for Justice and Peace, Dayton, OH.

Baumman, P. & Hammami, R. (1989). *Annotated bibliography on Palestinian women*. The Arab Thought Forum (al-Multaqa), P.O. Box 19012, East Jerusalem, Via Israel.

Binson, D. & Ameri, A. (1990, August). *The Palestinian movement and the role of women's organizations: 1978 to 1990*. Paper presented at the American Sociological Association Annual Meetings, Washington, D.C.

Collins, F. (1991, July). Palestinian economy in chaos after Gulf War. *The Washington Report on Middle East Affairs*, pp. 23, 54.

Dubrow, N., Fernando, S., Brauer, M. F., & Mellor, P. (1991). *Report on the mental health of Palestinians in the West Bank and Gaza Strip*. P.O. Box 5386, Nicosia, Cyprus: Palestinian Association for Mental Health.

Ellis, M. (1991, April). *Jewish progressives and the Gulf War*. Paper presented at the conference, Linkages in the Middle East: Opportunities for Justice and Peace, Dayton, OH.

Emery, M. (1990, November 13). New evidence. Two startling videotapes support Arab charges. *Village Voice*, pp. 1, 25-29.

Friedman, T. L. (1989). *From Beirut to Jerusalem*. New York: Farrar Straus Giroux.

Friedman, T. L. (1991a, April 10). Israel backs plan for single session on Mideast Peace. *New York Times*, pp. 1, 7.

Friedman, T. L. (1991b, April 12). Baker-Assad talks called inconclusive. *New York Times*, p. 3.

Giacaman, R. (1989). Palestinian women in the uprising. From followers to leaders. *Journal of Refugee Studies*, *2*(1), 139-146.

Haddad, Y. (1980). Palestinian women: Patterns of legitimacy and domination. In K. Nakhleh & E. Zureik (Eds.), *The sociology of the Palestinians*. London: St. Martin.

Hamdani, L. (1987). A Palestinian woman in prison. In M. Salman, H. Kazi, N. Yuval-Davis, L. al-Hamdani, S. Botman, & D. Lerman (Eds.), *Women in the Middle East*. Atlantic Highlands, NJ: Zed Books Ltd.

Harkabi, Y. (1988). *Israel's fateful hour*. New York: Harper & Row.

Hein, F. A. (1990). Personal communication from unpublished 1988 dissertation results, Ain Shams University, Cairo, Egypt.

Kazi, H. (1987). Palestinian women and the national liberation movement: A social perspective. In M. Salman, H. Kazi, N. Yuval-Davis, L. al-Hamdani, S. Botman, & D. Lerman (Eds.), *Women in the Middle East*. Atlantic Highlands, NJ: Zed Books Ltd.

Linn, R. (1991). *Fighting by the memory–Holocaust metaphors and symbols in the moral dilemmas of Israeli soldiers*. Manuscript submitted for publication.

Maksoud, C. (1991, April). *The new world order: An Arab assessment*. Paper presented at the conference, Linkages in the Middle East: Opportunities for Justice and Peace, Dayton, OH.

Martin, J. (in press). Nonviolent dimensions of the *intifada*. *Journal of Third World Studies*.

McDowall, D. (1989). A profile of the population of the West Bank and Gaza Strip. *Journal of Refugee Studies*, 2(1), 20-25.

Nixon, A. E. (1990). *The status of Palestinian children during the uprising in the occupied territories. Part one: Child death and injury*. Radda Barnen: Swedish Save the Children.

Palestine Human Rights Information Center. (1991, February 17). *Palestinians under curfew: Israel's prisoners of the gulf war*. P.O. Box 20479, Jerusalem via Israel: Author.

Palumbo, M. (1987). *The Palestinian catastrophe. The 1948 expulsion of a people from their homeland*. Boston: Faber and Faber.

Payson, P. L. (1991a, May/June). Figure it out. *The Washington report on Middle East Affairs*, p. 37.

Payson, P. L. (1991b, July). Figure it out. *The Washington Report on Middle East Affairs*, p. 55.

Rahib-Petry, J. (1991, April). *The Palestinian woman: A history of struggle*. Paper presented at the conference, Linkages in the Middle East: Opportunities for Justice and Peace, Dayton, OH.

Regan, G. (1990). *Israel and the Arabs*. New York: Cambridge University Press.

Roberson, M. K. (1990). *Palestinian mental health services: Present and future*. Unpublished fact-finding report, University of Dayton, Department of Psychology.

Rodan, S. (1991, 25 June-July 1). Shamir slow to get message of U.S. anger. *Middle East Times*, 9(26EE), pp. 1, 14.

Sabbagh, S. (1991, March). Behind closed doors. Palestinian families under curfew. *The Washington Report on Middle East Affairs*, pp. 15-16.

Said, E. (1989). The challenge of Palestine. *Journal of Refugee Studies*, 2(1), 170-178.

Salman, M. (1987). The Arab woman. In M. Salman, H. Kazi, N. Yuval-Davis, L. al-Hamdani, S. Botman, & D. Lerman (Eds.), *Women in the Middle East*. Atlantic Highlands, NJ: Zed Books Ltd.

Sharon vows to expand settlements. (1991, April 11). *New York Times*, p. 3.

Sosebee, S. J. (1991, July). How to explain American apathy over Israeli killings of Palestinian children? *The Washington Report on Middle East Affairs*, pp. 24-25.

Swann, R. (1989a). Reflections on the symposium and its significance. *Journal of Refugee Studies*, 2(1), 1-4.

Swann, R. (Ed.). (1989b). Palestinian refugees and non-refugees in the West Bank and Gaza Strip [Special Issue]. *Journal of Refugee Studies*, 2(1).

United Nations Economic and Social Council, Commission on the Status of Women. (1990). *The situation of Palestinian women in the occupied territories* (Report No. E/CN.6/1990/10). New York: Author.

Wagner, W. (1990). Letter to the editor. Tell it like it is. *The Washington Report on Middle East Affairs*, 9(5), p. 4.

White, P. (1991, March). West Bank curfew: "I just want to go out in the sun and play." *The Washington Report on Middle East Affairs*, pp. 14, 85.

World Health Organization. (1990). *Health conditions of the Arab population in the occupied Arab territories, including Palestine* (Document No. A43/INF. DOC./1, 12 April 1990). New York: Author.

Women in Exile and Their Children

Maria Bylund

SUMMARY. The article gives examples of interactions during psychological consultations with exiled mothers and their children. They exemplify different coping styles to problems of traumatic loss and separation from old families and social networks, loss of cultural and professional roles, and problems of identity and self-esteem. The observations are discussed in relation to the women's personality test profiles and their anamnestic material. Three typical styles of transactional defense in relation to their children are defined. These styles—"binding," "delegation" and "expulsion"—are also related to the risk of associated typical behaviors in the second generation, such as gang behavior and certain types of criminality. The usefulness of the Exner Rorschach in evaluating the (often overlooked) resourcefulness of analphabetic peasant women is touched upon. Finally suggestions are given regarding factors and treatment modalities that could facilitate the exiled women's process of working through their trauma and establishing new coping styles and networks that could provide fertile soil for constructive development in themselves and their children.

She was a small fragile woman with a calm angular face and erect posture. She gave a proud impression. She had been referred for psychological consultation due to excessive menstrual bleeding and other gynecological problems. There she stood in my waiting room with a one-year old child in her arms and no interpreter. I spoke her language badly, she mine even worse. After struggling with this common problem for some time an

Maria Bylund is a Clinical Psychologist teaching Developmental Psychology and Psychopathology at the Research Center for Children's Culture at the University of Stockholm. She supervises Creative Arts Psychotherapy projects at the Loewenströmska Hospital as well as at the Psychosomatic Unit, National Institute of Health Insurance Hospital, Nynäshamn. She also maintains a private practice in Stockholm.

onlooker may have perceived us as talkative, giggling teenagers sharing a secret. We had established a common ground where we were equals. A psychoanalyst would perhaps have said that we had established a hypomanic defense alliance. Maybe that was true, maybe not. In any case the little boy in her arms seemed to like the atmosphere, relaxed and started playing "peek-a-boo." "Doctor liking you, doctor liking you" she said repeatedly while hugging him and giving the impression, that this reflected on her own feeling of being accepted.

But when we began to talk about the possibility of her coming to see me on her own–the little boy had at the same time started to take an interest in my jewelry–she suddenly started to try to nurse him, now with a very harsh and stiff expression on her face. "You mean he should sit out there with my sister while you and I talk in here?" It was quite clear that she would not allow that under any circumstances.

During the sessions to come I also learned why: In her country of origin, she had been sitting one evening nursing this child, then only one month old. Her three older children were sleeping in another room. Suddenly the house was surrounded by police and military and in the big upheaval as the family and neighbors gathered and battled, one of her brothers had seized her in his arms and escaped with her and the baby on a motorbike. That was the starting point of a long journey, not yet over. Her brother was still alive, a soldier in her country's military service. Her husband had disappeared that night. She believed he was in prison, possibly tortured, possibly dead. The three small children she believed–or hoped–lived with the neighbors.

She had managed to arrange her living situation in this new country, so that she earned her room and board by helping an old couple in their household chores. Their eggs would boil for hours and the iron in her hands would suddenly stop over the cloth and burn a big hole in the material while her thoughts and attention wandered off to her children 5000 miles away. Her hosts had helped her talk to lawyers, to Red Cross staff, to embassy officials. But children of political prisoners were not one of her country's priorities . . . Rather the contrary it seemed. "It's the struggle to get them here that makes me survive," she often said. "How happy I will be when they come. Now my little son is all I have, all I have from my whole family, from my whole people." Little wonder that she wanted to keep this child tightly in her arms.

Looking at this woman's projective material, there were no indications that she would bind her child too strongly due to her own psychological profile. Rather that binding was caused by her feeling of traumatic loss and separation. During the period of our work she was able to let the boy engage in age-appropriate interest in other people and in the surrounding world, and he developed very well.

BINDING

In cases where parents in exile have their own developmental weaknesses, there is a great risk that the process of working through the grief of losing loved ones in the home country will be disturbed. The separation from the old family and social network of belongingness in the home country can thereby never be finalized, allowing new ties to be developed in the new country. Also, among such mothers there seems to be a tendency to overly intense binding of their children.

Mr. and Ms. J. had escaped together with their three children. They are very proud of how fast they managed to get into the job market. Yet the employment they could get was far below their level of education. They felt ashamed and tended not to contact other people from their own country. Both mother and father worked several jobs to be able to obtain a standard of living of which they would one day in the future not feel ashamed to invite other people to their home. They lived this way for many years, nurturing the memory of the identity they once had, while starving socially and emotionally. When the children were 14, 17 and 18 the husband suddenly died from a heart attack, and Ms. J. developed a severe idiopathic pain syndrome which brought her to psychological testing. Ms. J. at this point had intense pain in her back and her arms, which made it impossible for her to work. She complained intensely that the children did not help her enough and in fact gave her further problems. The 18-year old daughter refused to talk to her. She even refused to be in the same room as her mother. She left the room and went into another one and locked the door if the mother came in. The 14-year old boy tended not to come home at all, but ran around with gangs in the streets. He was often absent from school. All through his school years he lacked concentration and was over-active. As Ms. J. had left a lot of the disciplining of the children to her husband, and as she had no close friends and only fairly distant relationships with her companions at work (which she had not been able to attend for more than a year) she felt very much lacking in support for herself and was exasperated by the children.

The psychological tests of Ms. J. indicated that she was quite a dependent personality. One of the tests she was given consists of a picture of a separation situation presented repeatedly in a series of very brief time exposures. These start below the threshold of conscious perception and become successively longer, ending with an exposure time where most people see the picture appropriately. Ms. J. had initially very strong psychosomatic reactions to this procedure and never managed, not even on exposures longer than normal, to perceive the picture appropriately. What Ms. J. saw, when she saw anything at all, was a woman with a dog on a leash, "so the dog could not run away." It would seem that the 18-year old girl's action of locking herself away from the mother could be a reaction against the over-strong unconscious binding tendency in the mother.

The boy, on the other hand, who had been born shortly before the exile, and to a large degree brought up by his sisters while his parents were constantly working, seemed all through his childhood to have had difficulties processing emotional stimulation in ways other than motoric activity and acting out. To deal with the sudden loss of his father he would have needed much support, which nobody was able to give him. On the contrary, both the sisters and the mother turned to him for both emotional support and leadership of the family. So he ran away–escaping, and making the social authorities aware of the fact that he and his family needed help.

DELEGATION

Both the women described above seem to have had a tendency to keep their children "on a tight leash" so they would not be abandoned by them also. However, to an even larger extent, exiled women seem to rely on the child's ability to learn to handle the new world far more quickly than they do themselves. A representative of this latter group is Ms. H. She was referred to me with multiple psychosomatic symptoms including severe intractable asthma. Her husband had earlier been diagnosed as having idiopathic pain syndrome and was receiving anti-depressive medication which helped somewhat. Even though the family had a fairly large social network of other families from their home country, they had no relatives here, and were quite worried about the family members in their own country. They had both been in the new country for three years. Ms. H. herself had two years of school in her country of origin, her husband four. However, since his arrival in this country, he had been working only with other men from his country of origin, so that he spoke the new language quite badly. She on the other hand, had through the childrens' friends and their families, come in contact with people from many other countries and cultures and that way had to rely on trying to use the new language as a common means of communication. (Often the situation is the opposite: the woman is at home with the children and does not learn the new language.) Ms. H.'s vocabulary actually seemed to be a mixture of the different languages represented in this international group of women. It was a language totally its own, including words from many parts of the world and, even though strange, quite understandable. The family is Muslim and Ms. H. had learned that the man was the one to decide upon important matters and that she should obey him. Quite often she ran into the intricate situation that she more quickly and thoroughly understood the situation, the meaning of which she then had to try to convey to him without offending him or letting other people in the environment notice that she was the more capable in the couple. The husband however seemed to know this all too well and compensated by criticizing all her mistakes in grammar–even those she did not make–at the same time that he made excuses for her as she had had so little schooling in her own country. To show that it was not competence or effort that was of importance–but chance–he had taken to gambling, which of course upset her.

Ms. H.'s way of trying to deal with what seems to be problems of competence in the adult system was to idealize and rely very heavily on the small childrens' ability to learn the new language and the new culture. She arrived at her first psychological evaluation, not with an interpreter as requested, but with her whole family, claiming that her seven-year old daughter normally was the one to interpret for them, and therefore they did not need an additional interpreter. The seven-year old daughter–a very beautiful, alert and curious child–was the oldest of four siblings, all of whom seemed very capable and were speaking the new language well. She told me with what seemed to be great warmth, joy and pride about the different childrens' deeds, particularly the girl's, whom she talked of as "my Fatma." "She's taught me to read and write your letters, so now I can go to the store myself without the risk of buying washing powder instead of children's porridge, in case there isn't a picture on the package" she said laughing. "We're going to let her read a lot so she can become a nurse or perhaps a doctor when she grows up," she continued with great enthusiasm. Little Fatma nodded while handling the younger children.

At this point in our "family conversation" the four-year old found a toy guitar in my office and pretended he was a TV rock star. As I understand some of the language I thought I heard a text which was very different from both rock lyrics and childrens' tunes: "The prisons of Diarbakir, heroes and martyrs, heroes and martyrs" he shouted at the top of his lungs, with gestures imitating Michael Jackson. I questioned if I had understood the language right, and little Fatma quickly informed me that I had and about the different persons in their family who sit in the prison of Diarbakir and why. "Ali got there too," said the 6-year old boy. "Because he had helped his brother grease his gun when he was a guerrilla soldier, but they let him out after three months because he was just 13. I'm going to become a lawyer when I grow up and get them all out of prison," he said, inumerating the different members of the family who were political prisoners. "I'll go there and shoot them with my big 'banger' and kill them with my karate chop" the four-year old boy exclaimed before seven-year old Fatma shut him up. "Maybe they will manage" the father said, explaining that if so they will be the first to be "learned people" in their whole family of several hundred people. It was evident that both parents looked forward to that prospect.

These children, and many others in families like this, seem energized and vitalized by the importance and the hopes the parents tie to them. The question is though, how will these children be able to carry through with only minimal parental support and guidance, and with the burden of being the educators and translators for their own parents? Many of these parents, having abdicated many of their own functions of guidance and control to their children during their childrens' latency period, change quite unexpectedly, from the child's point of view, adopting a totally new attitude when the child, particularly if a girl, reaches sexual maturity.

Another Fatma I have met was born in exile. She seemed to have been "the right hand" of her mother, performing many of the social functions in the family. She was very bright in school, aiming to become a physician. After her first date with a boy in the new country, she was suddenly taken abroad and married off to a man from her own country of origin. She was then 14 years old (the parents had lied to the authorities to be able to marry her). When I saw this Fatma, at the age of 22, she had four children of her own. She had not been able to finish high school. In the periods between her pregnancies she had had short-term but very heavy cleaning jobs at an hourly wage, during one of which she had fallen and hurt her back badly. This woman's projective material was very similar to that found amongst younger teenagers. There were also many indications that suggested experiences of no or defective support and of betrayal.

EXPULSION

It also seems that many of the children, who in adolescence gather in groups and gangs with their own laws, are children who during their latency years have learned that they are the ones who know about the world and teach the parents, not the other way around. Therefore, they have great difficulty understanding that they cannot set rules for the society in general. Eklund (1982), for example, found that there are exiled children who tend to carry out criminal acts even though their personality structures–judged by the Rorschach Exner Comprehensive System–indicate that they are less severely disturbed than most of the non-exiled children with the same symptoms. The former can also quite often change to a social style of development if the adult world can provide appropriate authority and limits. The risk here, however, seems to be that the parents cannot take back the authority they earlier have given away. They feel exasperated in relation to the child, ashamed and humiliated in relation to family, relatives and society in general. Unable to handle this narcissistic damage, they do not reestablish their parental functions but instead label the child as being of bad character or "evil" and expel him or her.

One woman, Ms. E., was actually expelled as adult. She was the head of the cleaners attending the toilets at a big department store chain. In an incident where she had surprised some drug addicts who evidently had planned on staying overnight at the toilet, she got beaten up quite badly. The employer, however, claimed that her injuries were inflicted on her before her exile, and the whole description of drug traffic in his stores was only a falsification made up by an unreliable person. Her projective material showed an individual who was a well functioning, resourceful woman with a reflective problem-solving style, well integrated emotions, and with sufficient capacity to meet present stimulus demands. It also indicated a woman who had experienced a major emotional loss. A parallel blind rater, who at the same time happened to be evaluating the Rorschach protocols of a group of middle managers due to be laid off due to industrial cut-backs, presumed that the protocol of Ms. E. belonged to this group and that the "four years of education" was a typing mistake really meaning 14. In the rater's fantasy Ms. E. was a divorced or widowed, somewhat sad, elegant business executive of 32.

In reality Ms. E. was not at all elegant. She was a small wiry woman, looking older than her age, with square body and broad hands showing the signs of physical labor. Below the folded Muslim head cloth, two curious black eyes looked steadily at you while she told her story. She had entered the country as a teenager together with a brother and a sister. The rest of the family had come before, as the family got separated during the escape and the older siblings were left behind. The rest of the family was given political asylum, but as she was already 18 and had been engaged by the family to a man in her country of origin, the authorities did not regard her as belonging to the family and therefore decided she should be deported. At that point Ms. E. was hidden by a family in the new country for almost a year, during which time she seemed to have made very close ties to people here. She was finally granted permission to stay in the country and could marry her fiance who had also come and settled down here. After about 3 years however, he, without her knowledge, took their child abroad to his family of origin. He came back and explained that he was no longer renting their apartment as he was going to live with another woman, and that she'd better go back to her own parents. Ms. E. instead went to the police and to a lawyer, reporting the husband for kidnapping and filing for a divorce. At this point, her family of origin disowned her "as none of our relatives had even thought of divorce." Ms. E. first reacted with shame, telling nobody about what had happened and trying to sleep over at work, in laundry rooms, etc. She rather soon, however, contacted the family who had hidden her earlier. She proceeded to live with them once more, received help with her divorce proceedings, and finally, against all expectations, managed to get the child back. The child was now seven and Ms. E. remarried a man she had picked herself. She was still disowned by her family of origin.

GRIEF AND CREATIVE TRANSFORMATION

Even though there are reports in the literature (Raez, Martinez, Niño de Guzean, & Rossel, 1990) of Rorschach protocols indicating high functioning and resourcefulness among immigrant peasant women, what Ms. E. had managed seems extraordinary. When asked what she had experienced as helpful, during the time of waiting for deportation/asylum and during the years when her child was away, she in both cases talked about the comradeship and the activities among the refugees, the family she had been hiding with, and the friends of the latter. She spoke with great warmth about "a co-hider" who was a musician from another continent. These two women had got a big group of people together to improvise scenes from their lives, and then put together a musical to be performed at a human rights festival they decided they would organize when they got their permits to stay–a project they brought to fruition. "You know" she said, "it was a little like getting my old country here again. In one scene I played my brother who was shot and that gave me a feeling of being with him in his hard times, in his death. You know, that's the important thing: to be able to be together with those you love when it's tough. And I didn't feel so guilty any more that I survived and he didn't. And Miranda played 'the grief singer' and we did it as we do in my country, you know, where 'the grief singer' comes and sings the story of the whole life of the dead person and we all sit around and cry and fill in our own memories. Everybody cried for someone. Your folks here cried too. And I've seen at the performances we had later that you people understand how we feel. You cry, too, when the police come and shoot the children, and you cry when the funeral singer comes, and still it's only play and you've never been through it in reality. That makes me feel that you understand, that you share our struggle and that we've something really important for which we can struggle together and achieve a result. We still organize a festival for human rights every year, and the work goes on."

Even though Ms. E. was still sad about not being able to meet her dear ones–the ones left behind in the old country, the ones killed, the ones who refused to see her here–it seems that she had been able to go through a thorough grieving process and to replace that lost group of relatives with new deep ties. Maybe that enabled her to use her own resources effectively. Those refugees who had not been able to grieve lost relations and the old lost network seemed prone to "trying to stop time" and denying the loss of group belongingness by developing transactional defensive styles of binding, delegation or expulsion in their relations to their children, with detrimental effects for the whole family.

Ms. E.'s story also seems to point to the importance of having the experience of struggling together with other emotionally involved people for a shared and valuable goal. Could perhaps her and her friends' musical project become the prototype for a music-dance-drama group treatment modality for people who have lost their old network?

A song from one of Ms. E.'s human rights festivals can perhaps best describe the situation of many an exiled woman:

They seized our children
They burned down our homes
They left us to the desert
to waste lands without soil.

Children murdered
by famine
Anxiety our food.

So come sister come
let's act
Let's use our time.

REFERENCES

Eklund, L. (1982). Invandrarungdom: En riskgrupp för kriminalität? (Immigrant children: A risk group for criminality?) BRÅ-S-1982-3, Stockholm.

Raez, M., Martinez, P., Niño de Guzean, I., & Rossel, Z. (1990). Étude de l'identité des femmes des secteurs urbano-marginaux de Lima-Peru. XIIth International Congress of Rorschach and Projective Techniques, Paris (to appear in *Rorschachiana XVII*, Hans Huber Publ., Bern).

Rape and Domestic Violence:
The Experience of Refugee Women

Amy R. Friedman

SUMMARY. Despite the fact that women and girls make up over half of the world's 18 million refugees, little attention or resources have been dedicated to meeting their needs. Although all refugees face health and protection problems, women are susceptible to additional problems as a result of their gender. Women and girls who flee their home countries to escape violence and persecution are particularly vulnerable to sexual violence. Rape is a common experience for refugee women, and the resulting trauma has life altering affects for both the women and their families. Often male refugees suffer from "heightened male vulnerability" as a reaction to witnessing torture, violence or rape. This, combined with the additional stress of resettlement in a new culture, often leads male refugees to resort to domestic violence as a way of reestablishing control and gaining power. Since refugee women are the pillars of their families, domestic violence and rape trauma present serious obstacles to the self-sufficiency of refugee families. It is the responsibility of health care providers in both the international community and in countries of resettlement to significantly address sexual violence and its repercussions on the successful resettlement of refugees.

INTRODUCTION

More than 18 million refugees in the world today have left their homes and fled for their lives leaving behind war, persecution, or internal conflicts.[1] It has been estimated that 75% of the total refugee population consists of women and girls (Overhagen, 1990, p.3), and in some regions

Amy R. Friedman is currently Administrative Assistant/Bookkeeper at Refugee Women in Development (RefWID), Inc., Washington, DC. She has a BA in Sociology with a Program in Women's Studies from Brandeis University.

65

women comprise a greater majority of the refugee population. According to Sima Wali, Executive Director of Refugee Women in Development (RefWID) in Washington, D.C., women and girls comprise 80% of the more than 5 million Afghan refugees who fled from the recent Soviet invasion.

Women are not only found in disproportionate numbers, but often find themselves with sole responsibility for large families after losing their husbands to war or abandonment. In 1986 the Refugee Policy Group reported that two-thirds of all families in the three largest camps in Ethiopia were headed by women, 50% of these women were widows, and 50% were "grass-widows"–women whose husbands were alive but have been fighting or have abandoned them. Figures are similar among Indochinese refugees: 80% of the Khmer households along the Thai-Cambodian border are headed by women. Being the head of a household is particularly demanding since refugees tend to have large families. Among refugees in Somalia, the average household consists of 8-9 persons, including 2-3 adults and 5-6 children (Taft, 1987).

Although women make up the majority of the refugee population, most of the programs and services offered to refugees are developed, implemented, and administered by men. The result is a system which has little regard for the majority of its users. Most refugees live in unsanitary conditions where epidemics and disease are common, water supplies are contaminated, and food resources are insufficient. For a variety of reasons however, women face particular hazards as a result of their gender, and in 1980 the United Nations High Commissioner for Refugees designated women a "particularly vulnerable segment" of the refugee population.

The following is a summary of the problems which refugee women encounter, both abroad and in the U.S., and some recommendations through which the international community and service providers can begin to address these issues.

THE EXPERIENCE OF RAPE AMONG REFUGEES

One of the most serious risks for refugee women, one which is rarely addressed by the health community, is the problem of rape and sexual violence. Refugee women, many of whom are widowed or young, have few structures to protect them. Women and girls who flee their home countries to escape violence are vulnerable to sexual violence along every step of their journey. Although this problem is no secret, the international community has failed to develop adequate measures to protect refugee women from such violence.

DURING WAR

The rape of women and girls during war is nothing new. Rape is a military strategy used to humiliate and demoralize an opponent. Since women are a symbol of honor in many societies, they are not the only targets of rape. "In conflicts between different political or religious groups, sexual violence against women has been used as a means of aggression towards an entire section of the community or as a means of acquiring information about the activities and location of family members" (Siemens, 1988, p.22). As a form of torture, men are often forced to watch while their wives or daughters are raped. In such circumstances the humiliation of the woman and helplessness of the man are the desired results. It is often as a result or in fear of such torture that refugees flee from their countries.[2]

DURING FLIGHT

Escaping their home countries, however, in no way means escaping brutality. Refugee women are subject to sexual violence and abduction at every step of their escape, and are particularly vulnerable when crossing borders to seek asylum.[3]

It has been noted that approximately 44% of the "boat people" who arrive in Thailand are subjected to attacks by pirates (Taft, 1987, p.29). During these attacks women and girls are the primary target and are often subjected to multiple rapes and/or abduction. The women are usually taken off the boat and forced onto a pirate boat. They are raped repeatedly, often by gangs of men, and are then pushed overboard and left to die. If they are not pushed into the water, they may be passed on to another pirate boat for the same torture or taken to an island where they are forced to work as slaves.

Although pirate attacks in the waters of Southeast Asia are the most well-known and well-documented incidences of violence against refugees, refugee women's vulnerability has made them targets of similar violence along escape routes in many other parts of the world. At a workshop on Women Refugee Claimants held in Toronto, Canada on April 4, 1990, attorney Ninette Kelley provided some harrowing statistics concerning women refugees. In Djibouti it is estimated that virtually every female refugee who enters the country is raped at the border and at other times during her stay. In Mozambique, refugee women are often raped and abducted by Renamo guerrillas who take the refugees back across the border to act as slaves for the rebels (1990, p.5). In Central America, cayottes–men who are paid large sums of money to assist refugees in fleeing from their homelands into neighboring countries–often rape women and girls in exchange for safe passage (Wali, 1990).

Recently, the forced prostitution of Afghans has gained international attention. According to Wali, the women and girls are forcibly abducted at the border of Afghanistan and Pakistan and sold to Pakistani brothels. The tragedy is that most of these women are unaware of their fate, and think that they are being escorted to refugee camps. Since many are unaccompanied young girls and widows, no one is left to protect them or to monitor their movement (or disappearance). Although no official studies have been undertaken, it is estimated that thousands of Afghan women have been sold into prostitution in Pakistan. During their visit to Pakistan in 1990, a delegation of the Women's Commission for Refugee Women and Children based in New York heard numerous stories confirming this outrage (Wali, 1991).

As remarkable as it may seem, thousands of women survive such circumstances. They arrive at refugee camps expecting to find safety.

IN CAMPS

While refugee camps exist to provide a safe haven for those who have fled for their lives, they often provide little protection, and in fact can be dangerous places. Refugee women are often subjected to violence by the very people who are supposed to protect them. Stories of rape by camp authorities and military guards are common. Without protection, women are often unable to leave their camp homes to collect food or other necessities (Kelley, 1989).

In addition, refugee women in camps are often sexually harassed by men from their own ethnic communities.[4] The system of assistance in some regions encourages this condition. Relief agencies in Southeast Asia distribute food to women and children only, assuming that men will receive supplies through their families. Often men steal food from the women, and in some cases threaten or sexually harass a woman, and then vow to protect her (or stop the harassment) in exchange for food (Brahm, Soland & Swain, 1986, p.5). In certain Moslem regions such as Pakistan, where women are traditionally forbidden from having contact with male strangers, refugee women can receive food and services only through familiar male intermediaries (Taft, 1987). In such cases the survival of a woman and her children may depend on her ability to bargain with the men. Once again, refugee women are left vulnerable to sexual harassment and violence, and have no choice but to submit in order to survive.

IMPLICATIONS

The raping of refugee women is planned and unusually brutal. While most victims of rape in the United States are attacked by an individual man, many refugee women are gang raped or raped repeatedly, often for days at a time. They are often in situations where they witness additional rape, either the rape of a family member, friend or acquaintance. For many of these women, rape is the most frightening and humiliating experience they have lived through and carries serious implications. The experience is so traumatic that many victims consider or commit suicide.

In addition to the emotional trauma of being victimized, many women sustain physical injuries, contract venereal disease or become pregnant as a result of rape. Health resources are limited; most relief workers have not been trained to recognize either the physical or emotional symptoms of rape trauma. Even if they do identify victims, refugee workers are scarce and few have the training to recognize such problems and approach them in a culturally appropriate manner. Women usually receive no medical or emotional treatment and are left to confront the issue alone, without the traditional support structures of home.

This situation is worsened by the religious and cultural attitudes surrounding rape. Most refugee cultures relegate women to a submissive role where they are considered the property of men. For women who come from Asian or African cultures their value as women is based on their virginity, and goodness is synonymous with purity. Because women are considered to be the property and "honor" of men, rape victims are considered "ruined" and are ostracized by their communities. They lose all value in society and are rejected by their families who feel they have been shamed. This is further supported by the Islamic, Buddhist, Taoist and Catholic religious philosophies in which "fate" plays a large role. Rape victims of Muslim faith believe that rape is a punishment for some sin which they have committed. Similarly, Buddhist rape victims attribute their tragedy to "karma," or destiny. Thus, in addition to being ostracized by their families and societies, refugee women who have been raped often blame themselves for their tragedy and feel ruined and ashamed (Wali, 1990).

In response to these feelings, women refugees who have been raped are often unwilling to disclose their experiences to refugee workers. "A Winnipeg study found that over 1/2 of rape victims and 94% of other sexual assault victims didn't tell any professional outsider about the assault" (Pope, 1990, p.8). Instead of seeking help for rape, often women will approach a relief worker with psychosomatic symptoms related to her experience. Symptoms of post-traumatic stress are similar to those of nonrefugee rape victims. They include depression, loss of appetite, anger, a sense of hopelessness about the future, fear of strangers, or feeling dirty. Much like other rape victims, a woman may be deeply disturbed if left alone, or she may feel uncomfortable having other people near her. The worker must be trained to recognize the situation and respond appropriately. Understanding such cultures and religions and their ideologies regarding rape is central to the role of the refugee worker in determining appropriate intervention mechanisms.

Like rape victims, male refugees also suffer psychological damage which can affect their emotional well being. Once out of immediate danger a refugee man may be angry for the horrible crimes which he has witnessed and feel guilty for having been unable to live up to his expected role in society and protect himself and his family. After witnessing massive episodes of pain and torture, the psychology of violence may numb him and, like children who have been abused, make him more likely to resort to violence himself.

RESETTLEMENT

Upon resettlement refugee families face a variety of challenges adapting to a new society. For most refugees this is their first experience in an industrialized country, and traditional social patterns often become confused. The stress involved in this process is further elevated by the psychological and emotional traumas which result from the refugee experience. Refugee men often feel victimized by their experience and feel that they have failed in their obligation to protect their families. This vulnerability, compounded by the frustration of resettlement, often leads refugee men to resort to domestic violence to recover power and control.

ESCAPE TRAUMA

Once a refugee family has successfully arrived in the United States to resettle, the physical and psychological impact of its past experience can hinder its move to self-sufficiency. The term "escape trauma" has been used to refer to the scars left from the experience of fleeing one's country to escape persecution.

Refugees are likely to have lost children. A survey conducted in a Cambodian refugee camp in Thailand found that 80% of women in the camp had lost three-fourths of their children in the past four years. In

Sudan, a survey conducted in March 1985 found that 34% of the women in one camp had lost at least one child in the previous four months (Berry, 1985, p.36). As most refugees have lost family members through war, persecution or illness (i.e., epidemics, starvation), they often arrive with feelings of guilt at having survived when so many others did not. This guilt only compounds the grief traditionally associated with the loss of loved ones.

Refugees also face the distress of leaving their homeland with no knowledge of when, or if, they will be able to return. They often try to recreate their culture in countries of resettlement, waiting for the time when they can return home. This is particularly painful if a refugee has lost social status once held among their community. In addition, most refugees have lost the traditional support system of their extended family, and are forced to find new emotional support.

Escape trauma can be serious, and can be responsible for a range of symptoms including severe depression, anger, hostility, nightmares, insomnia, and waking memories (Mollica, 1988). Thus, memories of destruction and devastation can be both long-lasting and debilitating.

ECONOMIC OBSTACLES

In addition to psychological obstacles, most refugees arrive in the United States with little or no money and depend on limited federal assistance. Like millions of others, they can easily become caught in the cycle of poverty. A shortage of affordable housing and childcare, and lack of accessible health care are just a few of the economical obstacles refugees face. Employment is often hard to find, especially with language barriers. Even refugees who were well educated are often forced to resort to unskilled labor in order to survive.

SOCIAL ROLES

In their home countries women were responsible for the family and home, and primarily associated with other females or male family members. In countries of resettlement where it is difficult to support a family, women are often forced to work outside of the home for the first time. This is the most common alteration in family roles and responsibilities, and can create tension within the family. Especially for a male refugee who is unemployed or underemployed and whose sense of identity is already challenged, his wife's offer to work may be perceived as an indication that she is ignoring familial responsibilities and has lost respect for her traditional role.

Women are also confused by their new roles. Suddenly they are responsible for a job in addition to their caretaking responsibilities. When refugees arrive in the United States, they are often amazed at the independence of American women. Everyday chores like going to the grocery store often entail learning new skills including using public transportation and dealing with family finances. These activities are made more difficult since refugees are expected to learn a new language.

Contributing to this frustration, many women report feeling anxious about their children's assimilation into American culture. While refugee women are left isolated and struggling, their children are swept into the school system and immersed into a culture which their parents find unfamiliar. Refugee women feel their culture and traditions slipping away. Some complain that their children spend too much time watching T.V. and not enough time helping their parents or grandparents. To them, this is a sign that traditional methods of respect are being eroded by laziness and materialism. They also worry that their children will become involved in drugs and/or violence. The cultures from which most refugee families in the United States originate place great importance on families and familial responsibility. Refugee women often feel that they have lost control over their children, the only thing of importance still intact in their lives.

IMPLICATIONS

With the confusion of social roles and frustration of economic difficulties, the stress of resettlement can be overwhelming. For refugee men, the experience of war and escape leave psychological anxieties regarding their personal strength and sense of identity. Men who have been victims of persecution, especially men whose wives or daughters have been raped in their presence, feel a sense of failure at not having been able to protect themselves or their loved ones. Often termed "heightened male vulnerability," this feeling is exacerbated by resettlement trauma and financial struggles. In response, many refugee men turn to domestic violence as a way to reestablish control and increase their power.

This is especially true if a woman has been raped. Men are more likely to abuse a rape victim as her status in the community has been lost. Women also blame themselves and feel that they do not have the rights or resources to oppose such treatment.Refugee women who have relocated in the United States are not aware that domestic violence is illegal. Although the problem is widespread, it is often kept a secret as the result of the social, political, and religious customs in which refugees have been raised. Women believe that domestic problems are private and should not be discussed with non-familial members. Since such silence exists, refugee women feel isolated and are unaware of how widespread domestic violence actually is.

If a woman does discuss her situation, it is usually in private with either a female relative or close friend. However, these women are unaware of available resources and act more as support than as a solution. A refugee woman may consult a community leader such as a priest, or an elder who is widely respected. In most cases, however, these leaders also feel that domestic violence is a private matter and advise the woman to respect her husband and obey his decisions. Thus the women are left with no other choice but to return home and accept the situation.

Although awareness regarding the seriousness of domestic violence among refugee communities has increased and community groups have been created to assist refugee victims of domestic violence, there is a general reluctance to approach such help as it carries negative connotations. In his article on post traumatic therapy, Richard Mollica discusses several reasons why refugees avoid mental health resources. In many societies, especially among Southeast Asian cultures, there is an extreme stigma associated with mental illness. "Many refugees" explains Mollica, "associate shame and humiliation with their perceived need to seek help for a 'broken mind or spirit'" (1988, p.300-1). Apart from cultural barriers, many refugees have a well-founded fear of endangering their immigration status. Both within the camps, where refugees who have been diagnosed with major psychiatric disorders are denied resettlement, and in the United States, where refugees fear that their citizenship may be threatened, refugees avoid any association with mental health resources which they feel could threaten their immigration status (Mollica, 1988).

Refugee women are the pillars of their large families, caring for both children and the elderly. When a woman's health is endangered, the health of her entire family suffers making the move to self-sufficiency difficult. Both rape trauma and domestic violence have side effects which threaten the women's ability to care for their families. Refugee women's health and protection needs must be addressed not only by the international community, but by mainstream health practitioners in countries of resettlement as well.

RECOMMENDATIONS

In order to appropriately address these issues, a comprehensive plan must be developed. Protection overseas, and domestic violence in the United State must addressed by both international and domestic health providers.

OVERSEAS

Although refugee women who have been victims of rape are unlikely to discuss their experiences, there are steps which service providers in the camps can undertake to identify rape victims. The first and most obvious sign that a woman has been raped is physical injury. Even if she seeks help for a physical injury, however, a refugee woman is not likely to disclose what happened. Service workers must be trained and willing to recognize the symptoms and devise an appropriate response.

In an innovative chapter written for a soon-to-be-published handbook addressed to workers inside refugee camps, Sima Wali (RefWID) outlines some methods for recognizing victims of rape. Once a refugee worker recognizes that a woman is suffering from symptoms of rape trauma, background records can help to clarify her situation. For example, if a refugee's records indicate that she crossed the South China Sea in a boat and she appears to be suffering from rape trauma, it is likely that she was either raped or witnessed the raping of others by pirates.

As a result of the cultural attitudes toward rape, women who have been victims are often ostracized by their communities. When families learn that a woman has been raped, she is considered worthless and a source of humiliation for them. Listening closely to community members can reveal whether a woman is being ostracized or isolated by her community. This is a good sign that she has been raped.

Through this handbook, it is hoped that workers will get a better idea of how to recognize rape victims. Once a refugee worker has established that a woman has been raped, the chapter gives some suggestions on how to respond appropriately. Most important, considering the ostracism placed upon victims by their community, Wali stresses confidentiality. The victim must feel that she can trust the worker to keep her ordeal a secret. It must always be assumed that the woman has not revealed her experience to anyone, as refugee victims often keep rape a secret from their families, even their husbands (Wali, 1990).

IN COUNTRIES OF RESETTLEMENT

In many cases, mainstream health workers are the first people to come in contact with refugee victims of domestic violence. Like refugees in camps, refugees in the U.S. often seek medical help for psychosomatic symptoms related to rape or resettlement trauma. In order to effectively address the problem of domestic violence within refugee communities, mainstream workers need to be able to identify such symptoms and know what resources are available to the victims. Training about refugees and their experience is essential for health workers, especially those working near areas with high refugee populations. As with refugee workers in camps, the first step is education. Training on domestic violence should be incorporated into mainstream programs such as medical and nursing schools, and those likely to come in contact with refugees should be given additional training in dealing with refugee families.

Bicultural workers must be incorporated to assist mainstream (non-ethnic) service providers. Refugee women are more likely to be open and comfortable with women of their own ethnicity. This can also help address language barriers between refugee women and counselors.

In response to this need, RefWID has developed and tested a model for training refugee and mainstream service providers. RefWID has conducted training sessions across the country focused on teaching service providers culturally appropriate methods to working with refugee victims of domestic violence. The sessions are based on a manual entitled "Understanding Domestic Violence within US Refugee Communities" which is the outcome of the development and successful pilot test of a training program (Richie, 1988).

Educating the refugee community is another important step towards reducing domestic violence. Unless victims use available resources, intervention mechanisms cannot work. Successful education depends both on the ability of refugee women to speak out about their situation, and the willingness of the community to listen. Refugee women must be given the resources for empowerment, including leadership and organizational training, to enable them to better communicate with each other. By breaking their isolation, refugee women will realize that domestic violence is a widespread problem which together they can defeat.

Since refugee women often approach community leaders for advice, these leaders must also be educated about domestic violence and rape trauma. Whether they are religious leaders such as monks, or social leaders such as respected elders, their attitudes toward domestic violence and rape trauma set a precedent for the rest of the community. Leaders must be educated through culturally appropriate methods concerning the legal aspects of domestic violence, and the implications of traditional attitudes which place blame on the victim.

CONCLUSION

Domestic violence is a problem which can impair any family's self-sufficiency. For refugee families who have escaped terrifying and life-threatening situations to resettle in a new country, the trauma of escape and stress involved in acculturation can provoke the use of violence against women.

Refugee women who have resettled in the United States are a resourceful element commonly overlooked. They flee their homes amidst gunfire, cross dangerous and life-threatening borders, and provide care for large families within a system which provides minimal assistance. Their mere survival is a symbol of their strength. Despite suffering horrifying problems, refugee women demonstrate remarkable capabilities in creating better lives for themselves and their families.

Refugee women are the emotional support of their families and communities. They are responsible for educating and transmitting culture to their children, and caring for children and the elderly. When these women are consulted and included in the development process, their families move more quickly and successfully into economic and social self-sufficiency.

The health of refugee women must be addressed by the international community, as well as by health care professionals in the United States. A comprehensive method must be undertaken in order to effectively address issues of protection for refugee women. (1) The international community must be willing to dedicate the necessary attention and resources to prevent sexual violence. (2) Mainstream health and social workers in the United States must be trained to recognize and appropriately address the issue of domestic violence among refugee families. (3) Refugee women need access to the skills and resources necessary for self-empowerment. Only when health care professionals recognize their role in extending services to refugee women can comprehensive programs be developed.

NOTES

1. According to the 1961 Convention relating to the Status of Refugees, a refugee is any person who, owing to a well-founded fear of being persecuted for reasons of race, religion, nationality, membership in a particular social group, or political opinion, is outside the country of his/her nationality and is unable or, owing to such fear, is unwilling to return to that country.

2. Although rape is often used as a form of torture, it is not included in the 1961 Convention relating to the status of refugees. As a result, women who are in danger of sexual assault/rape cannot claim that they are in fear of being tortured, and may not be granted refugee status.

3. Refugees, by definition, are outside their country of origin. The issue of rape, however, is relevant for displaced persons, or those who have fled similar situations but are still inside of their own borders, as well.

4. Although it is rarely discussed as an issue of protection, refugee women are also faced with rape by their own husbands.

REFERENCES

Berry, A. (1985). Declaration on training. Proceedings, *Refugee women: A round table organized by the United Nations High Commissioner for Refugees* (pp. 36-38). Geneva, Switzerland.

Brahm, S., Soland, M., & Swain, P. (January 1986). *The rape experience of refugee women resettled in the United States.* Manuscript, Washington, D.C.: RefWID.

Kelley, N. (April 1990). Refugee women and protection: criteria and practices for determining refugee status. *Summary of comments made at the CRDD working group on women refugee claimants: Training workshop for members, RHO's and legal services.* Toronto, Canada.

Kelley, N. (1989). *Working with refugee women: A practical guide.* Geneva: United Nations High Commissioner for Refugees.

Mollica, R. (1988). The trauma story: The psychiatric care of refugee survivors of violence and torture. In F. Ochberg (Ed.), *Post-traumatic therapy and victims of violence* (pp. 295-314). New York: Brunner/Mazel.

Overhagen, M. van. (1990). Introduction. M. van den Engel (Ed.), *VENA Newsletter: Refugee and displaced women* (V2, n2, pp. 3-6). The Netherlands.

Pope, L. (April 1990). Refugee protection and determination: Women claimants. *Summary of comments made at the CRDD working group on women refugee claimants: Training workshop for members, RHO's and legal services.* Toronto, Canada.

Richie, B. (1988). *Understanding family violence within U.S. refugee communities.* Washington, D.C.: RefWID.

Siemens, M. (1988). Protection of refugee women. *Refugees* (pp. 21-22). Geneva: United Nations High Commissioner for Refugees.

Taft, J. (1987). *Issues and options for refugee women in developing countries.* Washington, D.C.: Refugee Policy Group.

Wali, S. (1990). *Female refugee victims of sexual violence: Rape trauma and its impact on refugee resettlement.* Manuscript, Washington, D.C.: RefWID.

Wali, S. (1991). *Rape trauma and its effect on refugee women and their communities.* Manuscript, Washington, D.C.: RefWID.

Soviet Jewish Refugee Women: Searching for Security

Deborah Fuller Hahn

SUMMARY. In the following article, you will meet some typical Soviet Jewish refugee women. Three came to America more than a decade ago, the others within the last eighteen months. Although they are from different regions and diverse backgrounds, their stories bear a common thread of the effects of living under totalitarian rule. They suffered anti-Semitism on the streets and sexual harassment in the work place. Yet even wife battering, overcrowded living conditions, and daily governmental repression would not induce any of them to seek professional help. Stress and trauma were never to be mentioned outside the family.

The Soviet Union is a vast country, glasnost and rebellions not withstanding, that is still ruled with an iron fist. Women in such a system bear the daily burden of that society. Almost every woman is employed full time outside the home, while she is expected to care for and maintain the family within the home. It is a country where everything from food to household items is difficult to obtain and there are few consumer goods to buy, even when money is available. A Russian proverb sums up the situation: "Women do everything! Men do the rest."

Working with Soviet Jewish refugee women has been both a joy and a remarkable learning experience. As President of the Jewish Family Service of Broward County, Florida, I was charged with the responsibility of resettling refugees when they arrived in our community. When my term of office expired, I assumed the position of chair of the Resettlement

Deborah Fuller Hahn is Past President of Jewish Family Service of Broward County, FL, life member of the Women's Division of the Ft. Lauderdale Jewish Federation, and a member of the Board of Directors of *Lilith* magazine. She is a freelance journalist.

Committee. I have had the unique opportunity to become acquainted with many women who have emigrated to America. They were born and bred in such diverse places as Leningrad, Odessa and Latvia, as well as Lithuania, Kiev and Moscow, and other cities and towns too difficult for an American tongue to easily pronounce. They originate from a variety of backgrounds and represent all ages and stages of life. The women I have chosen to discuss are very different individual people, yet they have common attitudes and similar ideas about life in the Soviet Union and the role of women in that country. Although the names have been changed, the stories are authentic. Their common goal in America is to find the security so elusive in the land of their birth.

One beautiful Sunday afternoon, I invited a group of our resettled refugee women to my home for coffee. The setting was relaxed and friendly. As we sat on the terrace and enjoyed the sun, it seemed more like an afternoon with old friends than a professional meeting. After a few moments, they ignored the presence of my tape recorder and spoke freely of their lives in the Soviet Union. I had prepared a series of questions that guided the discussion. At times, I had some difficulty in keeping the conversation in English rather than Russian. But I continued to marvel at the command of English in this group of people unable to speak the language only a few short years ago. These women have all become friends in their adopted community of Coral Springs, Florida. The one exception is Faina. Her story was told to me at a separate time.

It is hard for anyone raised in the freedom of the United States to comprehend living with the fear and anxiety of a totalitarian regime. Adina recalls that her earliest memory is that of her father, now 82, telling her that someday she would leave the country. He said it was a "bad system, especially for Jews." When she was a youngster, growing up in the city of Kishinev in Moldavia, she did not always agree with him. Under her parents' protective roof she felt safe. Once she was married, however, she recognized that everywhere Jews turned they faced hardship and anti-Semitic discrimination. Eleven years ago she, and her family, decided it was indeed time to leave. It was too late. By the end of 1979 the government of the USSR had closed the gates. In 1989, her older daughter Luba, now a married woman of 20, applied for an exit visa with her own husband. Adina realized the wisdom of her father's words and understood her own daughter's action. The doors were again beginning to open, if only a crack. It was possible to dream of a better life. The entire family left everything–jobs, friends, and most of their possessions–in Kishinev and started on a long, frightening journey. The traveling party consisted of Adina, her husband, Igor, their 12 year old daughter, and married daughter and son-in-law, with his parents, his grandmother and Adina's elderly parents. Unexplainably, they were also permitted to bring the family's small dog.

Their exit visas and papers in order, the group of ten people and the little Scottie boarded a train to Czechoslovakia. It was a harrowing experience, filled with apprehension and uncertainty. A week later they were in Vienna, where they were told they must go to a certain small town outside of Rome. It had been a popular Italian summer resort called Ladispoli. Now thousands of Soviet Jews waited. Here they spent several months until the representatives of the United States Immigration and Naturalization Service (INS) and the Hebrew Immigrant Aid Society (HIAS) were able to place them with our community in America. They arrived in Florida on December 20, 1989, during the height of the Christmas tourist season. Five pieces of luggage were lost en route. Allowed to take only two suitcases per person from the Soviet Union, they had been severely limited in the kinds of things they could pack. The USSR officials had told them exactly what could be taken out of the country. Family pictures were on the list of the many forbidden items. "Someone might have been photographed standing near a secret installation." Adina remembered, "All my life I had certain things . . . the government now says I cannot keep them. I must leave a piece of myself behind. My whole life was being put in two bags." Precious space also had to be used in the family's suitcases to carry food for the journey. Money was likewise limited. It was to be spent very sparingly. Each person leaving Russia is only permitted to carry the equivalent of $90.

Adina's parents were practicing Jews, in Moldavia, before religion was outlawed during the Russian revolution 70 years ago. When Adina was married she had a secret "Jewish wedding" in her parents' apartment, in addition to the usual state ceremony. Twenty one years later it was considered dangerous for her eldest daughter, Luba, to have such an indulgence. The young couple was married at the official Moldavian wedding hall.

Adina had been an economist in the Soviet Union. She held a very responsible position with a large industrial firm. She and her fellow workers belonged to a women's workers union. When asked if she belonged to any other groups, women's clubs or women's organizations, Adina cited only the workers' union. After work, members would get together and talk about common problems. Their discussions centered mostly on ways to obtain "hard-to-get goods" for the families. Personal problems were never mentioned. She confided, "No one wanted to be labeled as needing mental or emotional help. You could never risk the stigma of being seen as upset or under stress. It could lead to dismissal.'' If one needed advice or help with personal matters it was kept within the family or close intimate friends. This attitude is very common among women born in the Soviet Union. When asked her opinion of ''going for professional help'' Adina replied, ''I think you have to work it out with yourself.'' Today, in south Florida, she is employed as a bookkeeper and confides only in her daughter, Luba.

Regina arrived in the United States on August 2, 1979 with her husband, Alex, and two sons of three and five years old. For one year, they had tried to obtain the necessary permission to leave the Soviet Union. She and her husband, an accountant, lived in a private house with their two children in the Ukraine. For six years she was a practicing dentist in a small village near her home. Eleven invitations had been sent to the family from relatives in Israel–not one was received. These invitations were required by the Soviet government as proof of ''family reunion.'' It was generally believed that without one there was no exit. Suddenly, in the spring of 1979, Regina and Alex were issued visas allowing them to go to America. They had taken the chance on a direct application to the United States several months earlier. They were given exactly two weeks to pack their two suitcases each, say their goodbyes, settle their affairs and reach Moscow–it was a traumatic time. She recalls, ''We were the last to leave, the doors shut immediately after us. My family applied eight weeks later and were denied.''

Most of Regina's family remained in Russia in 1979 and became ''refuseniks.'' Refuseniks were not only the famous activists whose trials were widely reported in the world media–they were also the ordinary people who requested exit visas and were refused permission to leave. Although most refuseniks never made any headlines, all were subjected to ''special'' harassment in the work place. Very often they lost their jobs as ''enemies of the state.'' Their children were taunted at school for being ''unpatriotic and dirty Jews.'' Alex's brother, Boris, and his wife, Dina, arrived in America just four months ago, after ''living in refusal'' for over a decade. Today once again, as they did in the Ukraine, the two families live only a few blocks from each other. Dina spends much of her time at ESL (English Second Language) classes and has started working. She has a wonderful role model in her sister-in-law, Regina.

Regina remembers that they were welcomed very warmly into the Jewish community of Jacksonville, Florida, when they came to America. Her first job was as an assistant in a dentist's office. She longed to be a professional dentist again. With the help of scholarships, she enrolled in school to obtain an American license. For a while, it was difficult to go back to being a student. Persistence paid off and when she again became a licensed dentist, she was able to buy a small practice in Broward County, Florida. The family relocated once more. Today, she is very successful in her career and helps newly arriving refugees. Her husband has become a stock broker, a pursuit unheard of in the Soviet Union. Regina admits that even with her professional training and over a decade in America, she keeps her personal problems to herself. She still does not comprehend why anyone would seek professional therapy. She admits that this is likely ". . . a prejudice left over from years under the Soviet system. I was probably brainwashed. But," she continued, "there is much I need to yet understand about American ways, and am I learning more all the time."

Svetlana is 33 years old. She came to America from Kiev eighteen months ago. She and her husband, Sasha, have two children, six and seven years old. Her parents and two brothers remain in Russia. They have been waiting for their exit papers for over one year. She also misses the family pictures they were forced to leave behind, especially those of her children as babies. She said, "The government changes its mind every day. What is true today is not true tomorrow. It is hard to trust anyone." Svetlana, who was trained as a teacher, was the principal of a kindergarten in Kiev. She has a diploma in psychology from the university, yet admitted that women in the Soviet Union could not go to a psychologist. "Women, especially Jewish women, in Russia, talk only to their families or intimate friends. Most will try to solve any problems alone." She related a story of a close friend. In Svetlana's own words:

"Natasha was a very intelligent and beautiful young Jewish woman who felt that she needed some professional help. She went to a psychoneurologist who made out of her a case. He sent her to an asylum. There they used shock therapy on her. They destroyed her, completely. She was not a person anymore. She needed only someone to tell her, 'You are young, you are smart, you are nice, you are not sick.' She needed these words to tell her to get better. Her parents were divorced. She lived sometimes with father and sometimes with mother. She was not happy and decided, 'I am sick. I have to go to a doctor.' She believed the doctor could make her feel better about herself. She didn't know that once you get into an asylum you never get out. As soon as you get there . . . this is it. It's over. So everybody's afraid. It is really very common."

Ludmila considers herself an American. She has been in this country since 1979 and last year received her United States citizenship papers. She left her native city of Odessa in the Ukraine after a 15 month struggle to get the exit visas. Although the family was denied three times for various reasons, including a trumped up charge of being "a security risk," they were finally allowed to emigrate. Ludmila's husband decided that they should head for the United States.

Ludmila says, "All my life I wanted to be a teacher, but at the time, in Odessa, there was no way a Jewish girl could get into a teaching institution. I got into the engineering college because my father knew someone. I got a job as an engineer. I was supposed to draw things . . . I don't know . . . I hated it. Mostly I would be expected to get things for my boss. He was a married man and he had me run his errands. I waited in long lines for eggs, or to pay his bills. I would spend whole days in lines for my boss, yet I was called an engineer."

"If I have a problem today, in my private life, I would only speak to my husband or Anya. My son was having a difficult time in school, but the school psychologist didn't understand him. He couldn't know what we have gone through. Personal understanding is very important to me."

Faina came to south Florida from Leningrad. She worked as a hairdresser in the Soviet Union, although she has a graduate degree as an architect. It was extremely difficult for a woman, particularly a Jewish woman, to obtain employment as an architect. There was much money to be made as a hairdresser, especially in tips from foreign visitors. But anti-Semitism was, and still is, rampant on the streets of Leningrad–and it is officially sanctioned. She never felt secure. As the years went by, she worried about the safety of her teenage daughter. Faina decided it was vital they leave Leningrad. She arrived in the United States in June of 1989 with her daughter and young son, her elderly mother, and husband, Anatoly. Faina had just turned 34 years old. Since she had held a second job as a guide in the Hermitage Art Museum in Leningrad, her English language skills are excellent. Three months after her arrival she obtained a Florida license and a job in a local beauty salon. Meanwhile, Anatoly was experiencing difficulties with the English language and could not hold a job. One day Faina called me for lunch . . .

Over a friendly cup of coffee, she confided that Anatoly was a heavy drinker and had struck her on more than one occasion. He had promised to change his behavior when they came to America, but this was not the case. She felt that if I could find him a job perhaps it would stop. I urged her to go to a therapist and explained the benefits of counseling. If she would see a counselor at our agency she would be assured of confidentiality and she certainly would feel better. After much resistance she agreed to make an appointment. This was the first of several appointments she would schedule and cancel. Finally she decided to move to New York. Her husband convinced Faina that he could find a job in a bigger city, and would then give up the Vodka. She told me, "Look . . . I don't need help. He does. If he didn't drink he wouldn't be so mean. He's okay when he's not drinking. Sometimes he can drink for several days. Then the kids hide and my mother comes to work with me. If we go to New York there will be more opportunity for him. We will be alright."

Faina telephoned recently, late at night, from her apartment in Brooklyn. During a drunken binge, Anatoly had beaten her so severely that she called the police. He was told to move out. One week later, in defiance of a restraining order, he broke into her home and beat her ailing 79 year old mother. The 15 year old daughter climbed out of a bedroom window and ran to get help. Anatoly was jailed for less time than her mother was in the hospital. I asked Faina if she was going for personal help or counseling and offered assistance in finding a suitable program. Again she refused, still insisting it was not her problem, but his. Although ordered by the judge to do so, she does not know if Anatoly will go for treatment. It is also possible that he might carry out threats made against her and her family. It was very clear that calling the police and going to court was a difficult move for this woman. Perhaps in time she will be able to accept the special assistance that she needs.

Anya's grandmother was the driving force in her family. She was a very strong woman who led the family in a decision to leave their home in Moscow even before the Yom Kippur War in Israel in 1973. This is generally conceded to be the first time Soviet Jews felt they had a place to go which would welcome them and be free of the daily terror of anti-Semitism. With great difficulty, Grandfather used to listen, in secret, to "The Voice of Israel" on the radio. If anyone found out about this deed, the entire family could be arrested. Even when Anya was a child, she always knew of her parents' and grandparents' desire to go to Israel. They became a three-generation family of refuseniks.

Six years later she met Vladimir. He was also a refusenik and more than a few of his friends had been thrown in jail for "illegal" activity. The young couple knew each other only three weeks before they married, but they had a common goal–to leave the Soviet Union. Vladimir wanted to go to America. Anya says, "I could not stand that country any more. If he wanted to go to America it was fine by me." They applied for exit visas the day after the wedding and received permission three months later. Anya liked to sew. She recalled that at the border, Soviet Customs officers confiscated some dress patterns that she had taken with her. "Did they look like military plans," she asks?

Today, Anya is a resettlement case worker with Jewish Family Service.

In spite of the fact that she observes people being helped through counseling, she feels the role of the agency (in resettling) is merely to see that everyone has a home and a job. When asked, she commented, "Soviet women cannot relate to professional people in their personal lives. It is not part of their character. They never learned to trust "the system." The agency is, of course, part of that system." Nevertheless, in the ten years she has lived in America, Anya has come to believe that it is important to belong to a group. Explaining, " . . . we all need people who will cry with you and laugh with you and let you be yourself." She defines happiness as, "having a friend who understands you."

Sonia's husband was severely beaten in a vicious anti-Semitic attack in a back ally in Lithuania five years ago. The hoodlums broke both his knees while shouting, "This is what happens when Jews want to leave mother Russia." Immediately after applying for departure permits in 1979, Sonia and Yacov lost their jobs and their comfortable apartment. The local authorities refused to allow them any other living accommodations. They, and their young son, were forced to move in with relatives. For ten years, 13 people took turns eating and sleeping in two rooms. Yacov did menial labor to earn wages, although he was an experienced tool and dye maker.

In 1989 they finally received permission to emigrate. When there were waiting at the train station in Vilnius a man approached Sonia, swinging his fist at her face. He broke her nose, all the while screaming, "Take this with you, Jew." Yacov and Sonia are sure that both attacks were perpetrated by the KGB. It was many months before Sonia would venture outdoors alone. She is still painfully shy around people that she does not know.

Stories such as these are very typical among the Soviet Jewish women who have emigrated to this country. All of the women told of the long lines they stood on each day for the most basic necessities of life. After a full day of work, they were obliged to wait for hours, sometimes with little or no success, in lines to obtain items such as shoes for the children or meat for the table. The hard lives that these women lived in their native land make them appear at least 20 years older than their counterparts in the United States. Yet every one of them spoke of the future with hope. Freedom of choice is a new and valuable concept. Their common desire is for security. To each individual, "security" is of a very personal nature. Some yearn for economic security. Almost all have university degrees. They need to be productive citizens of their chosen land. Others pray for peaceful lives, secure from the harassment and fear of governmental authorities. They all ask for religious security, so that their children can be taught their own heritage without fear of imprisonment or persecution. They are just discovering customs, and enjoying ceremonies that were formerly unavailable to them. Perhaps, in time, these women will leave the traumas behind and learn to trust themselves and others. Only then will each person be able to live up to her full potential.

Displaced Women in Settings
of Continuing Armed Conflict

Michael D. Roe

SUMMARY. Based on interview data and observations primarily from Central America and the Philippines, this article reviews the psychosocial adaptation of women forced to flee their homes due to armed conflict, but who remain in settings of war violence. The pervasive danger and fear in such settings impedes progress toward psychological and social equilibrium. These women experience terror, a spectrum of war-related emotional traumas, gender and family role instabilities, and sexual vulnerabilities. These women may also experience empowerment in the midst of armed conflict through the formation of new communities in which they share the leadership, through filling essential roles within these communities, and through conscientization, in which they both analyze and take action against political and economic oppression and gender subordination.

Emelinda is a middle aged campesina (peasant farmer woman) of El Salvador. She and her immediate family fled Chalatenango in late

Michael D. Roe, PhD, is Professor and Chair of Psychology at Seattle Pacific University. He embraces an "action research" orientation for confronting questions in cross-cultural life span development. He has worked with and has been mentored by refugee peoples around the globe, and considers it a serious responsibility to help make their experiences known and their voices heard.

This article reflects the author's observations in settings of violent displacement, as well as the observations of committed colleagues in Central America and the Philippines. Many of these settings must remain unnamed and these colleagues anonymous for their protection. For similar reasons, pseudonyms are used in the case examples. The tenuous nature of life and liberty in armed conflict regions was tragically substantiated in the 1989 assassination of our valued colleague, Salvadoran social psychologist, Ignacio Martin-Baro. He was an unfailing voice on behalf of the violently displaced in his country.

1985 after the military killed a number of her siblings including her sister, who was also raped and mutilated. Emelinda's family moved into a closed refugee camp outside the capital, San Salvador. Following a few months of camp life they moved onto their own land purchased with a loan from a church. They lived independently on their land for two months until May 23, 1986, when the army came and captured Emelinda's husband. He was injured during the capture, held incommunicado in a clandestine jail, and tortured for twelve days. He was then incarcerated in political prison for crimes unknown to him. During the period her husband was incommunicado, Emelinda and the children remained on their land. Repeatedly the army came to their home and threatened her and her children. Soldiers had already sexually abused a woman nearby, and Emelinda was terrified that she too would become one of their sexual victims. She and her now broken family moved back into the refugee camp.

Fely is a middle aged peasant farmer of the Philippines. She was the elected leader of her village, a Base Christian Community (BCC) in Cotabato Province of Mindanao. On May 12, 1988, following a military-insurgency battle nearby, soldiers entered Fely's village to confront her and the other women. (The men of the village had fled from the soldiers into the surrounding forests and hills, because of their greater risk of being killed. In fact, that same day three men were pulled from their Nipa hut homes in a neighboring village, beaten, and shot to death by soldiers.) Fely was warned that any inhabitants found in her village when the soldiers returned would be killed. The following day, May 13, 1988, the soldiers did return and burned the village to the ground. Fely refused to consider herself helpless. Although displaced, she remained in the region and joined with a local human rights organization to file a formal complaint of human rights violation against the military for its actions.

The telling of Fely's story occurred among the burned ruins of her village, two weeks following the incident. She had already begun her formal action against the military. She stood straight, and with a determined look on her face, spoke of the violence against her people. In her words and actions, Fely was clearly demonstrating self-efficacy (Bandura, 1982). The telling of Emelinda's story occurred in her husband's cell in the political prison, also two weeks following her incident. This was her first contact with him since he was captured. She sat quietly with grief worn face, head down, leaning forward, with her arms folded over her stomach. In many ways her demeanor and posture were characteristic of Schaef's description of women in identity turmoil, protecting their "caverns" (1981, p. 34). In her silence and retreat, Emelinda was demonstrating helplessness (Wortman & Brehm, 1975), at least at that point in time. (Emelinda's story was not at an end. The refugee camp to which she and her children fled was proactive in its programs, and a few years later they returned en masse to the land in a resettlement program.)

The experiences of Emelinda and Fely are representative of millions of women worldwide. They demonstrate the *vulnerabilities* and *potentialities* of displaced women who remain in settings of armed conflict.

WHEN SAFE HAVEN IS NOT FOUND

Violent displacement is the experience of a vast portion of the human population. Reports from the U. S. Committee for Refugees (1990), the Office of the United Nations High Commissioner for Refugees, and the United Nations Relief and Works Agency for Palestine Refugees in the Near East (UNICEF, 1986), indicate over 15 million people meet the criteria for *refugee* status; that is, over 15 million people have been forced to flee their homes and seek asylum in other countries. Although more difficult to determine, it is estimated that at least as many people are *internally displaced* worldwide (UNICEF, 1986). In other words, forced migration is the experience of approximately 30 million people.

Models of forced migration tend to reflect the *refugee* experience. Although their stages vary, these models generally focus on the period before flight, flight itself, reaching safety, resettlement or settlement, and then adjustment or acculturation (e.g., Guendelman, 1981; Stein, 1986). Such models are limited in their application to individuals who flee but never reach safety or for whom safety is tenuous at best. These individuals include many who are *refugee* women in asylum settings, but who face harassment, rape, physical violence, obligations for sexual favors, and so on, from residents and in some cases officials of the asylum countries (Amnesty International, 1991). They include many *refugee* women and their families who face border incursions and the subsequent armed violence of those same forces from whom they fled in their home countries (e.g., Dilling, 1984). They include many *refugee* women and their families who live under constant fear of deportation back to the settings of armed conflict in their home countries (e.g., Aron, 1990; Roe, 1987a). Individuals who never reach safe haven also include the vast majority of *internally displaced* women throughout the world.

PSYCHOSOCIAL EFFECTS OF ARMED
CONFLICT AND DISPLACEMENT

Continuing Terror

When safe haven is not found, displaced women in settings of armed conflict constantly face the reality that those forces from whom they fled can pursue them. For example, Nelia was a peasant farmer woman from Leyte Island in the Philippines. Due to work on behalf of the Aquino government, local supporters of former president Marcos branded Nelia and her co-workers "communists," and they became targets of local armed civilian bands known as vigilantes. At first they were forced to flee their land for the safety of a local town only at night. As the vigilante attacks became more severe, they fled their island completely to Manila on Luzon Island, and eventually to Cebu City on Cebu Island. The vigilantes followed. At the time Nelia's testimony was taken, June 18, 1988, she was incarcerated in a political prison on Cebu, ultimately the result of those vigilantes' testimony. Similarly in Guatemala, the government has practiced relocating informants from villages in armed conflict regions to settlements of the internally displaced, so that their informers could continue to testify against these victimized people (Manz, 1988).

This accessibility of displaced women to armed forces places them at risk for control through the systematic use of terror. Terror is a tool which can shatter what little personal and social equilibrium exists among these displaced persons. It is used to intimidate and discourage organizing, to disrupt community life, to dissuade support for the insurgents, and to force people to flee conflict regions (see Protacio-Marcelino, 1984; 1986; Roe, 1987b; in press). In El Salvador, the military terrorized a group of displaced campesino women and men living in the conflict region of Usulutan, with the threat that the day a soldier died in their area, the military would return and kill everyone in the settlement. In a closed refugee camp near San Salvador, random shooting outside the camp caused residents to run around frantically. Julia, a campesina washing clothes in the river which ran through the camp, began to weep, she then screamed and fainted.

Psychosocial Trauma

Displaced women in settings of armed conflict display the spectrum of emotional responses to war trauma which has been documented among children and adults of both genders around the world (e.g., Northern Ireland, Cairns, 1987; Fraser, 1973; Southeast Asia, Lin, Tazuma, & Masuda, 1979; Liu, 1979; Uganda, Dodge & Raundalen, 1987; Mozambique, McCallin & Fozzard, 1990; Israel, Baider & Rosenfield, 1974; Palestinian settings, Punamaki, 1986; Central America, Lykes, Costa, Iboraa, Maciel, & Suardi, 1990; McCallin, 1988; Roe, 1986; Philippines, Protacio-Marcelino, 1984; Roe, in press). These emotional responses include psychosomatic illnesses, depressions, grief, attitudes lacking futurity, sleep disorders, lethargy, nervousness and tremulousness, the complete symptomatology of clinical Post Traumatic Stress Disorder, as well as other psychiatric complaints. For example, Maria is a middle aged campesina who lived with her eleven year old daughter in an open settlement of about 10,000 displaced people in El Salvador. Fear permeated this settlement because of frequent military incursions. Maria was forced to flee her home in the countryside when five of her children were intentionally killed by soldiers, the youngest of which was her eight year old son. Her eleven year old daughter witnessed the killings and was traumatized. Maria suffers severe emotional disturbance and spends most of her waking moments weeping.

Maria's experience revealed an important relationship between emotional trauma to war and settings of continuing armed conflict. Her lack of safe haven exacerbated her immediate emotional trauma, complicated her recovery of psychosocial equilibrium, and increased her vulnerability to further stresses. In fact, she was particularly vulnerable to the systematic use of terror in her settlement by the soldiers.

Another trauma of displaced women in settings of armed conflict is surviving a "disappeared" husband. Emotionally, the uncertainty does not permit a complete grieving process to occur, even though few victims of "disappearance" survive. Economically, the woman is effectively widowed but may gain no access to what resources may be available to survivors. In Guatemala, for instance, the National Coordinating Committee of Widows has charged their government with withholding compensation to a widow unless she both claims that her husband's disappearance or death was due to insurgent forces, and she ceases to investigate her husband's case (Amnesty International, 1991).

Gender and Family Role Instabilities

Displacement due to armed conflict commonly results in the dissolution of community and family systems. Known social parameters, norms and expectations often become replaced with adaptations quite alien to past cultural and social values. This is particularly so in regards to gender roles. In the experiences of Fely and Nelia described above, it was the women who remained in the villages to face the soldiers while the men fled into hiding in the countryside. This was in contrast to their social expectation of "man as protector." Emelinda and Maria and Julia described above all lived in refugee settlements where women far outnumbered men, as is common in refugee settings throughout the world (e.g., McCallin & Fozzard, 1990). Emelinda and Maria were both single parents attempting to fill mother and father roles, and to deal with increased economic hardship resulting from the loss of a family breadwinner. This was in contrast to their social expectation of "man as provider." It is not uncommon for women such as these to express concern over their ability to fulfill both parental roles and adequately care for their children, and again this is evidenced in other settings of displacement (e.g., McCallin & Fozzard, 1990; Protacio-Marcelino, 1984). Consistent with these experiences of role instabilities, are the findings of the late Salvadoran social psychologist Ignacio Martin-Baro (Personal communication, Universidad CentroAmericana, San Salvador, June 6, 1986). Through intensive interviews with violently displaced campesino women and men, Martin-Baro found that they perceived one of their greatest needs to be the fulfillment again of adult gender roles. Martin-Baro considered the loss of those roles to be a significant contributor to the lowered self esteem he noted in those he interviewed.

The gender roles discussed above reflect traditional expectations associated with patriarchal social systems. As will be presented below, the short term instabilities and consequent difficulties experienced by such violently displaced women can evolve into opportunities to move beyond traditional gender boundaries and experience new levels of empowerment (see Giacaman, 1989).

In some refugee settings, traditional gender roles appear to provide at least short term adaptive advantages for women. Such settings included a closed refugee camp for Nicaraguans in Honduras which was almost entirely dependent on outside aid, and a refugee camp in El Salvador where residents had relatively more freedom of movement, but little to no work was available on either side of the camp boundaries. Also in this Salvadoran camp, cooperative arrangements for distributing work were discouraged by the government. In both settings, men had little access to traditional adult male roles, and consequently many were idle. In contrast, women continued to practice the traditional adult female roles of food preparation, housekeeping, and child rearing. The *short term* nature of this seeming advantage must be emphasized, for both settings tended to nurture high degrees of dependency in camp residents. Ultimately such dependency can be quite debilitating to both men and women, hindering their reentry into independent living. A Salvadoran refugee in Nicaragua aptly described this debilitation, when she called it the "decomposition" of dependency.

The dissolution of community and family may result in other outcomes, for example the removal of societal protections for women, leaving them vulnerable to physical abuse and sexual exploitation by men in their refugee settlements (e.g., McCallin & Fozzard, 1990; Roe, 1986). Perhaps most dramatic of these outcomes is when violently displaced persons are victimized by oppressors who are family members. Cora and her husband were among the Leyte Island displaced discussed previously. They fled Leyte following a military strafing of their home and field, and increased intimidation from neighbors who were vigilantes. They were imprisoned in Manila, where Cora gave birth to an infant who died two months later. Socialized in a culture with strong familial values, Cora felt particular need for family support during her flight and subsequent imprisonment. Unfortunately, she felt she could not communicate with her mother and brothers, because she was afraid of them. Her mother and brothers had been forced to participate with the same group of vigilantes who caused her violent displacement.

Sexual Vulnerability

Sexual humiliation, threat of rape, and rape, are common experiences of displaced women in settings of armed conflict (Amnesty International, 1991; Goldfeld, Mollica, Pesavento, & Faraone, 1988). Rape is "a conscious tactic of warfare" and in its horrific demonstration of power relations between the aggressor and victim, it is the "ultimate metaphor" for armed conflict (Reardon, 1985, p. 40). The pervasiveness of rape in armed conflict indicates a preconditioned readiness among combatants to use sexual aggression against women. Reardon (1985) argued that this readiness derives from two sources: Permission and dehumanization. That is, social or political legitimation to carry out the act, coupled with rationalizing a lesser value of the victim of the act. Numerous examples of "permission" and "dehumanization" exist in armed conflict settings. One example of "permission" was provided by Amnesty International (1990) in testimony before the U. S. Senate Foreign Relations Committee. In discussing Peruvian military operations in regions of armed insurgency, Amnesty International (AI) testified:

Peruvian Officials told AI representatives visiting Ayacucho in 1986 that rape was to be expected when troops were based in rural areas, that it was somehow "natural" and that prosecutions could not be expected. (p. 7)

An example of "dehumanization" was provided by the Salvadoran military in its basic training. The following chant accompanied calisthenics in a military base in San Salvador; it was overheard by a nurse working with the violently displaced in the region (Anonymous, personal communication, San Salvador, June 1, 1986).

We rape women. We shoot babies. Soldiers never die.

As the soldiers were becoming desensitized, those within hearing distance were becoming terrorized.

Rape of displaced women in armed conflict settings is utilized to accomplish a variety of purposes. It is used in physical torture and humiliation, intimidation and coercion, reprisal, and in demonstration of power distinctions. Rape is often faced alone, and involves helplessness, humiliation, lack of self esteem, and victimization. It is not surprising that Punamaki (1986) found all five of these characteristics associated with events perceived as most stress producing by the displaced women she studied.

At midnight on April 12, 1986, two Salvadoran soldiers dragged a 14 year old campesina from her home and gang raped her. The girl and her family were working land adjacent to a refugee camp in El Salvador. The land was owned by the camp, and its produce helped feed the camp residents. This one violent act physically tortured and humiliated the girl; intimidated both her family and a neighboring family, forcing them to flee; terrorized the refugee camp, disrupting its tenuous equilibrium; and graphically displayed power over the powerless.

EMPOWERMENT IN ARMED CONFLICT AND DISPLACEMENT

Reestablishing Communities

The previous sections revealed the great tragedies associated with violent displacement and armed conflict, and appropriately so. War can only be characterized as tragic, with non-combatants and combatants alike victimized. Among victims empowerment can occur with the building of new communities, even in settings of continuing armed conflict.

Under circumstances where community breaks down, effective psychosocial intervention into war traumas begins (and may end) with community development in its fullest sense, what Ignacio Martin-Baro called sociopolitical therapy (Lykes, 1990). In this process social systems are again established with known boundaries, social norms and expectations; however, the new social systems do not reflect traditional power relationships of the past. In this community development, women are not relegated to support positions, but share with men in idea generation, program initiation, and leadership (see Giacaman, 1989). Resulting communities take on a variety of forms, such as the "nuclear communities" formed among internally displaced in the sprawling and impersonal barrios outside urban centers, or the refugee camps administrated through self government and maintained through work cooperatives, or entire villages of displaced persons formed into Base Christian Communities where faith and community organizing go hand in hand (see Roe, 1988).

Displaced women in these communities reveal an identity which is grounded in their experiences with each other, as they work to break out of and eventually change, the oppressive systems in which they live. Lykes (1989) describes this as *social individuality*; that is, "a dialectical understanding of individuality and sociality grounded in an experience of social relations characterized by inequalities of power" (p. 166). According to Lykes (1989) this sense of self in social relationship and sociopolitical context, results in reconstructed definitions of mothering and care. This reconstruction in turn leads to collective actions to confront injustice, as has been accomplished by such groups as the Mothers and Grandmothers of the Plaza de Mayo in Argentina, the Association of Families of the Detained-Disappeared in Chile, the Mutual Support Group for Relatives of the Disappeared in Guatemala, the Committee of Mothers and Relatives of Political Prisoners, the Disappeared and the Assassinated in El Salvador, and so on. Supporting Lykes' analysis, Punamaki (1989) found that displaced Palestinian women perceived the *collective* facing of events related to their political struggle as least stress producing, even if the events in which they were participating had the potential to be life threatening.

Less formal in organization, this social sense of self was also revealed in the corporate refusal of violently displaced Guatemalan women to form a civil patrol in the model village of Chacaj, Huehuetenango, despite pressure from the military (Manz, 1988). Again, less formal in organization, this redefinition of mothering and care was revealed in a Palestinian mother's reconceptualizing of her personal maternal role within her collective role in the *Intifada* (Khass, 1989). As Khass (1989) described, she was standing outside an Israeli military court waiting for her son to be led in. When asked if she needed assistance, she replied, "No, not at all. Listen my dear, we have been paying this price for many years. Now for the first time, the world knows about it" (p. 147). And then when asked if she intended to bail her son out, she replied, "Oh no. I'm not going to give any money to the Israelis. Not a penny. I only want to see my son passing by. That's all" (p. 148).

Filling Essential Roles

Juanita was 23 years of age when she fled the horrors of El Salvador to become a refugee in Nicaragua. When she arrived in 1982 she was withdrawn and fearful. She was quickly processed through a refugee camp in Esteli, and then joined her sister and others to form a Salvadoran cooperative to cook and sell native Salvadoran food. Later she joined a sewing cooperative, and at the time of this interview in 1986, she had taken a position administrating a Salvadoran refugee child development cooperative in Managua. She was a well adjusted, vital and contributing member of the Salvadoran refugee community.

Cooperative efforts in which the violently displaced organize themselves according to their own needs and priorities can be quite successful in meeting physical, safety, and psychosocial needs. For example, in a closed refugee camp in El Salvador cooperative arrangements covered areas such as child care, agriculture, food preparation, sewing, and carpentry. In this camp, cooperatives facilitated the development of new communities by distributing responsibilities so that all were contributing to the survival and well being of the settlement. Cooperatives were used to help assimilate newly arrived displaced people by providing the recent arrivals with integral roles in the community and by providing them with an immediate peer group of cooperative members. The Salvadoran psychologists working with this camp reported important psychosocial consequences from this assimilative role, for people violently displaced from armed conflict tended to arrive in states of confusion and grief and often remained withdrawn and isolated from others unless purposefully drawn into the community (Anonymous, personal communication, El Salvador, June 4, 1986). Cooperatives also contributed in quite practical ways by teaching skills necessary to the settlement and often marketable on the outside, by increasing work efficiency, and by distributing material and human resources. In addition, they helped teach organizing skills, and provided opportunities to nurture leadership abilities in both women and men. These latter points, as well as the autonomy which resulted from community organizing, unfortunately marked this refugee camp for increased repression (see Roe, 1987b). The gang rape reported earlier was directed at this camp, and was a consequence of the camp's autonomy.

Among essential roles in these new communities are those which intervene into children and family needs. Child development is one such area of intervention. For example, one closed refugee camp in El Salvador provided parent education which included child development, and day care for children from birth to seven years which included nutrition, medical, and psychological programming. In another closed camp in El Salvador a day care center for approximately 200 children from three months to five years was run by 17 mothers who had been trained in child education and child health.

Paraprofessional training of mothers is also occurring for intervention into mental health issues of their children and families. A Filipino psychologist reported that the Children's Rehabilitation Center in the Philippines was training parents to be paraprofessionals and program designers for those children who were traumatized by the armed conflict (Anonymous, personal communication, Child Rehabilitation Center, Quezon City, Philippines, June 2, 1988). Although not in a conflict region, a similar program was being considered in Zambia among Mozambican refugee mothers (McCallin & Fozzard, 1990). In El Salvador, a group of psychologists who worked clandestinely with violently displaced people were training members of the displaced communities to be "mental health promoters," using group processes to work with such issues as self esteem, cultural elements in the social environment of campesino women and men which were damaging to their psychosocial health (e.g., religious fatalism), and Salvadoran sociopolitical realities (Anonymous, personal communication, San Salvador, June 7, 1986).

The impact of such paraprofessional training is evidenced in a variety of ways. There is the direct impact of the psychosocial intervention on the traumatized children. There is the empowerment felt by the adults as they realize they are not helpless, but can intervene in their children's lives. Finally, as children often are barometers of their parents' status, there are also the indirect positive effects on children whose parents now perceive themselves as efficacious, and communicate this in their attitudes and actions (see Baider & Rosenfeld, 1974; Punamaki, 1989).

Conscientization

Conscientization or consciousness raising is also an integral part of programming in these new communities. Both the Filipino village in which Fely was the elected leader and the neighboring village where she took refuge following the violence were Base Christian Communities, in which faith, community organizing, and conscientization were all integral elements (see Barreiro, 1982; Torres & Eagleson, 1981). These communities of Filipino displaced analyzed the socioeconomic and political situation of the Philippines, their experience of oppression, and avenues for social change. Similarly the mental health programs promoted by the group of clandestine Salvadoran psychologists mentioned earlier sought to achieve three goals, all of which supported the conscientization process. The first goal was for these campesino women and men to gain in self knowledge and self esteem. The second goal was for them to understand their victimization in the social, political, and economic realities of El Salvador. The third goal was for them to make decisions for community action (Anonymous, personal communication, San Salvador, June 7, 1986).

Finally, it is recognized that conscientization must not be limited to political and economic analysis and action; it must also include personal-social analysis and action. That is, true empowerment of violently displaced women requires action against political and economic oppression *and* against gender subordination. At times it can be difficult to articulate an agenda which encompasses both areas of action, as was demonstrated at the United Nations' International Women's Year Conference held in 1975 in Mexico City. Domitila Chungara, a woman from the tin mines of Bolivia, joined in deliberations with women from around the world. When she stated that "for us, the first and principal work was not to fight against our *companeros* but with them to change the system" (Arias & Arias, 1980, p. 84), she found herself in conflict with many women who accused her of only thinking about politics and ignoring feminist issues. She in turn was frustrated with her accusers, because many of them had no comprehension of the poverty and oppression of her people. In discussing the struggle for national liberation of displaced Palestinian women, Giacaman (1989) warned that political and economic transformation does not guarantee transformation in the conditions and status of women. Using the example of the Algerian revolution, she argued that Algerian women signalled their own downfall when they called for a return to Arab-Islamic cultural values in the home. In discussing Third World women's perspectives on development, Sen and Grown (1987) likewise cautioned that "the struggle against gender subordination cannot be compromised during the struggle against other forms of oppression, or relegated to a future when they may be wiped out" (p. 19). Following from their own caution, Sen and Grown (1987) argued for new models of development which do not continue to disenfranchise the poor in general and women in particular, and for the recognition that empowering of women can provide new possibilities in economic development. They also argued for an understanding of feminism as heterogeneous, dynamic, and encompassing a struggle against all forms of oppression, including the political and economic. Eloquent in its simplicity and directness, Salvadoran Miriam Galdemez's statement for International Women's Day in 1981 captured both sets of priorities:

> The social structure in El Salvador is inhuman. It's important to say this because, yes, machismo, is a real problem, but nothing's ever going to change until we have the basic necessities of life: economic security; housing; health and education. At the moment most people don't have either. And we're never going to get them until we change the whole power structure in El Salvador. We must join with our men who suffer too, as well as fight for our specific rights. (Galdemez, 1984, p. 224)

In line with both Sen and Grown's (1989) call for no compromise and Galdemez's (1984) condemnation of machismo, the group of clandestine Salvadoran psychologists described earlier worked with both sets of priorities in training mental health promoters for the violently displaced in El Salvador. The mental health promoters, themselves members of displaced communities, were trained to explicitly address the anti-human machismo cultural values in their working with both women and men when analyzing the Salvadoran reality. In addition, these mental health promoters worked more directly with women to assist them in recognizing the pervasive quality of machismo, and how to defend themselves from being exploited by it (Anonymous, personal communication, San Salvador, June 7, 1986). Also in line with Sen and Grown's (1989) call for new models of economic development and the empowering of women in those models, were the new communities in armed conflict settings discussed above. Community economic development was accomplished through collective and cooperative efforts, and women were in positions of community leadership. One Filipino woman who was a leader in the BCC movement, characterized their foundation as *pakikibaka*, which is Tagalog for "unity in shared struggle."

CONCLUSION

The impersonal nature of modern warfare, where assailants may never face each other and the consequences of ones violence may never be known, can lead to antiseptic, unrealistic perspectives on war. This appears particularly evident today in the U.S. following the so-called victory of the allied forces in the Persian Gulf. In contrast, the women's stories contained in this article demand that the horrors of war must not be minimized. Armed conflict produces local and personal human consequences of terror, confusion, grief, pain, and the dissolution of family and community relationships through death or flight. Displaced women in particular share distinct vulnerabilities in such circumstances.

Ironically, in the violence and destruction of armed conflict, social redemption can arise, as persons adapt by forming new social norms and expectations. For displaced women, this redemption can be experienced in the solidarity of new collective identities, in the empowerment which results from filling leadership positions and other essential roles in new communities, and in the conscientization process in which analysis and action against both political and economic oppression *and* gender subordination occur.

REFERENCES

Amnesty International. (1990, August). *Convention on the elimination of all forms of discrimination against women.* Transcript of testimony before the U. S. Senate Foreign Relations Committee, Washington, D. C.

Amnesty International. (1991). *Women in the front line: Human rights violations against women.* New York: Amnesty International Publications.

Arias, E., & Arias, M. (1980). *The cry of my people: Out of captivity in Latin America.* New York: Friendship Press.

Aron, A. (1990, April). *Central American refugee children in the United States: A mental health disaster.* Transcript of testimony before the U. S. Senate Subcommittee on Children, Family, Drugs, and Alcoholism, Washington, D.C.

Baider, L., & Rosenfeld, E. (1974). Effect of parental fears on children in wartime. *Social Casework, 55,* 497-503.

Bandura, A. (1982). Self-efficacy mechanism in human agency. *American Psychologist, 37,* 122-147.

Barreiro, A. (1982). *Basic ecclesial communities: The evangelization of the poor.* Maryknoll, NY: Orbis.

Cairns, E. (1987). *Caught in crossfire: Children and the Northern Ireland conflict.* New York: Syracuse University Press.

Dilling, Y. (1984). *In search of refuge.* Scottdale, PA: Herald Press.

Dodge, C. P., & Raundalen, M. (1987). *War, violence, and children in Uganda.* Oslo: Norwegian University Press.

Fraser, M. (1973). *Children in conflict: Growing up in Northern Ireland.* New York: Basic Books.

Galdemez, M. (1984). Interview with Jenny Vaughan and Jane MacIntosh. In Cambridge Women's Peace Collective (Ed.), *My country is the whole world: An anthology of women's work on peace and war.* London: Pandora Press.

Giacaman, R. (1989). Palestinian women in the uprising: From followers to leaders. *Journal of Refugee Studies, 2,* 137-146.

Goldfeld, A. E., Mollica, R. F., Pesavento, B. H., & Faraone, S. V. (1988). The physical and psychological sequelae of torture: Symptomatology and Diagnosis. *Journal of the American Medical Association, 259,* 2725-2729.

Guendelman, S. R. (1981). South American refugees: Stresses involved in relocating in the San Francisco Bay area. *Migration today, 9,* 19-25.

Khass, M. (1989). The effects of occupation on women and young people–some examples. *Journal of Refugee Studies, 2,* 147-148.

Lin, K. M., Tazuma, L., & Masuda, M. (1979). Adaptational problems of Vietnamese refugees. *Archives of General Psychiatry, 36,* 955-961.

Liu, W. T. (1979). *Transition to nowhere: Vietnamese refugees in America.* Nashville, TN: Charter House.

Lykes, M. B. (1989). The caring self: Social experiences of power and powerlessness. In M. M. Brabeck (Ed.), *Who cares? Theory, research, and educational implications of the ethic of care.* New York: Praeger.

Lykes, M. B. (1990, November). Reflections commemorating the continuing struggle of the Salvadoran people. In *Searching the silence: In commemoration of the November 16th assassinations at the University of Central America.* Symposium conducted at Boston College, Chestnut Hill, MA.

Lykes, M. B., Costa, E., Iborra, M. Maciel, R., & Suardi, L. (1990, August). Guatemalan Indian children of war: Multidisciplinary collaboration in action-research. In *Community approaches to mental health care for children of war.* Symposium presented at the 98th Annual Meeting of the American Psychological Association, Boston, MA.

McCallin, M. (1988). *Report of a pilot study to assess levels of stress in a sample of 90 refugee children in Central America.* (Research Report, unnumbered). Geneva: International Catholic Child Bureau.

McCallin, M., & Fozzard, S. (1990). *The impact of traumatic events on the psychological well-being of Mozambican refugee women and children.* (Research Report, unnumbered). Geneva: International Catholic Child Bureau.

Manz, B. (1988). *Refugees of a hidden war: The aftermath of counterinsurgency in Guatemala.* New York: State University of New York Press.

Protacio-Marcelino, E. (1984, November). *Stress and coping among children of political prisoners in the Philippines.* Paper presented at the Conference on Aid to Torture Victims and their Families, Copenhagen, Denmark.

Protacio-Marcelino, E. (1986, January). *Victims without voice: Human rights violations against children.* Paper presented at the National Conference on the Filipino Child, St. Theresa's College-D. Tuazon, Quezon City, Philippines.

Punamaki, R. L. (1986). Stress among Palestinian women under military occupation; women's appraisal of stressors, their coping modes, and their mental health. *International Journal of Psychology, 21,* 445-462.

Punamaki, R. L. (1989). Factors affecting the mental health of Palestinian children exposed to political violence. *International Journal of Mental Health, 18,* 63-79.

Reardon, B. A. (1985). *Sexism and the war system.* New York: Teachers College Press.

Roe, M. D. (1986). Psychosocial development of Salvadoran refugees in El Salvador. *Global Perspectives, 4,* 1-3.

Roe, M. D. (1987a). Central American refugees in the United States: Psychosocial adaptation. *Refugee Issues, 3,* 21-30.

Roe, M. D. (1987b, August). *Religion, terror, and control of the displaced in El Salvador.* Paper presented at the 95th Annual Convention of the American Psychological Association, New York, NY.

Roe, M. D. (1988, November). Role of community development in psychosocial adjustment of Central American refugees: Local church as agent. In H. C. Schreck (Chair), *The local church: A focus of community development.* Symposium conducted at the 87th Annual Meeting of the American Anthropological Association, Phoenix, AZ.

Roe, M. D. (in press). Psychosocial adaptation of Filipino *evacuees* in the Philippines. *National Social Science Journal.*

Schaef, A. W. (1981). *Women's reality.* Minneapolis, MN: Winston.

Sen, G., & Grown, C. (1987). *Development, crises, and alternative visions: Third World women's perspectives.* New York: Monthly Review Press.

Stein, B. N. (1986). The experience of being a refugee: Insights from the research literature. In C. L. Williams & J. Westermeyer (Eds.), *Refugee mental health in resettlement countries.* New York: Hemisphere Publishing.

Torres, S., & Eagleson, J. (1981). *The challenge of basic christian communities.* Maryknoll, NY: Orbis.

United Nations Children's Fund (UNICEF). (1986). *Children in situations of armed conflict.* Unpublished manuscript presented to the UNICEF Executive Board, New York.

U. S. Committee for Refugees. (1990). *World refugee survey: 1989 in review.* Washington, D. C.: American Council for Nationalities.

Wortman, C. B., & Brehm, J. W. (1975). Responses to uncontrollable outcomes: An integration of reactance theory and the learned helplessness model. In L. Berkowitz (Ed.), *Advances in experimental social psychology, 8.* New York: Academic Press.

Fifty Years Later:
Am I Still an Immigrant?

Rachel Josefowitz Siegel

I came to this country in the spring of 1939, when Europe was on the brink of the second World War. Hitler had invaded Austria and Czechoslovakia and was attempting to cleanse the German Race of undesirable non-Arians. Jews were systematically being exterminated in concentration camps and hard labor camps.

My Jewish family had previously migrated from Lithuania to Germany, where I was born, and then to Switzerland, where we lived with the constant fear of German invasion or of having our temporary resident's visas revoked. I was thirteen when my two brothers were sent to the US to study. I remember not knowing if I would ever see them again. I remember air raid drills, and the Jewish strangers we sheltered in the relative and temporary safety of our home. They had crossed the border illegally and were desperately trying to get visas, transit papers, whatever documents might get them to a safer country. They were learning languages, Spanish, Turkish, English, Hebrew, on the chance that one of these countries would let them in. I began to learn English.

On the surface my family was relatively secure. In this strange world of immense insecurities, we had some significant assets. We had Lithuanian passports, and the US quota for Lithuanian immigrants was not as tightly closed as the quota for German Jews. We had enough money to be able to travel and to relocate without immediate hardship. My father had also acquired considerable skills in manipulating the legal loopholes and bureaucratic inconsistencies of immigration officials and border guards. He knew when and how to bribe.

I was aware that my parents spent a lot of time planning how and

Rachel Josefowitz Siegel, MSW, is a Jewish grandmother who came to this country at the age of fourteen in 1939. She is a writer, lecturer, and clinical social worker. She practices feminist psychotherapy in Ithaca, NY, where she has lived for over forty years.

when to get us to a safer place. In the meantime, I continued in school as if the world was normal, the only Jewish child in my class of patriotic Swiss citizens. I spoke French, German-and Schwyzerduetsch like a native. I could and did easily pass; I often felt like one of 'them.' I loved the school outings and walking tours of the magnificent Swiss countryside. I still feel nostalgic when I hear the sentimental Swiss mountain songs I sang with my girlscout troop. I wanted to feel that belonged and that I too could claim allegiance to this tiny and idealistic haven of peace and democracy. My parents sometimes reminded me that 'they' could kick us out at a moments notice, and that if Hitler came, who knew which of my friends would turn on me. I was a displaced person, a child without a country long before I ever set sail across the Atlantic.

During those early moves from one country to another and from one language to another, it was simply expected that I would absorb the new language, and I did, and that I would continue to do well in school, no matter how often I changed schools and languages. On the whole I did that too with remarkably few periods of difficulty. I do remember though the utter shame and embarrassment of not passing the oral exam at age eleven, that separated the university bound children from the others. No one attributed my failure to the fact that we had that year moved from Lausanne, in the French speaking part of Switzerland to Zurich, in the German speaking part of the country, in which the entire curriculum was different. So I spent the next two years in a school for children who, like me, had not tested well and came, on the whole, from workingclass families with limited ambitions. I got migraines and dizzy spells, and my parents did not approve of the friends I occasionally brought home.

We moved again, back to Lausanne, where I was accepted in the college bound system on the basis of my earlier school record. I do remember feeling somewhat lost at first, not having realized that I would have some catching up to do. I needed tutoring to make up two years of Latin. By then the whole of Europe was in a state of prewar tension, and I felt very strongly that my parents had more important things to worry about than the particulars of my school adjustment. I realized that we would soon be leaving though I was not supposed to talk about it. I spent many hours walking around the town that I had come to love and that felt more like home than any other, silently saying goodbye, secretly mourning the anticipated separation.

When we came to America, I knew that I was an immigrant and that I must not act like a greenhorn. If I tried very hard, 'they' would not know that I had 'just got off the boat,' they would not tease me or take advantage of my ignorance. When people asked me if I was a refugee, however, I was not so sure. Refugees were other Jews who had lost everything, who came without worldly possessions, whose professional degrees were useless, who had to start over at menial or domestic jobs, and who had lost or were separated from other members of their family.

My family's lifestyle did not seem to have changed; my mother was still a homemaker, though much confused at having to learn yet one more language and set of customs; my father was still a businessman who had investments in the US and was able to support us. Though I sensed my parents' worries and insecurity, there was never a question about their ability to send the five of us through college. Being financially and physically comfortable, and having my entire family on this side of the ocean, made me doubt that I was a refugee. Yet to this day, I cannot find the words to describe how subtly and profoundly my life had changed.

It took many years, perhaps twenty, before I became aware of the immense pain and sense of loss that had been an integral part of my childhood. Even before I was uprooted from our home in Berlin at the age of six, I had known the earlier uprootings that my parents and older siblings had experienced. I had sensed the pervasive insecurity and non-belonging so typical of wandering Jews.

But I was not aware of all that when I was growing up. No one ever spoke of the challenges and the separations, the difficulties inherent in leaving friends and neighborhoods and moving from one school system to a new one. I was aware only of being privileged and very very lucky. The message I got, over and over again, from my parents and from friends and relatives, was that I had much to be thankful for and nothing to complain about.

Fifty years later, as I write this paper, I still feel the strange mixture of privilege and pain, I still think of myself as self-indulgent, if not downright selfish and arrogant when I write or talk about the realities of my refugee and immigrant past. How can I presume to raise my voice among those who have suffered so much more and been so much more cruelly displaced and persecuted. Intellectually I know that even the rich and privileged feel pain; emotionally I know that my early unnamed wounds have left deep scars, and that my need to heal has been legitimate. But I also know, both intellectually and emotionally, and beyond simply calling it survivor's guilt, that there is an immense difference, in kind and in degree, between what I have experienced and the experiences of concentration camp survivors and of refugees who have escaped and are still fleeing from the terrors of war, famine, political torture, and other mass migrations. It has been difficult for me to integrate the legitimacy of my feelings within the context of a lifetime of witnessing the unthinkable inhumanities of our age.

Since I feel that I should feel lucky to be alive and well, I am still surprised and taken aback when long repressed and previously unvalidated feelings emerge with unexpected strength and urgency, as they did in 1989, when my husband and I attended his fiftieth college reunion in Boston. While he was happily reminiscing with his classmates, I began to feel more and more alienated, as if I did not belong. At first I brushed it off, as a predictable reaction to being immersed in his former world, in which I fell back into the long-ago discarded position of decorative and silent wife. But there was something else going on. My discomfort had an edge of profound sadness and deep-seated anger, my sense of non-belonging felt like being unwanted and unsure about how to behave. The famil-iar Boston streets and landmarks reminded me of my first years in this country and my own college days. A flood of long-buried, unnamed feel-ings emerged.

On our way home, as we were driving along the Massachusetts Turn-pike, surrounded by the lush green rolling hills of New England, I heard myself saying "That's a beautiful country of *yours*."

Fifty years of living in America, loving the varied landscapes, breath-ing the air and swimming the waters, walking the beaches and the wooded paths, over forty years of citizenship, of voting, of raising an American family, making English my primary language, and still I say *yours*. Still I have moments or days of feeling like an immigrant, a refugee, especially now since I have become a widow.

Fifty years after finding refuge on these shores from the unspeakable threat of total Jewish annihilation, my subconscious still brings up feelings of not really belonging, being a guest not quite sure of her welcome, a foreigner uncertain of the social or linguistic subtleties of the new world. These feelings tend to get reactivated when I have been exposed to a more than usual dose of incidents that can occur when I am a woman in a man's world, an old woman in a youth-oriented culture, a Jew among non-Jews, and now a widow in a world of couples. Even today, widows, like Jews, are often treated like outsiders whose wisdom and life experi-ence are not valued. Often I feel 'other,' 'alien,' 'ignored,' 'left out,' and those feelings reverberate with memories of my childhood as a wandering Jew without a country.

Such immigrant memories, dreams, feeling states, or flashbacks also occur when I am in a learning situation that requires the acquisition of new language, or in situations in which what I know and what others know is not the same. This can happen, for instance, when Jewish friends speak of their childhood in the Bronx as if I too must surely have played softball in an empty lot. At such times I feel as if their words and mine have different connotations, different associations that are not being acknowledged. I retreat into silence, or I try harder to make myself understood, while they, more likely than not, stare at me with incomprehension or try to convince me that we have more in common than think. It feels as if the burden of fitting in is on me.

When I came to this country, I heard repeatedly that I must become americanized as quickly as possible. Our American relatives had long ago changed their name from Josefowitz to Joseph, why couldn't we? Why was I so stubborn about not wanting to anglicize either the spelling or the pronunciation of my given name Rachel?

I have felt great relief, in the last ten years, in reading the accounts of other Jewish immigrant women. Eva Hoffman (1989) writes eloquently of the many ways in which her very identity felt "lost in translation." Georgia M. Gabor (1981), after describing the horrors of surviving the holocaust, depicts the ultimate insult of being subjected to the judgmental attitudes and regulations of American would-be caregivers. Lore Segal (1958,1986), and the Jewish Women in London Group (1989), write about their personal experiences with English families who sheltered them and who expected the immigrant teenagers to show appropriate gratitude and to try harder to assimilate to the host country. Their stories convey the displaced child's feelings when her benevolent hosts were unable or unwilling to recognize or to legitimize the refugee's need to maintain her own identity and to mourn her losses. These writers recount the same sense of bewilderment and exclusion that I felt among kindly Americans who were putting themselves out to welcome me in their own, unknowingly ethnocentric fashion.

Recently, since my husband's death two years ago, my immigrant memories have been vividly reactivated by a poignant similarity of feelings. Suddenly separated from my partner of forty-six years, and from the familiar daily patterns of our combined lives, I now often feel sad and alone, as I did then, among others who have not shared my loss. As an immigrant and as a new widow I have also felt enormous fluctuations between the frustrations and the pleasures of coping with new challenges. I swing between feeling stupid and vulnerable when confronted with unfamiliar legal or financial documents and decisions, and feeling elated and surprised when I realize that I have indeed done a good job of coping with a task I never tried before. I have felt intermittently dumb, unable to function at my accustomed level of competence, or strong and resilient and pleased at my ability to comprehend and to adjust.

In both situations, the demands on my capacity to change were externally imposed on me and my need to learn, and to adapt felt urgent and occasionally overwhelming. In both cases my experiences set me apart from those who had not shared a similar life event. And yet, the skills that I acquired as a child, in adjusting to one country after another, are serving me well now in late life, in this most profound adjustment of all, to the land of widows and single women, where widows, like Jews are not always welcome, where my wisdom is not always appreciated, and where these realities tend to be denied.

In her last year of life, my mother got agitated and anxious near the end of each of our visits. As we, her middle-aged children, scattered over two continents, prepared to return to our homes, she expressed an urgent, almost desperate need to decide, again and again, where she should be. "Ich weiss nit uf wesser Welt ich bin" she would say in Yiddish; "I don't know know where I belong," or literally, "I don't know in which world I am." It was my sense that she was not only preparing for her own death, but that she was reliving the agony of separating from loved ones, and of fleeing from the terror of persecutions. When her life and that of her children had depended on getting away, she had learned to cope by uprooting herself and moving to a different place. Now that she was again confronted with death, she felt the urgency to move once more.

That phrase seemed to carry the message of her life, which I had absorbed into my own sense of self. I too had often felt that I did not know where I belonged.

In my mid-fifties, after my mother died, I became aware of an inner shift in my own sense of belonging. I began to feel that I did belong, to some extent, in each and all of the places that I had ever called home, rather than feeling that I did not really belong in any of them. I felt a shift to feeling less deprived and more enriched by the early exposure to different cultures and different languages, less injured and more strengthened by successive adaptations to new circumstances. Now when I travel, the transitions from one place to another, from one country to another, are less difficult; when my children return to their respective homes, the pain of separation is less acute; when I sense that I have been left out or excluded, I am less devastated.

I no longer feel like a homeless person. And yet, the fears, the anger, and the loneliness of my immigrant days still lurk beneath the surface, still emerge when least expected. The imagery and feelings expressed in my dreams connect the present to the past. While the pain of my recent widowhood is intensified by memories of previous wounds, my present grief has actually helped me understand and further the healing of much earlier loss.

REFERENCES

Gabor, Georgia M. (1981). *My destiny: Survivor of the holocaust.* Arcadia, CA: Amen Publishing Company.

Hoffman, Eva. (1989). *Lost in translation: A life in a new language.* New York: E.P. Dutton.

Jewish Women in London Group. (1989). *Generations of memories: Voices of Jewish women.* London: The Women's Press, Ltd.

Segal, Lore. (1958). *Other people's houses.* New York; Harcourt Brace Jovanovich; (1986) New York: Ballantine Books.

SECTION III:
WORKING WITH REFUGEES:
THE CHALLENGES AND REWARDS

The Balancing Act:
Plight of Afghan Women Refugees

Sultana Parvanta

SUMMARY. This case study reports the story of two Afghan women who left Afghanistan and became refugees in the U.S. after the Soviet invasion and takeover in 1979. The fight and flight for life for the refugee women and children have been very difficult, involving countless hazards and complications. The women usually did not imagine that leaving their homes for safety was only the first leg of a difficult journey demanding patience, stamina, flexibility, and strength of will. They continually face personal, social, cultural, psychological, and economic challenges. Their old values clash with different ones in their new environment. In order to deal with these daily dilemmas and conflicts, the women confront a balancing act with values they had taken to be non-negotiable. The current socio-political and cultural conditions faced by the Afghan women refugees worldwide are in many ways in total conflict with what they

Sultana Parvanta, PhD, is an Educational Consultant and Migrant Education Specialist at Region 3-Chapter 1 Rural Technical Assistance Center for PRC, Inc. in Atlanta, GA. She is also an Adjunct Professor in the Division of Educational Studies at Emory University.

113

perceive as the preferred and perhaps the only way of life. Their lives are further complicated by the wounded pride of the men in their lives.

INTRODUCTION

The Soviet Union invaded Afghanistan 13 years ago in the Spring of 1979. The forceful, violent takeover by Soviet military with the backing of the Communist regime in Kabul that the Soviets had created earlier, led to a blight that is burning the very texture and fabric of life; destroying the intricate patterns, tones, designs, and images that a people had created over centuries and called their own.

The invasion created millions of Afghan refugees seeking safety in Pakistan, India, Iran, Europe and the United States. Five million Afghan refugees, more than 80% of whom are women, children, and elderly men live across the border in Pakistan. A refugee camp in Peshawar is referred to by one journalist as a "dreadful refugee camp that spawns crime and violence of every kind" (*World Monitor*, September 1990, p. 16).

According to a recent eyewitness report, the funds and support systems for the camps have been terminated. More people die now due to ill health and abuse than ever before. The situation of women and children in the refugee camps is becoming desperately serious. The sources for survival are diminishing.

The camps are filled with sick people, many with life threatening diseases. According to nurses from the camps, most women have serious health problems, and are abused in many ways. These issues are not addressed or discussed openly.

The women in the camps do not know their neighbors. There are no social and communal relations and no trust as they knew before. They have no means of going back and starting anew. People inside Afghanistan are also starving. The fields are mine-ridden. The villages are gone. The cities are over-crowded and high inflation has reduced people's purchasing power to near zero. Women in the refugee camps in the border town of Peshawar between Afghanistan and Pakistan have no place to go, and are faced with dire isolation–condemned to a painful existence.

In the mist of these difficult, unfamiliar, and hostile circumstances the Afghan women demonstrate that they too are warriors. Their Jihad (holy war) is through courage, bravery, art, stitchery, and eighteen-hour work days. They do not talk much about their problems. They remain pragmatic as they deal with what is immediately at hand, believe in God, and trust in their beliefs.

Case Study

In this case study, stories of two Afghan women who became refugees provide a brief glance at their lives before the invasion, their misplacement from their homes and country, their flight to safety, and their continued struggles in their new environments.

These factual stories will also provide an insight into the Afghan women refugees, struggle for adaptation to their new environments, and their social, psychological successes and failures as they reach out for life–for continuation of the old ways of life even as they clash with the new.

The difficulties these women deal with daily in their new homes provide a glimpse of what they consider to be most stressful, as well as the ways in which they cope with these conflicts. Their trials, errors, failures, disappointments, triumphs, and glories provide lessons for all women worldwide.

The schematic structure of this case study follows the natural progression of the women telling their stories, transcribed and translated by the author. The stories are told by two women, one in her late twenties and the other in her late sixties.

First Story

Before the Russians came, people in Afghanistan led happy and relatively orderly and peaceful lives. We went to school daily for half a day. We would then return home and tend to immediate matters of keeping the house, going to the market, preparing meals, washing clothes, tending to our small gardens, and making tea for guests. We would all gather to share meals that took a long time to prepare.

One day in the market we heard that the Russians had come. The rumors were substantiated as people's lives began to change drastically. We heard that the forces moved into the city at night. Local people did not see the massive movement of military forces.

As we talked about the new situation, and heard more about this unbelievable, uneasy, and scary news, we began to see families in turmoil as they were losing loved ones. Fathers, sons, brothers, and in some cases women were taken to jail, beaten, tortured, and many remained unaccounted for.

People began to experience hard times. Even going to school and back became frightening. The fear of unjust treatment of civilians by military and police was debilitating. No one wanted to be outside of the house unless it was absolutely necessary, for fear of apprehension, punishment, and random firing by police and military who were known to shoot at a whim in the name of keeping peace up, and rebellion down.

In my family the feelings were unanimous. We did not like the new government and their attack on the people in the name of socialist revolution that was supposed to be good for us. The government moved quickly and changed all familiar symbols.

Our school uniform was changed from black to red. The flag and its emblem was altered to reflect the new revolutionary vision. The unwritten laws of segregation on the basis of party affiliation were enforced. It was clear that if a family did not join and support the new communist party, they were considered traitors, a threat to the new regime, and had to be dealt with severely. This meant elimination.

My two brothers were against the new system, and did not support the new government. They also knew that the Afghan army was rebuilding and was going to draft them. They did not want to serve in the communist army. They fled the country to join the opposition forces that were forming in the eastern regions, on the Pakistan boarder.

Their departure created a new problem for the family. Most young men who left for the border joined the opposition forces called the Mujahedeen or freedom fighters. We were afraid of being punished for their absence. This fear accompanied a new challenge for the economic survival of the family since they both were the bread winners. They had worked in a small farm that was owned by my father. My dad was an elderly man who suffered from respiratory ailments. My mother, also in ill health, was a housewife with three daughters in school.

As the social, political and economic conditions were deteriorating, my parents decided to leave the capital city, go to Pakistan to insure our safety, and be near my brothers. We hoped that they could still help out with the family finances.

My elderly father, my mom with her high blood pressure and arthritis, and we the three girls, left the city quietly at night as we walked to the edge of the city to embark on our journey on donkeys and horses.

We travelled for eight days across difficult pathways through mountains and valleys. One of my brothers met us after two days to help us through the journey. We trekked only at night since the day journey was considered too dangerous. During the day Russian helicopters scanned the countryside to spot "traitors" and spoil their escape.

The trip was horrendously difficult. The nights and days were so cold that I felt I was losing my fingers and toes. We just could not get warm. We were told not to have fires. During day time the sun shined but we could not enjoy it. We had to hide in dark caves and behind large rocks.

During night travel we could not see where we were going. We would fall down on rocks and on thorns. The two men who helped us through the trip were rugged and oblivious to the elements.

On the fourth day of this treacherous journey, we ran out of food. There was nothing to eat. We had brought food for a few days only, thinking we would find some on the way. But as we reached villages and one of the guides would go out to get food, he would find the villages deserted and mine-filled. This situation was particularly difficult on my father who was already weakened. We had no food for the remainder of the journey. The cold and starvation were unbearable. But the worst fear we all had was what will happen if we get caught by the military?

On one occasion we ran into a woman and her three young children. We asked her for food. She said that she had no extra food to give us and that she had seen many hungry travelers lately. Her village was destroyed and she had lost her food support system and her children were hungry. She seemed disoriented and confused about what to do, where to go, and how.

On the eighth day we approached the border town with a sense of relief, high hopes for comfort, and visions for a better life. Alas! The dreams were soon to be shattered and empty.

For the first few days we had to stay with a relative in a crammed two room structure. There were no tents available and the hotels were either full or too costly. We found my other brother and with his help moved to a small shack, using the remainder of the family savings to pay for the lodging and immediate food needs. There were no jobs to be found. The local people were hostile and did not make efforts to make us feel welcome. The flood of Afghan refugees was placing an immense burden on the shoulders of the local community.

After one year of search for work our efforts paid off. My sister and I found sewing jobs. We sewed clothes for a program that was giving them to the refugees. Our weekly wages were the sole source of income for our family in Peshawar. Meanwhile none of us could attend the girls' school in the area. We did not have enough money to pay for our education. My sisters and I really missed school.

The weather was hot. There was no electricity during the day and sometimes none during the night. My dad's breathing condition was worsening. We had never experienced such high temperatures and humidity before. During the day my sisters and I would take turns using a straw hand fan to fan my dad so that he could breath easier.

The refugee health clinic was a sham. The medicine and food that were donated by international relief for the refugees did not reach the targeted audience. The initial shipments of medicine and food would get sold in the black market for high prices to the Pakistanis. The locally-made cheap medicine would be purchased with half of the money and would be given to the refugees who were sick at the clinic.

The poor health and hygiene conditions were complicated by the oppressive control of some of the men in the area. These men were mostly affiliated with the freedom fighting factions (the Mujahedeens). They wanted to insure decency and Afghan pride by protecting the women from local abuse. However, they ended up as the abusers and controllers. They forbade us to leave home unless it was absolutely necessary. The purpose for leaving home more than three times daily was questioned. We were not allowed to go out without our veils or with western clothes on. The large veils had to reveal only the eyes. This was a new condition to me since I had never wore the veil when I was in Kabul.

Three years of hard work, poor conditions, isolation, humiliation, and poverty gave way to a glimmer of hope. We were told that since my mom had once worked in a U.S. affiliated program during the census count, there was a possibility that our application would get accepted for refugee status in the U.S.

We eagerly proceeded with the paper work. We went through the proper channels, and with the assistance of one of the relief agencies through a church, we were considered for a refugee visa. We moved to Islamabad to be near the offices so we could attend expeditiously to the needed and extensive paper work. Our application went through and we were granted refugee status and prepared for our departure.

The excitement was immense but accompanied by a sense of trepidation. In the midst of excitation, we only half listened to my father's sense of doubt and caution about a hasty move to a far away place, a long way from Afghanistan. He feared we might never return to our land where we were needed the most. Soon we were in a plane heading for the U.S.A. to make our new home in Louisville, Kentucky.

Now, I am in the U.S. I work hard and much. Working hard is not new to me. Yet there is a distinction between working hard here and in Afghanistan. Here I work so that I can pay for rent, car payments, and food. After the work is done and daily responsibilities are met, I find that there is no time left to really enjoy my family. My regret is that my dad passed away, and during his last days, I could not take time off from my work. I did not want to lose my job. Consequently, I was not able to spend as much time with him during his last days as I would have liked to.

I feel that with so much hard work I should be able to save money and visit relatives in other cities. But I cannot find the time, nor the money, nor the energy to do so. My life is all work oriented. There is no real joy and pleasure.

My problems are associated with lack of money, little time with family, and lack of time to really learn the language. Where do I get the time and energy to learn English?

In order to deal with these problems I have to keep myself strong; maintain strength in mental, physical, and financial domains of my life. Now I don't know when and if I'll get to return to Afghanistan. Meanwhile, I need to take care–accept my present circumstances, and deal with them effectively. I try to remain objective. I have much to be thankful for. However, there are moments when I wonder and ask why did I come here? Did I have a say in the matter? What if I had stayed? How do I deal with my feelings of regret, guilt, and disappointment?

In order to remain strong I pray daily for assistance in maintaining my heart convictions and my devotion to my spiritual beliefs. I also pray that I don't get old fast. I am afraid of getting old here. I don't like and approve of isolating old people. What will happen to me, then?

The most difficult issue for me is my feelings of unhappiness. I worry about my future and the future of the thousands of refugee women and children left in the camps in Peshawar who do not have anything, and the world has forsaken and forgotten about them, including myself. I deeply worry that in the world today we still make wars and create refugees. This is intolerable. I think and worry about these issues constantly.

My message to other women, particularly Afghan women who want to hear me, is: Be strong. Do not lose your strength and insight that are embedded in you and supported by culture. Remember that lack of education, inflexibility, shortsightedness, ethnocentrism, tribalism, intolerance, and closed-mindedness led to the downfall of Afghanistan. Let us prevent wars, promote education, practice and promote honesty, honor differences, and teach peace, cooperation, and peaceful coexistence.

Women must remember that strength and patience are important. We must further develop, cherish, and honor our relation to our deeper Self, and keep close to God.

Second Story

In Afghanistan, before the revolution, life was calm. My husband was an assistant governor in a northern province. We had a jeep and my children went to school. Then the revolution came. My husband was dismissed from his position and we moved to the capital.

In Kabul, we were wondering about our situation. Life was getting uncomfortable. We felt uneasy and uncertain about our lives, work, and school. One night, only a few weeks after our arrival, we heard a knock at the door.

Two men dressed in civilian clothing pushed their way into the sitting room asking for my husband. As he entered the room, the men told him to come with them "for tea." Outside there was a car with two other men. They had military uniforms, and one was the driver. They rode off, the dust rose–leaving me, my daughter, my five sons, and two daughters-in-law behind. In bewilderment we wondered if he would ever return from this unfriendly invitation to tea.

Soon after this incident, our house was repeatedly searched by military police. We were never told what they were searching for. At times the houses in the entire block would be searched. The only people in the neighborhood who seemed to have had any prior knowledge of these searches were the shop keepers. There were times when they would whisper, "Tomorrow there will be another long search. Get what you may need for the next few days because the store will be closed for search and seizure."

Weeks lent themselves to months and we had no news about my husband or his whereabouts. We continued our search for him. We asked officials in the ministries of interior and defense, and at the municipal offices if they could tell us about the fate of my husband. No response. We waited patiently and hopefully. There were no signs of him or of his name anywhere.

During my daily quests to the various offices, I learned that there were hundreds of other women who were also in my predicament; searching for their loved ones. Our demands for information grew louder. Women were getting impatient, fearing the worst.

In the weeks that followed we were threatened and told to go home. The women continued to raise their voices. From then on we were always surrounded by military men with machine guns. On this one occasion we were told that in the weeks to follow the government was going to release some information about the political detainees.

The following week the number of searching women increased many fold. The number of guards with machine guns also increased. The chief of police spoke through a microphone announcing names of people they considered "traitors" for having fled the country for Pakistan. My husband's name was on that list. The women were shocked about such lies. They knew, just as I did, that the men had not left the country. It was obvious they had destroyed these men and did not have the courage to confess to their crimes. The feelings of loss, chaos, and confusion are indescribable.

The bus ride home with my youngest son was sheer hell. I did not know what and how to feel. I wondered what is next? Who is next? My sons? My brothers? Who else?

I got home and didn't know how to break the news to my children. They all had been hoping and praying that we find their father alive. Now that hope was gone. He was killed and we did not even get to see his body. The unnatural circumstances surrounding his death made the mourning incomplete. Even during our mourning we felt restricted. We could not cry loud, ask questions, and blame the system as we would have liked to. We were afraid of further punishments. I was terribly afraid for my five sons.

Soon after the invasion the government radio announced the enactment of emergency military draft for all boys from ages 16 and up. My sons and I were clear that we did not want them to serve in the military, fighting a war against their own people and dying at the hands of their own countrymen.

Within one week of the announcement, I hired a man who was to take my three older sons out of the country through the mountain ranges. The operation began immediately that night. The hired man was basically going to smuggle my sons out of the city and out of the country. There were no preparations to be made. No one was to know of the plan, not even very loved neighbors.

Three years passed. Our only source of income was the money I received from selling what we owned. Even selling was difficult. Not many people would buy things for fear of cooperating and assisting people who were against the government and were preparing to leave the country. I tried to sell my house three times and each time the buyers would go back on the deal and change their minds. At last I practically gave it away for nothing.

My sons who were in Pakistan would send word repeatedly and insist that we must leave. They wanted me, their wives, and young children to join them in the border camps. I knew that I had to take the rest of my family to safety and comfort. The next step was to join my sons. But how?

I knew that our house was being watched. The surveillance was done openly. Sometimes the watcher would knock on the door and ask for water! I had to be careful not to let this spy think that we were selling our belongings and preparing to leave. We actually left most of what we owned behind unsold, including the land.

During the night I, my daughter, two daughters-in-law, and two young children left our home and city through the back roads. Our guides for hire were three men who were to take us to Pakistan. They took us through uncharted paths to avoid the military camps and personnel. We had two donkeys and one horse. We walked for fifteen days. The bread we were carrying was getting as hard as rock. I would soak the hard bread in water in order to make it consumable. Our food, though rationed, was running out.

My daughter-in-law gave birth to a little girl on the road to freedom and safety. She delivered her little baby in a dark smoke-filled room with three other women assisting us in birthing at a half ruined village. We made a little basket to carry the new baby in.

My young daughter and my grandchildren were always frightened. Any sound would make them jump and they would turn pale. They were tired, hungry, exhausted, and frightened. My daughter-in-law, the new mother, was weak and very depressed. Her milk stopped flowing. She was unable to breast feed her baby. We took a day of detour to find the baby some milk. We worried that the infant might die of hunger.

Fifteen days of hardship on the way from Kabul ended and we reached Peshawar. We met my sons. We all had bleeding feet and hands. All the children were ill for weeks afterwards.

My sons were involved in the resistance movement. Our request for food and shelter was granted through the organizations run by the Mujahedeens and their relief resources for the refugees.

We heard that people who had relatives in the U. S. could apply for refugee visas through the consulate in Islamabad. We immediately moved to Islamabad and began the procedure of applications through a church-related resettlement program. We had a good chance for relocation because I had a brother who lived in California.

Our application process took two years. Meanwhile we all lived together: my sons, daughter, daughters-in-law and three grandchildren. None of us was employed. The assistance we were receiving from the Mujahedeens was for bare minimum essentials. In order to remedy the situation, I began to cook beans and prepared molasses juice to be sold in two carts for street vending. My sons would take the carts in the morning and sell food on the streets. In the evenings, after dinner we would all prepare the carts for the next day.

The news of our acceptance for resettlement to the U. S. finally arrived. However, the acceptance was granted only to me, my daughter and my two unmarried sons. We had to separate from the rest of the family with the vision of reuniting in the U.S. We left Islamabad after two years and six months.

When we arrived in California we were still in a state of shock. Our new shelter was a nice, clean and modern two bedroom apartment. All immediate necessities such as towels, bedding, utensils, clothes, and furniture were already provided. We were given food stamps. The food was good and fresh, and we liked the weather in California. I felt relieved to be alive and for my family to be out of immediate danger from the violent and unfriendly forces that were sweeping our country. I am thankful that I did not lose my sons to the war. Actually it was not a war. It was an evil ideological storm that destroyed all in its path.

I still remember the plight of other women who lost more than their homes and husbands. I feel lucky in comparison to some other women who are still in the camps, burdened by tremendous losses, struggling daily with little hope.

Presently all is well with me on the surface, but I still feel a deep pain in my heart. I miss my country and my familiar earth. However, I treasure this new country and the freedom and comfort it has given me. Most important, I am grateful that this country allowed my sons to come to safety. Their safety was the primary reason I left my home in the first place.

I tell my children that they should take advantage of being here and benefit from the good educational system. I tell them that in the old days in Afghanistan it was such a big deal to go to American schools. Only the very rich could have had this privilege. Now that my children have this good opportunity they should further their education, learn the good things of this culture and retain the good ones from their own heritage.

Daily I take time to pray for all. I pray that God may lead us all on the path of peace, not war and violence. I pray that people of the world find it unthinkable to take a break from compassion and kindness. War and conflict are destructive and promote extensive and prolonged suffering for many.

For women it is important to remember to have patience despite difficult times, to cooperate and reach out to those who are needy. Being far away from my familiar surroundings and faces, language, land, and religion is difficult. Here we have food, shelter, comfort, and freedom. What I miss is a free Afghanistan. I know that in order to build a new free Afghanistan men and women have to work together, shoulder to shoulder.

Many Afghans here face difficulties of a new kind. Many couples are separating in divorce. Young people do not spend enough time with their families. Young girls experience relationships with men early and before marriage. This used to be an unacceptable and shameful behavior. Parents are worried that they are losing control over their children. One man who had beaten his son to discipline him for bad behavior was forced by the police in California to take a parenting course in order to learn proper parenting. This Afghan father's pride is broken.

People are nervous, passing through uncharted territories in their psyches. They don't know who they are, what is happening to their families, where they are heading, and how and where to fit into this mosaic of American society. The questions are many and the answers are hard to find.

SYNTHESIS

There are of course thousands of other stories of Afghan women refugees from varying socio-economic backgrounds. This study has focused on two women who went through the stages of being stable and happy inhabitants of their nation, to fleeing to a bordering country and observing the displacement and degradation of their people thrust into a "refugee" status, to their flight to the United States as "refugees."

Many women went through another intermediary stage of being stationed as refugees in Germany, France, Italy, and other European and Asian countries before arriving in the United States. The vast majority of Afghan refugees (about six million) are still spread out in Pakistan and Iran. Most of them are living in poverty and deprived conditions, hoping and dreaming to come to the United States or to go back to a peaceful and rehabilitated Afghanistan, while they realize that neither of these possibilities could come into fruition in their lifetimes.

The fight and flight for life for the Afghan people, particularly for women and their children, has been a very difficult trial. The journey to freedom, particularly for women, was perceived by loved ones to be the most difficult due to hazards on the way to a better life. The odyssey was seen as the only alternative path where potential for hope and survival existed.

The women refugees usually did not, and perhaps could not, imagine that leaving their homes for safety was only the first leg of a difficult journey that would demand exquisite patience, acceptance, stamina, and strength of will. The new situations and transitions for which these women were neither skilled, nor prepared proved to place a broad range of demands on their physical, emotional, political and psychic perceptions. The range of new demands has made social adaptation and adjustment extraordinarily difficult for most Afghan women refugees.

The Afghan refugees, particularly the women, are continually faced with social, cultural, and economic adjustments and cross cultural clashes. In order to deal with these daily dilemmas and confrontations, the women have to come to terms with bartering values they had taken to be nonnegotiable. The women have to perform a balancing act of learning how to barter values–to delineate the parameters and comfort zones for this exchange and evaluate the worth and quality of the values being bartered.

The current social, political, and cultural conditions faced by the Afghan women worldwide are in many ways in total conflict with what they had come to know and perceive as the preferred and perhaps the only way of life. Their present lives are further complicated by the wounded pride of the men in their households and the difficulty of the men in accepting their wives, mothers, or sisters working at jobs which are often difficult and demeaning.

This study in a sense is a pilot for a more encompassing study which would try to fathom the psyches of women refugees who are at diverse stages of their "refugee" status. A further and deep inquiry into the problems of women refugees, their present circumstances, and the their roles as future mothers of a new generation in this country and abroad, is worthy of serious and extensive consideration.

This endeavor could also include explorations of the psychological and cultural problems that are faced by refugee men who have survived the violent and harsh political realities that have lead to their misplacement as well. Many refugee men suffer from the added burden of guilt. They feel condemned from having run away from war and from saving their country, and the innocent people.

Implications for Psychiatrists, Psychologists, Social Workers, and Counselors

The numbers of refugee women are increasing world wide. The recent turmoil in the Middle East and Eastern Europe is adding to the influx of refugees entering the U. S. In addition to the logistical needs for food, shelter, health, education, and language training, the psychological needs of refugee women with wounded hearts should be addressed. Are we ready to serve, repair, and nurture the psychological wounds of refugee men and women? How are we training our front-line service providers to serve this population with enormous emotional and psychological problems? Do our current paradigms for psychotherapy and counseling take into account the unique needs of refugee women, and their families?

On the global scale women refugees from other corners of the world–Middle East, Eastern European countries, Vietnam, Laos, Cambodia, Ethiopia, Guatemala, El Salvador, Haiti, and many other countries–share fates similar to the Afghan women refugees. In order for Westerners, in the residing countries of the refugees, to understand the psyche of refugee women, several factors must be taken into consideration. Here are four main questions that come to mind when dealing with a refugee woman:

1. How does the woman refugee perceive and respond to the transition from a culture of extended families and large support groups to one of nuclear families and lack of community support? Women refugees do find a lot of support in their host countries from social workers, refugee organizations and compassionate individuals. However, this kind of support is quite different from their communal villages or neighborhoods back home.
2. How does the woman handle the drastic changes in her socio-economic status? In many cases she and her family have gone from relatively affluent living conditions in their country, to utter poverty on their way to Europe or the United States, and finally to relative and uncertain economic security by working at hard jobs for long hours in the Western countries. Though they may reach comfortable lifestyles in their host countries they often do not acquire the social and cultural status they had back home before their displacement commenced.
3. How does the woman deal with the transformation from being part of the majority in her culture to becoming a "minority" in a foreign culture? Is she preoccupied with being "accepted" by the dominant culture? How does she feel about and relate to other minorities in her new environment? Does she empathize with other refugee women from other countries and other deprived minorities in her new country of residence? What should be done about this insufferable isolation?
4. How does the woman deal with her family relationships, with her daughters, sons, siblings, parents and in-laws during this transition period? In most cases the women have come from matriarchal but patrilineal family structure. They are thrust into the Western societies which in principle tend towards egalitarianism between the sexes, but show the tinges of a patriarchal history. How does the woman in particular deal with the men in her family with their wounded "male pride" and with women in her family in the face of "sexual liberation?"

These questions expose the different problems of refugee women from the problems of the women in their new host countries. Certainly anyone who has endured a major unplanned change and tragedy in one's life is subject to grief, disorientation, anger, and fear, and needs loving support.

But getting that support is more difficult for refugees because the kind of support systems they are used to in their native culture are now gone. Professional social service workers and relief agencies, while essential and well meaning, cannot match or replace the family, customs, and symbols with which one's psyche has bonded for one's whole life so far. Thus to be more useful to refugees, service deliverers in the host country need to have in addition to clinical skills, an understanding of and respect for cultural differences.

Another important difference that is essential to bear in mind is that refugees in the host country is the result of usually years of determined effort. So although they are broken and needy in many ways their journey has also brought out their strengths, and they must be honored for this. The women refugees who have endured the horrors of war, dislocation, loss of loved ones, hunger, humiliation, and still opted for life and safety of their children are not weak women. They have confronted and have walked passed the insane and inhuman conditions brought on them by greedy policies, and short-sighted politics that have lost a sight of balance and wholeness. These women have proven that the dignity of human spirit and reverence for life are far greater and are worthy of enormous sacrifices.

To treat these refugees as merely needy, helpless, pitiable people is an insult. They have proven themselves, probably more than most who are now in the nominal positions of helpers.

Thus two points suggest themselves. One, the refugees should be consulted on their needs and desires, and encouraged to help themselves as much as possible. To offer support services to these women without giving them the right and the chance to articulate their needs is to demean their accomplishments. Two, these refugees can have something of their own to give and teach from their hard won victory if the new host helpers are open to also receiving as they administer aid. Thus aid to refugees should be in the form of cooperative nature.

Another point about the kind of aid needed could follow the motto: The more holistic and concurrent the better. Just as with homeless people in this country, refugees need both material and social-psychological assistance at the same time. They go hand in hand. One single from of aid cannot solve all the problems. They need a job *and* counseling, medical attention *and* language study, housing *and* transportation, etc. Refugee women and children have great needs that necessitate a coordinated approach to service delivery.

A final and crucial need is to balance aid and self-help. The basic needs must be satisfied, but at the same time care must be taken not to make the refugees dependent. Consideration should be given to provide the resources and services that can contribute to breaking the cycle of dependence. Services delivered are most useful when they are deliberately planned and targeted to address the immediate health and adjustment needs and also can enhance self-reliance, and self actualization in the refugee's new environment.

To return to the two women, reported here: their stories are certainly traumatic and deserving of our compassion. But they are not tragic, for these women are heroines. They did what they had to do against great difficulties to bring themselves and their families to a foreign country and the possibilities of a new safe life. They gave up everything and risked their lives, and they survived.

The ordeal is not over for them yet, and they can use our assistance if it is appropriately given out of respect for who they have already proven themselves to be. Who are these refugee women? They are women who have come to us on a long journey. Along their journey they have been given the gift of strength, resourcefulness, forbearance, and capacities that only they know they had to muster. They came to us now with these gifts, in addition to their pains and needs. Can we receive them? At the close of the Twentieth century, all of our lives are changing–beyond our control. In a sense, we all could be "refugees." These women who have "been there" can be resources in our communities. By approaching them with the attitude of mutual exchange we can all benefit. America has abundant material resources to give and share. We should be thankful for the dignified human spirit that these Afghan women refugees can bring us in return.

Traces of Khmer Women's Imaginary: Finding Our Way in the West

Sokhany Sieng
Janice L. Thompson

SUMMARY. This paper presents the voices and reflections of two women who worked together in a community mental health project with Cambodian women. The first person narrative of Sokhany Sieng recollects her story of migration to the United States and her insights into the lives of refugee women in America. The discussion by Janice Thompson examines the ethics of feminist practice with refugee women and explores questions of colonialism in the use of feminist scholarship in multicultural work with refugee women.

ON MY WAY TO THE WEST

When I was a child, I had two great desires in my life. First, I wanted to reside in the West. In Cambodia, we studied French from grade four. In school, some of my teachers liked to talk about the freedom of the West. We also studied about French civilization. When at home, I read my father's magazines. I was intrigued and attracted to western culture. I also wanted to become an educator. I thought the value of education was very important for me. In Cambodia, women are raised to rely on men. For instance, if we wanted to have a good life or happiness, we were taught that we have to find a husband who has a good career and who can make decent money. Conversely, I saw that those women who found men

Sokhany Sieng is a 36 year old Khmer woman. She is the mother of two children who live with her and another child who lives in Australia. She is a part time student at the University of Southern Maine.

Janice Thompson is Associate Professor at the University of Southern Maine where she teaches in the School of Nursing and in the Women's Studies program. She earned her PhD in Nursing at the University of Utah.

as the primary resource in their life had never been happy. I had learned in school to believe in self-reliance.

(ខ្ញុំទំព័រ៩ខ្ញុំ) មនុស្សគ្រប់រូបអាគ្នា តែកាលណាផ្តកផ្តួលលើជីហរអ្នកដទៃហើយគឺមនុស្សនោះ រស់មិនដែលបាន ប្រកបសេចក្ដីសុខអស់មួយជីវិត ។

Unfortunately, I was born into the wrong place and the wrong family, which prevented me from accomplishing my desires. My parents were conservative, especially my father. He did not allow my sisters and me to attend school too long or to become educated. He was worried that we might be involved with men. And Cambodian culture does not encourage women to become educated.

Even though I was strictly raised, I never gave up my dream. After my parents forbade me to attend school in the late 1960's, I kept studying at home by reading books everyday. My favorite books were psychology and philosophy. I sometimes talked with my sister about my fantasy of leaving Cambodia for the West. But she never supported me and she criticized my idea, saying that I was thinking about trivial matters.

In 1975, I attempted to leave Cambodia for France, but my effort was futile. That year Cambodian communists took over the Cambodian government and this prevented me from going to France. About four years later, I had another chance to flee my country to Thailand. I stayed in Thailand at a refugee camp for about a year. Then I came to the U.S. in 1981 as a refugee.

បញ្ញាក្រៈបានបន្ថែមឲ្យខ្ញុំទៅប្រកបកិច្ចការងារជាកម្មករក្នុងរោងចក្រទាំងបន្ថិចិត្ត ។

My life in the U.S. is not as easy as I expected. I have to support my family. My plans to study seem always to dissolve because I have to care for my children. Even though I could not always afford to go to school, I tried to find another way to study and to improve my English. Once a week I studied the Bible with an American woman, in spite of the fact that I did not believe in the Bible. And I also provided my people with free help, taking them to see doctors, case workers, etc., and this also helped me with my English.

In 1985, after I got my divorce, I decided to go back to school to get my high school diploma. In 1988 I received my diploma from the Portland adult education program. Soon after this, I enrolled in the University of Southern Maine in Portland. At that time, my English did not meet college requirements. I had to study English as a second language for another year in order to attend regular classes at the University.

As a single parent with two children, I find myself financially hardly surviving. I am unable to attend school regularly because I cannot afford to pay for my tuition. Sometimes I don't have enough money to buy food. These kinds of problems really distract me from my studies.

In 1988, while I was attending college, I was employed by a local resettlement program as a part time interpreter for Cambodian women. My duties were helping women with social needs. During my work with Cambodian women, I discovered that it was very hard for them to start new lives in the U.S. For instance, they have to study a new language and new culture. And most of the women who I worked with have problems studying English. They told me that they had problems with concentration in school and they tried in vain to force themselves to go to school. Because language is fundamental, how could these women learn a new culture without language?

Even if women have good English, they still have a hard time growing accustomed to and learning this new culture. It is not only a language barrier or culture shock that we have to deal with. We also have severe problems which are caused by Cambodian genocide. The war left us with psychological scars. All of us have been suffering severely from being separated and being lost. Even if too many years have past, we are still haunted by memories of our families. And this event seems endless and drags on and on.

For example, at daybreak I am doing o.k. but whenever nightfall comes, I frequently have dreams about my family who were executed by Cambodian communists. I wake up at the middle of the night with emptiness surrounding me. I feel restless and cry for a couple of hours before I can fall back to sleep. And this memory takes me a few days to recover from emotionally. One woman I know has been in a severe depression since her husband was taken away. She has severe headaches and trouble sleeping. As an interpreter for these women, whenever I take them to see a psychiatrist or a counselor, I find myself wrapped up with their ordeals. I can feel the reflection of their dreams.

Our life in the U.S. is like a small boat which is floating in the middle of the ocean. We have no destination and no hope. We don't know how our future is going to be. Although I sometimes feel pessimistic about my future, I always try to overcome my obstacles. I never say die or let myself drown because of these obstacles.

ជីវិតជាការរស់ នៅ វិឆសេចក្ដីព្យាយាមនិងសេចក្ដីអំណត់ក៏ជាផ្នូវល្អានផ្លោះទៅរករសេចក្ដីសំរេចនិងសុភមង្គលបាន ។ បើ រស់នៅខ្ញុះសេចក្ដីរស់ហើយផ្ដេកផ្ដួលរង់ចាំតែវាសនា តើវាសនានឹងណានិងរត់មករកឃើង ។

One night I had a strong dream about being in a boat with a lot of Cambodian people in the Cambodian gulf. I dreamed that we were in the ocean and the boat began to sink. I heard people screaming but I was not afraid. And I had a feeling that my parents were with me. The boat did not sink and we came to a small fishing village-market off the coast of Thailand, with houses up on poles. We were able to leave the boat and walk through the village. We all felt free. I think this dream helped me to realize about myself, that I become stronger to overcome my obstacles.

FEMINIST PRACTICE WITH REFUGEE WOMEN: SOME THOUGHTS ABOUT COLONIALISM

In her most recent work, bell hooks (1990) notices

> how often contemporary white scholars writing about black people assume positions of familiarity, as though their work were not coming into being in a cultural context of white supremacy, as though it were in no way shaped and informed by that context. White scholars can write about black culture or black people without fully interrogating their work to see if it employs white western intellectual traditions to re-inscribe white supremacy, to perpetuate racist domination. . . . When this happens, cultural studies re-inscribes patterns of colonial domination, where the "Other" is always made object, appropriated, interpreted, taken over by those, in power, by those who dominate. (pp. 124-125)

My contribution to this paper is to examine more closely what it feels like to be involved as a white feminist in community mental health work with refugee women. I am a 39 year old white nurse, employed in an academic setting, married with two children. I believe that in the passages quoted above, bell hooks could just as well have been speaking about refugee women and in fact this is how I hear her as she confronts racism and colonialism in the feminist movement and in academic settings. I take seriously her challenge that it is important for white practitioners and academicians to interrogate their own work and to examine more closely the fields of power that are replicated or interrupted in multicultural work.

Sokhany and I worked together during a year-long project (1988-1989) in which we met with a support group of Cambodian women in Portland, Maine. The purpose of the project was to explore psychosocial adjustment among refugee women and to explore the cultural and symbolic traditions that influence their adjustment and their responses to trauma and assault.

Our work combined elements of community mental health and feminist research methodology.

The project was co-directed by myself, another white community mental health nurse, and Sokhany. We met every two weeks with a group of 12-16 Cambodian women in various settings, including the University of Southern Maine, their apartments, and at the beach. Our meetings lasted for three hours during which time we shared informal dialogue and food. Neither I nor the other nurse spoke Khmer. About half of the women spoke with us in English. In our discussion with the remaining women, we relied on Sokhany's interpretation. Sometimes I met individually with women and was able to listen more carefully to their recollections of their lives.

Language was an ever present tension in this work with refugee women. I was conscious every moment of the politics that were encoded in my use of an interpreter. I was conscious of the privilege I held in speaking in my native tongue while they spoke to me in English. bell hooks (1990) acknowledges this politic:

> the presence [of those who dominate] changes the nature and direction of our words. Language is also a place of struggle . . . We are wedded in language, have our being in words . . . The oppressed struggle in language to recover ourselves, to reconcile, to reunite, to renew. Our words are not without meaning, they are an action, a resistance. Language is also a place of struggle. (p. 146)

And Alenka Bermudez (1988) also notices this politic:

> I reserve the right to use the Spanish word to tell you: death to death and victory to life and combat and battle and machetes to life and courage and tenderness to life I reserve the right of the precisely exact Spanish word to name death and to name life as long as the blood holds itself suspended in our trees. (p. 27)

The personal choice to learn or not learn Khmer as a second language is a political one. Since in language, as in our bodies, we have our being, I feel the distanciation of translating a life history or a trauma history from Khmer into English. I felt complicit and frustrated since there were never enough hours in a day to learn more than a list of frequently used words. I realize now that to deepen my work with Khmer women, I must learn to speak Khmer.

Most of the women in this support group had been living in the United

States for more than three years. As a result, they were not being followed by case managers for social services. They ranged in age from late 20s to early 60s. All but one of the women were unemployed during the time of this project. All reported a history of heterosexual relationships. All but two of the women were widowed, divorced, or separated from male partners. One woman was married. All but one of the women had children, and 13 of the women had lost children in the war. I can barely write these words, because I still cannot hold the thought of these losses. All of the women reported histories of nightmares, headaches and dizziness. Five of them were being seen by a psychiatric resident and had prescriptions for antidepressants.

We spent the first half of every meeting discussing immediate material and social needs. These included health care and dental needs, housing crises, questions related to social assistance, assistance with family reunification, questions related to education and jobs. I was and am continuously alarmed and discouraged by shrinking resources and by the massive proportions, the sheer weight of what would have to be moved to make housing more available, education more meaningful, jobs more available and more fulfilling, etc. During these discussions I was reminded continuously of the context in which the women struggle. Of Maine's 1.2 million residents, 98% are white. As I move in and out of their communities, I am continuously reminded of the field of power which I occupy and I ask myself repeatedly, "Why am I doing this?" "What entitles me to enter their lives?"

The participants in this support group were referred by case workers, physicians, community health nurses, sponsors and other refugee women. Their participation was voluntary and they were free to attend whenever they wanted or stop attending whenever they wanted. We referred women to community resources and followed up on each of their requests in the weeks between our meetings.

During the second half of our meetings we explored gender and culture in Cambodia. We listened to Cambodian legends and myths. We asked about women's roles in Cambodia. We explored folk beliefs about health, sexuality and childbirth. Because of clinical reports regarding nightmares and sleep disturbances (Mollica, Wyschak & Lavelle, 1987), we also explored their dreams and dream interpretation in Cambodia. I recorded their dream narratives in handwritten field notes. I discovered that this sharing of dream narratives was a ground which held an extraordinary power for me. Cambodian women seem to respect their dreams as cues to events that are unfolding in their lives and as sources of wisdom and guidance. Some themes that recurred in their dream narratives included

(1) violence and searching for safety; (2) communications from relatives, spirits or ancestors (3) good omens/bad luck; and (4) sexuality or their relationships with men (Thompson, 1991).

As they discussed and interpreted their dreams, they also asked questions about American people, about life in our cities, and about our connections to the land. Most of the women had lived in rural villages before the war. Their questions were a gentle nudge that pressed me to examine my own whiteness and those connections to nature that many white people now sense as missing. I had not anticipated what a doubly conscientizing experience it would be to realize that these women have not just been "one time" victims of colonization. They are now totally disconnected from their land. I began to feel an ever deepening wound, the same awareness that happens when I realize that white people physically removed American natives from their land. I am reminded by Carol Lee Sanchez (1989) that "dominant Euro-Americans waste the resources and destroy the environment in the Americas because they are not spiritually connected to this land base, because they have no ancient mythos or legendary origins rooted to this land" (p. 345).

My experiences with refugee women in this group became a powerful ground of learning. As I listened to their reflections about their lives before, during, and after the war, I was reminded continuously of the recursiveness of colonization. I felt a profound sense of personal and collective responsibility for their displacement. This is the personal and political kind of consciousness that women of color have insisted we must confront (Bulkin, Pratt & Smith, 1984). I now wonder about how white feminist practitioners or academicians working with refugee women experience the dynamics of conscientization. It was important for me to understand that this dynamic was occurring in my work and that I needed to take care of myself. It was important to be connected to sources of support and supervision which nourished me. I paid attention to my own dreams, I noticed and located women's art and music, I refocused my community service efforts on state and local initiatives to increase support for refugee women.

As a feminist, I wanted to understand if there are fragments of the symbolic or traces of women's imaginary that heal the wounds of patriarchy. As a nurse, I felt the responsibility to ground my practice in feminist scholarship. My theoretical leanings always lead to the same (frustrating) intersections: socialist feminist analysis of class; postmodern feminist analysis of sex/gender and race in the construction of power; psychoanalytic feminist revisions of object relations theory. I have been influenced by the writing of Nelle Morton (1985, 1989) and Julia Kristeva (1982a,

1982b), by feminist revisions and criticisms of archetypal theory (Goldenberg, 1976, 1989; Lauter & Rupprecht, 1985; Wehr, 1987) by the feminist writings of women of color (Anzaldua, 1990; hooks, 1984; Lorde, 1983, 1984; Walker, 1989) and by revisions of object relations theory (Flax, 1990).

I notice that these are all western feminist writings and that they raise a question about my understanding of Cambodian culture, i.e., that I have just grafted a western feminist template onto practice with refugee women. I have tried to work through this theoretical and practical dilemma, although I believe that like the poetics and politics of ethnography, multicultural work will always involve incommensurable texts and their interpretations, many of which may only be fully and finally resolved by repressing conflict and imposing closure (Clifford & Marcus, 1986; Gordon, 1988). I did read and study ethnographic accounts and histories of Cambodia (Briggs, 1951; Chandler, 1983; Coedes, 1963; Crow, 1988; Ebihara, 1968; Kuoch & Skully, 1983; Sam, 1987). I studied color photographs of the land and sacred temples in Cambodia before the war. In particular, I wanted to understand how Theravada Buddhism and the "old religion" might be part of healing experiences for refugee women. But the more I explored Khmer Buddhism, the more skeptical I became about its teachings. I notice that I repeat the white feminist script: Khmer Buddhism emerges for me as another patriarchal religion and they all have that scent of death. I see also that I have become another carrier of postmodern thought in the west: cultural relativism does not translate into moral relativism for me. I have a deep skepticism of the counsel and advice Buddhist monks would give to refugee women.

As I listened to their life histories and their trauma stories, I heard suffering, losses, and sorrow that in my experience are unmatched. In each of the women's narratives, I heard traces of struggle and endurance, despair and power. But I also heard traces of women's imaginary. I heard desire and longing and seduction. I heard powerful symbols which mirrored struggles of the body. There were dreams of weddings with dark men, dreams of desire for men who were mixed blood Cambodian and American, driving around in pick-up trucks. There were dreams of indigenous female spirits blowing their breath through a woman's body and healing her when she was ill. There were warning dreams about leaving the city before more desperate economic times came. There were warnings about adolescent sons being eaten by tigers in America. And there were strange coincidences: a bird with its feet cruelly tied together flying into a woman's apartment and her connection with it as an omen; that just as she untied the bird's feet and set it free, she wondered who would untie her and set her free.

These traces of refugee women's imaginary emerged in a context, were shared in a situation that constantly reiterated the struggles of class, race, gender, sex, and power. I cannot say whether the effects of our work were clinically significant for any of the women. I am happy to know that many of them are still in touch with each other in the community. And I have become much more vigilant about the need for local programs that address the needs of refugee women in our communities.

I thought I was doing this work because there is a need for feminist practice for/with refugee women. I see now in retrospect that I was also doing it for myself. I want to insist that this is not voyeurism. The women I worked with were not objects nor was I. Their subjectivity was so very clear that it illuminated, enlarged everything, politicizing everything.

This was not a reactionary, apolitical experience. Feminist scholarship can ground a practice which is at the same time deeply strengthening and deeply political.

> . . . women need to dare to be mad, to dream, to envision the soul that might emerge from a free body. We need to speak and write the words that knock the winds out of the codes of the good society that have restrained us. To empower ourselves we need to use our own divinizing mirror that reflects our truth . . . But if like the men before us, we see only a partial image in the mirror, if all we allow ourselves to see is the good mother, we will find no more than an abstract and potentially violent ideal. If we do not split off part of ourselves, if we do not forget that we are split ourselves, perhaps our image can elicit an ethic that allows for a responsibility that is not only caring . . . but deeply and radically political. Perhaps we can discover a responsibility that looks in all directions for its victims . . . (Massey, 1985; p. 187)

REFERENCES

Anzaldua, G. (1990). *Making face, making soul*, San Francisco: Aunt Lute Press.

Bermudez, A. (1988). Guatemala, your blood. In D. Gioseffi (Ed.), *Women on war: Essential voices for the nuclear Age*, New York: Simon and Schuster.

Briggs, L. (1951). *The ancient Khmer empire*, Philadelphia: American Philosophical Society.

Bulkin, E., Pratt M., & Smith, B. (1984). *Yours in struggle: Feminist perspectives on anti-semitism and racism*, Brooklyn, NY: Long Haul Press.

Chandler, D. (1983). *History of Cambodia*, Boulder: Westview Press.

Clifford, J., & Marcus G. (1986). *Writing culture: The poetics and politics of ethnography*, Berkeley: University of California Press.

Coedes, G. (1963). *Angkor: An introduction*, Oxford: Oxford University Press.

Crow, K. (1988). *A theory toward therapeutic syncretism*, Salt Lake City: University of Utah, PhD Dissertation.

Ebihara, M. (1968). *Svay, a Khmer village in Cambodia*, New York: Columbia University, PhD Dissertation.

Flax, J. (1990). *Thinking fragments: Psychoanalysis, feminism and postmodernism in the contemporary west*, Berkeley: University of California Press.

Goldenberg, N. (1976). A feminist critique of Jung, *Signs, 2(2)*, 443-449.

Goldenberg, N. (1989). Archetypal theory and the separation of mind and body. In J. Plaskow & C. Christ (Eds.), *Weaving the visions: New patterns in feminist spirituality*, pp. 244-255, San Francisco: Harper Collins.

Gordon, D. (1988). Writing culture, writing feminism: The poetics and politics of experimental ethnography. *Inscriptions 3(4)* (pp. 7-24). Santa Cruz: University of California Santa Cruz.

hooks, b. (1990). *Yearning: Race, gender and cultural politics*, Boston: South End Press.

hooks, b. (1984). *Feminist theory from margin to center*, Boston: South End Press.

Kristeva, J. (1982a) *Desire in language: A semiotic approach to literature and art*. New York: Columbia University Press.

Kristeva, J. (1982b). Women's time. In N. Keohane, M. Rosaldo, & B. Gelpi (Eds.), *Feminist theory: A critique of ideology* (pp. 31-53). Chicago: University of Chicago Press.

Kuoch, T., & Skully, M. (1983). *Cambodian voices and perceptions: A collection of materials, experiences and crosscultural understandings*. Unpublished master's thesis, Goddard College, Plainfield, Vt.

Lauter E., & Rupprecht, C. (1985). *Feminist archetypal theory: Interdisciplinary revisions of Jungian thought*. Knoxville, Tenn: University of Tennessee Press.

Lorde, A. (1983). *Zami: A new spelling of my name*, Freedom, California: Crossing Press.

Lorde, A. (1984). *Sister Outsider: Essays and speeches*, Trumansburg, New York: Crossing Press.

Massey, M. (1985). *Feminine soul: The fate of an ideal*, Boston: Beacon Press.

Mollica, R., Wyschak, G., & Lavelle, J. (1987). The psychosocial impact of war trauma and torture on SE Asian refugees. *American Journal of Psychiatry, 144(12)*, 567-572.

Morton, N. (1985). *The journey is home*, Boston: Beacon Press.

Morton, N. (1989). The Goddess as metaphoric image. In J. Plaskow & C. Christ (Eds.), *Weaving the visions: New patterns in feminist spirituality* (pp. 111-118). San Francisco: Harper Collins.

Sam, Y. (1987). *Khmer Buddhism and politics: 1954-1984*, Newington Connecticut: Khmer Studies Institute.

Sanchez, C. (1989). New world tribal communities. In J. Plaskow & C. Christ

(Eds.), *Weaving the visions: New patterns in feminist spirituality* (pp. 344-356). San Francisco: Harper Collins.

Thompson, J. (1991). Exploring gender and culture with Khmer refugee women: Reflections on participatory feminist research. *Advances in Nursing Science, 13(3)*, 30-48.

Walker, A. (1989). *Temple of my familiar*. San Diego: Harbrace.

Wehr, D. (1987). *Jung and feminism*. Boston: Beacon Press.

From Helpless Victim
to Empowered Survivor:
Oral History as a Treatment
for Survivors of Torture

Patricia K. Robin Herbst

SUMMARY. A group of Cambodian women suffering from Post-traumatic Stress Disorder were treated at the Marjorie Kovler Center for the Rehabilitation of Torture Survivors in Chicago, Illinois. The community-based Kovler Center stresses the philosophy of empowerment. The term "survivor," connoting their strength, is used rather than "victim" in the multi-disciplinary holistic treatments approach. The average number of traumas experienced by the women were 6.5. Symptomatology included memory and concentration problems, low self-esteem, flat affect with detachment, feelings of not living a long life, avoidance of memories and feelings, nightmares, flashbacks, and somatic complaints. The somatic complaints included "heart attacks," headaches, dizziness, fainting and stomachaches. The technique used for treatment was the Oral History method. The women felt empowered and in control when relating their stories. At the same time, with education, verbalization had cathartic benefits. The Oral History serves as a denunciation of their suffering and gives some positive meaning to their experiences as well as brings them together into a support network. Previously forgotten memories began to be uncovered as the traumatic experiences were relived within the context of the Oral History. Trust, acceptance, release of anger and the reforming of a supportive network developed through the use of this technique.

Patricia K. Robin Herbst, MS, is a member of the Clinical Committee and Executive Committee, and Chair of the Research Committee at the Marjorie Kovler Center for the Treatment of Torture Survivors, a program of Travelers & Immigrants Aid, in Chicago, IL, and a Clinical Psychologist in private practice.

141

INTRODUCTION

The Cambodian women's group initially met on December 16, 1988. Since that time, the number and composition of the group has varied. Therefore, in data gathering, I have restricted myself to a core group of fourteen women who have been there consistently.

All but one of the women were widows upon arrival in the U.S. Only one of the widows has remarried. All the women were poor and came from a rural area of Cambodia, mainly from the province of Battambang. The majority of them are illiterate in Cambodian and semi-literate in English. All of the women escaped by walking through the jungles of Cambodia into Thailand with their children, often carrying one child on their back for days. Once in Thailand, they were placed in a refugee camp where they resided for an average of four years before resettling in the United States.

Twelve of the 14 women are single parents with an average of two children each and reside in a poor area of Chicago. One woman is married with no children. One woman is married and has two children.

The number of traumas incurred during Pol Pot's regime (1975-1979) and counted to-date is given in Table 1. I've used the term "counted to-date" since the losses are noted and listed as they come up during the therapeutic session. I do not ask the women directly to list all their losses and traumas, as such forced recounting negates their psychological time-table for resolution and is therefore disempowering. As a result, these figures should be regarded as a minimum rather than an accurate and final statistic. The losses are broken down into two areas, both of which are familial: the number of deaths or torture in the nuclear family which includes husband, children, parents and siblings; and the number of deaths and torture in the extended family which includes all other relatives. The x's in the table stand for unknown.

The average number of total losses per woman is 6.5. The total number of other traumas verbalized to date by the fourteen women is 90. This includes such traumas as being tortured, raped, seeing the massacre or torture of others, and starvation.

As stated earlier, all of the women in the group escaped into Thailand with their children by walking through the jungle of Cambodia. Their only food was what little they could find in the jungle. Besides starvation, they faced the constant fear of physical attack by Thai pirates who were known to steal, kill, and rape. If they were fortunate enough to find and pay a trustworthy Thai or Cambodian guide to lead them safely into Thailand, they still had to be fearful of stepping on one of the numerous land mines.

TABLE 1. Number of deaths experienced by Cambodian Women's Group in their nuclear and extended families.

WOMEN	NUCLEAR	EXTENDED
SP	10	4
IM	2	1
SY	2	5
HS	2	4
MC	5	5
TE	5	5
TR	10	x
HP	2	2
SC	10	x
SK	4	x
UM	3	x
CC	6	x
TT	2	x
CT	2	2
Totals	65	28

Upon entering Thailand, the women and their children were placed in a refugee camp for an average of four years before resettlement into the United States. The lack of freedom, lack of privacy, overcrowded conditions, sparcity of food and water, and the lack of useful activities made the camps a center of depression, violence and crime. Rape, robbery and other forms of violence were everyday occurrences and kept the refugees ever hypervigilant.

Living accommodations entailed one room, approximately nine feet by nine feet, in which an entire family would eat and sleep. In an attempt to enhance their families' meager food supply, many men slipped out under the barbed wire at night to scavenge for food. In the course of this scavenging, many of them stepped on land mines. As a result, there were and are a fairly high percentage of amputees in the camp.

Sleep was constantly interrupted by intruders looking for hidden gold or jewelry. One woman recounted how a robber entered her neighbor's shack. "They came and robbed her in the middle of the night and set fire to her place. When the guards heard the commotion, they opened fire on the robbers, but they escaped. Fortunately my house didn't burn down too." If they remained in a light sleep, they could run to the hospital, sleeping on the ground around the building, when they heard a commotion. The hospital was a safe place since security measures were tighter to protect the foreigners that worked there.

Rape was also a frequent occurrence in the camps. When questioned about their own experiences, however, none of the women admitted to having been raped. Pictures they've drawn, as well as behavior, however, leads me to believe that at least 50% of them have indeed been raped. Intrusive, emphasized object-like parts of bodies as well as frequent, heavy use of red on lips were prominent in many of their drawings. Normally, they had no difficulty telling me that something did or did not happen. When the question of rape came up, they all essentially became mute and started doing something else without looking at me or anyone else. Since Cambodians are very judgmental about women who have been raped, their reaction was understandable.

RESETTLEMENT IN THE U.S.

Upon arrival in the United States, the refugee faces innumerable problems. Primary is the fact that it is a forced rather than a chosen exile from their homeland. Even with six months of training in the Philippines prior to their entrance into the U.S., they have little knowledge of the English language. Finding a place to live, getting to a social agency to obtain funds on which to live, buying food in a grocery store, and managing transportation problems are all overwhelming tasks confronting these women upon arrival in the United States. Additionally, the women in the Cambodian group were all from rural areas and were resettled into a highly urban area. According to Sluzki (1979), a period of overcompensation, when a denial of the migration's subjective impact occurs, lasts for weeks and even months. That stage, according to Sluzki, is followed by a period of decompensation, ". . . a stormy period, plagued with conflicts, symptoms, and difficulties."

Since the United States government-sponsored resettlement programs last for one year, chances are that upon entering the decompensation stage, they are, at the same time, faced with lack of funds for rent, food, and transportation, and an inability to speak English well enough to provide for the financial loss.

Their facility with the English language remains minimal for years. Even though they attend English classes faithfully every day for a number of years, resultant memory and concentration problems from their torture experiences handicap the learning and retention of new material. Without facility in the English language, it is impossible to get a job that pays even a nominal salary. Therefore, they remain at poverty level. In spite of this, each of the women ambitiously obtains work wherever and whenever possible to supplement public aid.

Because of their poverty, their residences tend to be in a high-crime area in the city of Chicago. There, they are constantly vigilant against being mugged, robbed, and raped. The ongoing threat of violence triggers flashbacks to the traumas they experienced in Cambodia and intensifies their feelings of powerlessness.

Self-esteem is further diminished by the racial prejudice experienced by Asians in this country. This is further intensified by the fact that their coloring tends to be much darker than other Asians, the Chinese and Vietnamese for example. All of the women manifested a hesitancy and caution in relationships with Americans as a result of such experiences. Such encounters reinforce and continue the feelings of isolation and alienation incurred during the Pol Pot regime. The systematic destruction of the community's structure was effected by the encouraged betrayal of friends and family for a little more food to eat by the Khmer Rouge.

All of these ordeals are suffered essentially without a support system or network.

SYMPTOMOTOLOGY

After evaluation, each woman received a diagnosis of Post-Traumatic Stress Disorder (PTSD).

Memory and concentration problems make it very difficult for them to learn and retain English. Very few memories of their childhood and pre-Khmer Rouge life were available to recall. This both puzzled and upset them. Memories of traumatic events were, if present, disjointed and obscure in the recounting with important pieces missing. When I questioned them about their memory problems, one of the women replied "If someone sees a member of the family die, it would be easy for them to lose their memory."

Affect during the recounting of their traumatic experiences was usually flat. It was quite common for a woman to relate the deaths of her children and her husband with a blank look on her face and no affect. Detachment from both past and present experiences as well as from their feelings was apparent. One woman related in great detail an attack and robbery on her person with total detachment and no affect.

About 50% of the women verbalized concern over the fate of their children upon their demise. When questioned, many admitted to a belief that they would not live a long life.

Conscious avoidance of remembering the trauma and any concurrent feelings of pain was apparent with all of them. "Don't talk about it, it's over, don't cry, put it away," were typical remarks made to each other. One of the women expressed it this way: "Before I was working at my neighbor's house sewing, I cried every night. Now it's better . . . I keep myself too busy to remember anything."

Traumatic events are reexperienced in frequent nightmares and flash-backs. Each of the women suffered from disturbed sleep patterns. Nightmares were encountered by the majority of women on an average of twice a week. Typically the nightmares were direct replications of a trauma experienced by them. An example of this was given by a 36 year old group member. She had dreamed that she was in Cambodia and the war was still going on and many people were killed. She watched in horror as the corpses were eaten by the dogs. She also saw cows and oxen eating the corpses. When questioned as to the possible origin of the dream, she told me the following story. "As I was walking to Thailand, after the Vietnamese came, I saw many corpses of Khmer Rouge in a village that had been devastated by the Viet Cong. First I saw the cows smelling the corpses. Then the cows, the oxen, the water buffalos, and the dogs started to eat them. It was disgusting." A dream shared by many of the women in the group was that they were back in Cambodia and someone, usually the Khmer Rouge, were coming to get them. They would inevitably wake up in terror.

Perhaps the most extensive and common symptoms among the women were somatic complaints. Every woman suffered from frequent headaches. The second most common complaint was what they called "heart trouble" or "heart attack." In general these "heart attacks" involved psycho-somatic pain in the chest area and were usually associated with feelings of emotional pain of some kind. It was somewhat surprising at first to hear one of the young women tell me that she's not feeling well today because her heart attacked her. Dizziness, fainting and stomach aches were also experienced by the majority of the group.

Description of the Marjorie Kovler Center and the Nature of the Cambodian Therapeutic Group

The Marjorie Kovler Center is one of five formal centers in the United States working with survivors of torture.* The center is community-based. That is, it is located in the center of an ethnic neighborhood rather than attached to a university or medical school. Clients are seen as survivors rather than victims with emphasis on the empowerment of the survivor and his/her family through a multi-disciplinary holistic treatment approach.

Multi-disciplinary, holistic treatment is appropriate since the consequences of the torture damage the individual psychologically, physically, and politically. Torture not only affects the individual but the family, the community, and even the nation. Therefore rehabilitation has to restore not only emotional health, but restore the physical, spiritual, and community health, as well as the individual's capacity to exercise power and be an active citizen.

To accomplish this treatment goal, the Kovler Center has a large corp of volunteers divided into three areas: clinical, case management, and organizational. A core of 35 to 40 volunteers from the professions of psychology, psychiatry, social work, massage therapy, physical therapy, art therapy, pastoral counseling, occupational therapy, and forensic, family, internal, and other medical specialties make up the clinical section. The individual needs of the client determine his/her participation with a particular profession.

Case management provides help in settling into the new community. Case management volunteers help the survivor deal with important basic issues such as finding housing or a job, how to get around the city by public transportation, learning how to fill out forms for getting services in the hospitals, etc.

The organizational section is composed of people who help to maintain the structure of the Kovler Center by advertising, fund raising, and by giving support to and organizing the other two areas.

The most important tenet of the Kovler Center is empowerment. Symptoms, although painful, can be treated by physical therapy, psychotherapy, and other healing disciplines. Empowering the survivors, however, strikes

---

*Taken from an interview with Dr. Antonio Martinez, Coordinator of the Marjorie Kovler Center for the Treatment of Torture Survivors, February 1991.

at the central core of torture, the aim of which is to put the individual in a powerless position.

Oral history is one of the methodologies used in the Kovler Center to operationalize the philosophy of empowerment. At the present moment, there are two Oral History groups ongoing at the Kovler Center: a Guatemalan group of male and female survivors, and the Cambodian women's group referred to in this paper.

A person relating her history discovers her importance, discovers she is in charge. Therefore, in and of itself, oral history promotes an enhanced self-esteem. By asking for their histories in an holistic approach, we are implying that the trauma is only part of their experience. It sends the implicit message that survivors are more than victims: they are strong; they are survivors. They can use their strength to help in the recovery process. This "strength approach" makes the disclosures of the traumatic experiences easier. By relating the experiences in her own words, the survivor is being empowered.

Emma Kowalenko states, "No matter how it is blended with another discipline or disciplines, Oral History enables people to speak for themselves. Language externalizes as nothing else can. Thus Oral History provides a picture; not a mere report of the experience but the experience itself. It represents human experience as it has been or is being lived. When, during psychotherapy, stories are told, data from the individual's life are retrieved and pressures are relieved thereby increasing self-control" (Kowalenko, 1988, p. 2).

As noted by Ana Julia Cienfuegos and Cristina Monelli, Chilean psychologists working in a mental health program in Chile (1983), the testimony (i.e., oral history) provides the client with the cathartic benefits of verbalization as the elaboration of the traumatic experience is presented in her own words.

Within the context of the Oral History, the therapist can hone in on the symptoms of Post-Traumatic Stress Disorder (PTSD) as they arise and respond in a spontaneous way, without forcing the issues and thus revictimizing the survivors. The therapist is able to explain to the client that it is indeed a symptom common in people who suffer trauma and *not* a defect in the individual. "These are normal reactions to abnormal situations; it is not your fault." This statement enhances the client's self-esteem. The survivor's strength and survival are emphasized at all times.

To integrate their experiences, clients not only need to say the words, but to connect the affect to the experience. The facilitator's job, then, is to explain and encourage the necessity for the expression of feelings.

The Oral History brings people together to talk about their shared and individual experiences in a community. In this way, individuals regain strength by sharing those experiences in a supportive group. As the women hear stories similar to their own, the mutual display of feelings and support reestablishes a sense of community. By creating this common project of support and association, the survivors are explicitly and implicitly saying that they are in the position of being active agents again. The group is empowered. Their decision as to the employment of their histories, by putting them into a book, enhances their power. The Oral History then serves as a denunciation of their suffering and gives some positive meaning to their experiences. As such, it could then be used to help liberate their country or to help pass international laws so that their experiences will not reoccur.

In the Guatemalan group, they have decided to use their Oral History to fight a dictatorship. In the Cambodian group, their objective is to teach their children and the world about their experiences.

The Cambodian Oral History Group

Initially, the group of Cambodian women was requested to join an oral history group. The women were told that their memories of Cambodia were important and needed to be taught to others so the culture would not be lost forever. The memories would then be printed into a booklet to be passed down to their children as well as people from other cultures.

To effectuate the treatment goals, the group needed to develop a certain level of trust in the American, English-speaking therapist. To obtain this trust, the therapist must be incorporated into the group. This presents particular problems when an interpreter is used.

With the Cambodians, incorporation of the therapist was accomplished through the following three ways: (1) their recognition that the therapist, unlike many Americans, did indeed like them; (2) the elimination of an authoritarian role by the therapist and the creation of a community by fostering equality and; (3) the trust that the interpreter placed in the therapist. Once trust was developed, the therapist could deal with the emotional symptomotology as it arose. The work on the integration and resolution of the traumatic experiences proceeded as it would with English-speaking clients.

Even though I used all these direct methods to gain their trust, complete trust took a period of time to develop. While it was developing, however, I believed that with innocuous, nonthreatening questions about the past, their self-esteem would start rising. Meanwhile, these non-threatening questions would emphasize that their lives are more than the torture experience. My respect for and interest in their histories would further enhance their sense of self-esteem.

At the first session, the clients' low self-esteem was apparent as they expressed the belief that they were unimportant with absolutely nothing of interest to say. As one client stated, "I don't know anything–I have no education, I'm just a mother." This was counteracted quite naturally once they started describing their life and found that the group, as well as the therapist, were indeed interested in what they had to say. This immediately put the clients in the position of teachers, an empowered position rather than that of the helpless victim.

During the early sessions, another problem became apparent immediately. The clients didn't seem to remember anything about seemingly innocuous or even happy events in the past such as holidays or traditions. I was unsure whether to attribute this to the fact that the Khmer Rouge demanded they forget the past, "This is year zero!" they were told. Perhaps it was too painful to remember positive feelings and events, or perhaps their memories of events before the trauma were indeed gone because of the trauma. At this point in time it seems that the latter was most likely, indeed the culprit. Whichever was the cause of the problem, my first task was to explain to them that memory and concentration problems were a natural result of trauma, and that they were not stupid! Because of this initial piece of information, they very easily brought up memory problems in other areas of their life.

One way in which their memory problems were manifested was the difficulty they had in learning English. They requested that I help them practice English. As I attempted to assist them, it strengthened the bond between us. The Cambodians went to school every morning and complained that by the afternoon they could not remember anything that they were taught. "I must be stupid," was their automatic response. This gave me the opportunity to explain to them that their being unable to concentrate to learn English was a response to trauma. I did indeed practice English with them for a few minutes at a time, but I also requested that they in turn teach me words in Khmer. This kept me as a nonauthoritarian participant, rather than the "teacher" as they insisted on calling me. Because of this interaction, they could learn English easier.

This method does not reflect and trigger the "power versus powerlessness" structure of the torture experience. Instead, it created another tie in the bond that was forming between us.

After several sessions in which the supposed "innocuous" questions were unanswered and the group was lagging, I made the assumption that the memories were suppressed due to the trauma and that the newer experiences would be closer to recall. I proceeded to ask them about the relocation camps. They all immediately responded by relating a variety of experiences they had in the camps.

As this topic seemed to come to its natural end, several members touched on their torture experiences. I felt like a new level was about to begin, but their trust in me was still too tenuous. At that point, one of the women asked me if I was divorced and why. After some hesitancy, I told them about my divorce. Although this personal disclosure would have probably been inappropriate in my private practice, I realized that it was essential to their ability to trust me. At the end of the session, one of the women took my hand while the others all watched, smiling, and said, "You really do like us, don't you?" They felt that I was not like the other Americans but one of the group. My sharing with them proved my respect and trust for them. At the very next session, they were able to describe their torture experiences to me. At that moment they began to feel that we were all together in this common enterprise. It began to be a group of women working together.

In the course of these reminiscences, there were a large variety of responses both from the person relating her story and the group as a whole. Helping them recognize their own distancing techniques while accepting and indeed modelling that acceptance of their feelings was an important part of the treatment. During one particular story, the woman next to the story-teller was crying. Another was staring straight ahead, "unseeing." Someone was smiling and even laughing throughout, and several were talking to each other, not wanting to hear at all. A common remark was "This is now, that's over with, forget it." This had to be dealt with quickly and effectively so as to not revictimize the individual.

At one session, I tried to explain that suppression of feelings would cause a multitude of problems. A perfect example of what could happen if you keep suppressing feelings and avoided remembering the trauma was their physical complaints. They all seem to have somatized the experience in some way, especially with headaches. Again, this enabled me to point out how important the discussion of the trauma was. They seemed to have no difficulty understanding the connection between feelings related to the trauma and their headaches.

Recently, the group trusted me enough to let me teach them some relaxation breathing techniques. This was accomplished by showing re-

spect for the techniques that they used in Cambodia for ridding themselves of headaches. It was an "exchange" of techniques. Relaxation
technique will enable them to feel in control of their own bodies and less
helpless, which is a necessity for amelioration of symptoms and a sense
of personal power.

During their reminiscences, I modelled the normal therapeutic attitude
of acceptance and compassion. The other members began to exhibit the
same attitudes, recognizing that they were not alone. This helped reform
a feeling of community that had been destroyed during the Khmer
Rouge's reign. At times during these early sessions, I sensed a feeling of
isolation on the part of my clients. This was combatted by holding the
client's hand or by expressing physically and emotionally my compassion
for their emotions and experiences. This attitude was picked up by the
group, and they became readily available for each other at this point. With
the enumeration of their experiences and feelings came a sense of pride.
This was seen not only in their manner–they literally sat straighter with
heads held high–but in their use of my first name. Up until then, regardless of my insistence that I was "Pat," they continued to use the term
teacher when referring to me. This sense of equality was very empowering
to the group as a whole.

After several women had related their stories, there seemed to be some
hesitancy on their part to continue. It turned out to be due to their deep
sense of shame that "Khmer killed Khmer." They were very embarrassed
by this fact and believed they were the only people to whom this had
occurred. To combat this, I brought in a book on the holocaust, with
pictures. They all seemed to be very interested in this historical tragedy.
Next, I brought in a holocaust survivor to relate her story. In relating her
story, she stressed that all survivors were strong, good people–the righ-
teous who needed to tell their story. The Cambodians were not alone–others
did it to their own people too.

As the holocaust survivor's story unfolded, through an interpreter, the
group exhibited nervous laughter, smoking, blinking, shaking heads, and
spontaneous uh-huhs. This rapidly gave way to rapt attenion with heads
shaking in silent agreement and encouragement. When she was finished, she
asked if anyone could tell her a little bit about what happened to them. One
Cambodian woman proceeded, just as methodically, to tell her story. The
meeting of the feelings between the holocaust survivor and the group was
almost tangible. She would burst out, with raised hand–"Yes–they did that
to us too!" And at one incredible moment when she said, "The Khmer
Rouge killed people who were lazy," another Cambodian woman loudly
interrupted–"No! We were tired and starving–not lazy!"

"It helps to talk about it, we feel better that way, and we also talk about it to educate so that it won't happen again. I went through this and I'm a happy person with grandchildren, and you can be happier too," the holocaust survivor stated. This pointedly expressed the importance of their oral histories and the fact that they had the power to denouce what happened in Cambodia as well as educate the world about it. This was obviously very empowering to the group or community as a whole.

The expression and release of anger, which is very empowering, remained particularly difficult for the women. In their culture, a direct expression of anger is frowned upon. In an attempt to help them release their anger, Elisa Perlman, an art therapist, and I encouraged the women to draw a picture of someone they were angry with. The majority drew some semblance of what they felt were Khmer Rouge figures. That accomplished, the faces were pasted on a padded stick body and the women made bats. Although very hesitant at first, several became quite energetic in their beating of the figures along with verbal attacks. The following week, one of the women was able for the first time to discuss and feel anger openly at her husband. She asked to draw a face of him and with little encouragement proceeded to pummel him and make angry remarks to him. Several of the women followed suit in more personalized anger toward their husbands and teen-age children. The allowance of anger toward the Khmer Rouge made them strong enough to express this more personal anger. The nonprocessing of the abuse by the Khmer Rouge was not permitting them to talk about the abuse by their husbands. They could now say the abuse by the Khmer Rouge wasn't their fault.

The feelings of empowerment that developed from their release of anger were immediately apparent in behavior changes. The first change concerned their feelings about Cambodia. Prior to this, none of the women ever wished to return to Cambodia. After the anger, they all began expressing a desire to return to Cambodia to "help their people."

The other new development was their desire to speak directly to me in English as much as possible. Usually, they will not try to speak English to an American because they cannot speak it perfectly and therefore believe it will insult the American. They very assertively and with great confidence want to speak to me directly and not through the translator. To feel empowered in the new community, you need to make the assessment of the skills that you need and try to get those skills. Therefore, they need to learn the English language and be able to speak to Americans in order to have power in this community.

In closing, I'd like to leave you with three thoughts from the Cambodian women for all of us to remember, as a tribute to their strength and survival.

"I survived because I guess I had a 'strong heart.'"

"I collected the seeds that we used to feed the animals and cooked and ate them."

"My children helped me and supported me. I needed to get food for them so I stayed alive."

REFERENCES

Cienfuegos, A.J., & Monelli, C. (1983). The Testimony of political repression as a therapeutic instrument. *American Journal of Orthopsychiatry*, v. 53(1), 43-51.

Kowalenko, E.A. (1988, April). *Oral history as a therapeutic method.* Paper presented at Approaches to Mental Health Delivery: A Cross-Cultural Perspective Conference. Chicago, Illinois.

Martinez, A., PhD (1991, February). [Interview with Dr. Antonio Martinez, coordinator of the Marjorie Koveler Center].

Sluzki, C.E., MD (1979). Migration and family conflict. *Family Process, 18(4)*, 379-390.

On Trial in the Promised Land: Seeking Asylum

Nancy Grey Postero

SUMMARY. Refugees seeking asylum in the United States face a legal system insensitive to the emotional problems refugees commonly suffer. Refugees who have escaped persecution in their homelands may be unprepared for the stress of the political asylum process. They are often treated more like criminals than victims of political violence. Many experience renewed terror as they are arrested by armed officers, jailed, and put on trial. Lawyers and judges with little psychological training may further aggravate the stress by their inquisitory or adversarial behavior, or misinterpret the symptoms of trauma-induced emotional disorders and conclude that refugees are dissembling or untrustworthy. Under such threatening circumstances, refugees may be unable to reveal the facts necessary to gain asylum.

Mental health practitioners can help by explaining the psychological symptoms of trauma to lawyers and judges. Psychological evaluations of refugees have been successfully submitted in asylum cases to explain the refugee's seemingly aberrant behavior, to corroborate the refugee's testimony, and to provide a sympathetic lens through which the refugee can be seen.

INTRODUCTION

A uniformed man, gun jutting out from a holster at his hip, pulls a scared, handcuffed couple out of the back of the van, compelling

---

Nancy Grey Postero, JD, is a Journalist based in Prescott, AZ. She has been working for the last two years on "Vanishing Homelands," a series of documentaries for National Public Radio. For this article, she draws upon her ten years experience as an immigration lawyer in Tucson, AZ, as well as interviews with refugees, other immigration attorneys, legal workers, social workers, and counselors.

155

them into the station. He motions them to a bench. The two Salvadorans, a pregnant woman and her husband, tremble, and say nothing. More armed men come in, bringing others. A young girl is brought in, crying desperately. Then the armed men begin questioning them. Where do you live? Do you know this man, that man? Where did you meet him? When? Then, after hours of questions, the woman is taken to a van, alone, and driven away. Where is my husband, she asks. He's being moved away, she is told. That is all they will tell her. Sobbing, in terror, the woman looks back into the darkness where she last saw her husband. She wonders if she will ever see him again, if he'll ever get to see their baby.

A military base in El Salvador? A death squad preparing to torture a subversive? Another disappearance in the making? In fact, this is the experience of a young Salvadoran woman arrested this year in Southern Arizona by the United States Border Patrol. The situations are very different; but for a refugee fleeing violence in her homeland, the feeling resulting from being hand-cuffed, interrogated, and separated from her husband would likely be the same: extreme trauma. In her experience, armed men mean only death and fear. She can't understand that the Border Patrol agents are asking these questions as part of their normal processing of undocumented refugees. She doesn't know that men and women are kept in different holding facilities. From what she knows of men with uniforms and guns, separation from her husband means her husband will be probably be tortured or killed.

For many refugees fleeing violence in their homeland, arrest and detention by the Immigration Service mark the beginning of a long and difficult process–seeking asylum in the United States. They have survived the terrors of persecution at home, and made the terrible decision to leave their homes, family, and culture behind. They have made the long and often dangerous trip to the United States and have arrived exhausted, but alive, in what for many has always seemed like a promised land. Emotionally scarred from their experiences, they long for a safe place where they can start their lives over and find a way to deal with the pain and fear that hound them. They are often unprepared for the next trauma they must face: the process of applying for political asylum.

This article will describe the process refugees seeking political asylum in this country must follow, as well as the emotional obstacles they encounter along the way. This is not a scientific study; but rather, a collection of anecdotal data. What each refugee experiences is, of course, particular to his or her personality, coping strategies, support systems, and the specifics of the trauma-producing events (Mejo, 1990). Nevertheless, understanding the range of difficulties refugees face as they seek political asylum may be helpful to all those who hope to counsel them in their adjustment to their new lives. Further, while the issues in this article apply to both genders, a book on refugee women would be incomplete without a discussion of the legal process they face.

The obstacles described by refugees may be difficult for many of their North American care-givers to understand, not because we do not believe the facts, but because our own experience with the legal system may well have been completely different. Care-givers–be they psychologists, counselors, social-workers, physicians, nurses, or lawyers–tend to be comparatively well-educated, privileged members of our society. Although we have seen injustice, and are sensitive to race, gender, and class bias, many of us still believe, fundamentally, that the legal system works. For many refugees, particularly those fleeing persecution from governments the United States supports, the U.S. justice system hasn't worked at all. Instead of receiving the protection they felt they deserved, they were arrested, lied to about their rights, and accused of fabricating stories of torture just so they could stay and work in the U.S. Ultimately, thousands of legitimate political refugees were deported back to the dangerous conditions of their homelands, *Orantes-Hernandez v. Meese*, CV 82-1107, (C.D. Cal. 1988).* From 1983 to 1986, only 2.6% of Salvadorans and 0.9% of Guatemalans who applied for asylum received it, as compared with 60.4 % of Iranians, 51% of Romanians, and 14% of Nicaraguans. The overall rate for all countries or that period was 25.9%. (U.S. Committee for Refugees, 1986). A January, 1987 study conducted by the General Accounting Office is even more revealing. In cases in which torture was the basis of the asylum claim, it found the following approval rates: 4% for El Salvador, 15% for Nicaragua, 64% for Iran, and 80% for Poland. Only applicants from El Salvador had actually been deported (Congressional Record, 1987). (Both statistics cited in Immigration Project, 1990.)

The last few years have brought some relief for Salvadoran and Guatemalan refugees, who have received some of the harshest treatment over the last decade. Several court cases have documented discrimination against Salvadorans and Guatemalans, and resulted in court orders design-

---

*Legal cases are cited according to publishing guidelines in *The Blue Book: Uniform System of Citations*, (15th edition, 1991), published by the Harvard Law Review. This is the universally accepted authority for citation in legal writing.

ed to improve their treatment. For the many thousands of non-Central American refugees, however, the process has changed very little. This article will describe the treatment many refugees have experienced, and, unfortunately, continue to experience now. It will also explain the changes that have been put into place because of the lawsuits, and the results for refugees.

WHAT IS ASYLUM?

Prior to 1980, asylum laws in the United States were overtly ideologically-biased. Asylum was only granted to people fleeing persecution from communist countries or the Middle-East (Immigration Project, 1990). Although the U.S. had signed a 1967 United Nations treaty which called for protection of all refugees, and an end to their deportation to countries which would persecute them, it was not until 1980 that the U.S. finally brought its immigration law into conformity with its international treaty obligations. Under the terms of the 1980 Refugee Act, asylum is now legally available to any alien, who satisfies the statutory definition of a "refugee," regardless of their country of origin. Many observers believe, however, that in practice, U.S. foreign policy continues to dictate asylum determinations (Immigration Project, 1990).

The asylum process takes on extreme importance to refugees, because if they have no other legal way to immigrate into the country, such as through family members already here, asylum is the only way to avoid being sent home to face persecution or death. A refugee who is granted asylum may stay in the country indefinitely, and may apply to become a permanent resident after one year. They have legal status, and may work legally. Most important, they no longer need fear they or their family will be arrested and deported. They are finally safe. This allows them to begin the long process of normalizing their lives.

Refugees can apply for asylum from outside the United States, at the border, or once inside the country, regardless of whether their entry into the United States was legal. Refugees may file an "affirmative" application by voluntarily turning themselves into the Immigration and Naturalization Service (INS), and asking for asylum. They can also wait to apply once the INS has found them to be illegally in the country, and begins trying to send them home. In this second type of application, the refugee applies directly to the Immigration Judge (IJ) during the deportation or exclusion process.

WHO ARE REFUGEES?

According to Title 8 of the United States Code, sec. 1101(a)(42), a refugee is an alien who is unable or unwilling to return to his or her country because of persecution, or a well-founded fear of persecution, on account of race, religion, nationality, membership in a particular social group, or political opinion. (An alien cannot qualify for this status if he or she has persecuted others, has been firmly resettled in a third country, or has been convicted of certain serious crimes.)

Refugees applying for asylum must show they have been persecuted in the past, or that they have a well-founded fear of being persecuted in the future, should they return to their country. To prove a well-founded fear, the refugee must demonstrate both a subjective and an objective aspect of fear. First, the refugee must suffer from genuine fear, defined as apprehension or awareness of danger, and this fear must be the motivating factor in the decision to seek refuge in the United States (rather than economic reasons, for example). Second, this fear must be based in objective facts or events, so that a reasonable person in his or her circumstances would fear persecution.

By definition, refugees face persecution, which one court has described as harm or suffering inflicted upon an individual to punish them for their beliefs or characteristics. *Matter of Acosta*, Int. Dec. No.2986 (BIA 1985), *modified on other grounds, Matter of Mogharrabi*, Int. Dec.No. 3028 (BIA 1987). Whether a refugee has suffered past persecution, or has escaped in time to avoid it, fear is the common denominator among them. Refugees come fleeing all sorts of horrors: rape, torture, arrest, civil war, and massacres. As a result, many suffer from severe emotional problems, such as anxiety, depression, adjustment disorder, or Post-Traumatic Stress Disorder (PTSD) (Cunningham, Silove, & Storm, 1990; Mejo, 1990).

Mental health practitioners have documented these disorders, and the many symptoms–nightmares, edginess, emotional numbness–that plague these troubled survivors. Many, like the contributors to this collection, are exploring the most effective ways to treat refugees. At a minimum, providing a safe environment and slowly establishing a relationship of trust seem to be necessary for the refugee be able to reveal and overcome the painful experiences he or she has survived. As the following sections show, for many refugees the immigration process often serves the opposite function, causing them further stress, and deepening their emotional problems.

THE ASYLUM PROCESS: FROM ARRIVAL TO TRIAL

The Voyage to the New Country

Refugees find their way to their new land in many ways, depending upon where they come from, and their economic circumstances. Some Southeast Asians and Eastern Europeans come under government-sanctioned refugee programs, and enter with pre-documented refugee status. Those with financial resources may enter legally with student or tourist visas, and then stay after the permit expires. Other refugees fly into the country with fraudulent documents and are apprehended at airports. Still others, like Haitians, flee in boats and are caught out at sea, or land without permission and are then apprehended at the port upon arrival.

The vast majority of Central Americans come in illegally, across the southern border. For those who make the trip overland, it may take weeks of bus rides, train trips, and hiking across land filled with road-blocks of immigration officials ready to send them back to their countries. Some refugees are lucky enough to come escorted by "Sanctuary" workers, the church-based North Americans who help high-risk refugees flee danger. Some people come on their own, wading across the rivers at the borders, and dodging the robbers who prey on the vulnerable travelers. Mexico City is renowned among refugees. If you're caught there, they say, you're sure to robbed, raped, and sent back to the Guatemalan border (Friedland & Rodriguez y Rodriguez, 1987).

There is a thriving business in alien transportation, too. For a sum of money, ranging from a hundred dollars to several thousand, a *"coyote,"* or transporter, will take refugees across the Mexican desert into the United States. Often, the *coyotes* take the refugees' money, and abandon them in the desert. Women tell of rape by *coyotes*; children tell of being held hostage by *coyotes* until family members can send more money. Families are often separated on the trip north. Some may be caught by the Border Patrol, while others escape, each wondering about the fate of the other.

By the time refugees make it into the country, they are under great stress. They are exhausted and far from their homes, usually don't speak the language, and are acutely aware of the loss of the family and community support structures that they have depended upon. Uncertainty and fear of discovery mark every aspect of their lives.

Arrest and Detention

The lucky refugees are those who are never arrested and find their way to a new community to begin the adjustment to this new culture. They may find homes with other family members already here, or in towns with others from their country or village. Nevertheless, if they are illegally in the country, these refugees live "underground," hiding from police, fearing even a traffic stop, which would result in their being turned over to "*la migra*," as Spanish-speaking refugees call the INS. Some women live for years in abusive relationships, refusing to call the police because they fear one call will mean their deportation. The bulk of the employment available to refugees is illegal, subject to sub-minimum wages, and often involves abusive treatment. This is particularly frustrating to those who left professional or academic careers.

Many refugees find this life so stressful that they make affirmative application for asylum. In the early 80's, this meant being prepared to go to jail, and posting a bond to get back out. For the last five years or so, in most communities, the INS has allowed refugees who apply this way to remain out of custody without the posting of a bond.

But many refugees are apprehended. This may happen at any time or place–in factory sweeps, in restaurants, at a traffic stop. Most often, however, it is upon entry into the United States. The Border Patrol has underground sensors in the paths near holes in the international fence, and rounds up groups of illegal entrants every night. An arrest along the border may take on a war-like feel, as helicopters swoop overhead with blaring lights, and agents with ultraviolet scopes surround the terrified refugees. They are captured, hand-cuffed, put in vans, and taken to Border Patrol stations, where they are fingerprinted, photographed, and interviewed. Some convince the Border Patrol they are Mexicans, and are turned back across the border to try the crossing again the next night. The rest are taken to immigration detention centers to await formal deportation hearings.

An arrest would be frightening for anyone, but it is especially so for already traumatized refugees. In many cases, their persecutors have been military or police officers, and to be under their control again brings on great fear. The guns, interrogations, and institutional settings may cause a reliving of the traumas already endured. Two Salvadoran girls, sisters aged 13 and 15, described their experience to the church "sanctuary" workers who gave them refuge in Tucson last year. Both had been raped on their trip north, the younger was pregnant as a result. When they saw the officers running toward them in the desert, they decided not to run because they feared being shot in the back. They thought they would surely be raped again, so the older sister told the younger to sit down. "Maybe they'll just rape one of us," she said. "If you sit down, it will be harder for them."

Once in detention centers, refugees are split up, the men sent to one jail, and the women and children to others, often far apart. Often, no contact is allowed between them, causing great anxiety for all. These are jails, and the men are forced to wear institutional jumpsuits, and talk to visitors through iron grills and plexiglass. One infamous detention center in the Rio Grande Valley, in Texas, where refugees were often forced to stand for hours in the hot sun, was known simply as *"el corralon,"* the big corral.

Since immigration jails have limited spaces, refugees are often farmed out into county jails along with other inmates accused of crimes. Refugees often rage at this demeaning treatment, saying they aren't criminals, and have never broken the law. They are scared of their cell-mates, isolated, and have no information about what is happening to them. Many don't even know where they are.

Being in jail has often been made even worse by dishonest Immigration officers, who deliberately mislead refugees about their rights. In 1988, a Federal District Court, ruling in a class action lawsuit called *Orantes-Hernandez v. Meese, supra,* decried the "coercive effects of the practice and procedures employed by the INS" during arrest and detention, and ordered it stopped. For many years, the Court found, the INS lied to refugees, telling them that if they applied for asylum, they would be forced to stay in jail for months, without telling them about the right to bond. They failed to tell many of the right to asylum and coerced them into signing Voluntary Departure forms, which results in the refugees' immediate return to their homelands. Many people who expressed great fear of returning to their homelands signed the forms and were sent home.

The *Orantes-Hernandez* case focused exclusively on the treatment of Salvadoran refugees, but many other refugees also suffered from this treatment. Since then, advocates for refugees say, the INS has been better about advising all aliens of their rights, and the number of voluntary departures has dropped dramatically. Other conditions in detention centers have not improved, however, and detained refugees still have great difficulty in exercising their right to asylum.

To file for asylum, the refugee must fill out complicated legal forms, and describe the basis for the claim to persecution or fear of persecution. This means saying who persecuted you, and why. Those refugees who cannot afford bond, or who have no one to post it for them, must file asylum from inside jail. Many of the detention centers and county jails where refugees are housed are in very remote areas, miles away from cities where lawyers work. The few prison projects that exist to help refugees through this mind-boggling process are overwhelmed by the huge numbers of refugees who need their help. Volunteers and lawyers who manage to get to see the refugees are often allowed too little time with their clients, and the interview rooms are rarely conducive to confidential conversation.

Moreover, revealing their life-threatening secrets is one of the hardest things for refugees to do. They are often convinced that the information they give will be forwarded to their homeland and harm those they left behind. They have no way to judge if the person to whom they are telling these secrets is reliable or will turn the information against them. And, most importantly, their experiences are very painful to remember and talk about.

To be forced to reveal such things while in the threatening environment of jail, shortly after a traumatic arrest, is exceedingly difficult. Many simply can't do it without the time or the safe environment necessary to allow them to open up and tell the truth. Understandably, asylum cases prepared and heard from jail often fail.

Several changes have made the detention experience a little less difficult in recent years. In some areas, legal advocacy groups have formed to help in-custody refugees. Sympathetic legal workers who speak the refugees' language help make contacts with the refugees' families, find bond, and prepare asylum applications. Unfortunately, these groups are only available in some detention facilities, and most refugees must make due without them.

Then, in 1990, two important new benefits for Central Americans arose. First, Congress created a "Temporary Protected Status" for Salvadorans, which temporarily bars the detention and deportation of Salvadorans. Second, as part of the settlement of a class-action lawsuit, discussed more fully below, the INS agreed that all Salvadoran and Guatemalan refugees in detention would be released without bond. These two benefits place eligible Salvadoran and Guatemalan refugees in a special favorable position, but bonds are still required for all other classes of refugees.

Preparing the Asylum Case: The Attorney-Client Relationship

Once out of jail, the refugee must find a lawyer to help fight their case. Whether it is a sensitive, politicized lawyer from a refugee advocacy center; a naive volunteer lawyer from a big commercial law firm, doing pro-bono work; or a well-paid private immigration lawyer, this lawyer takes on an extremely important role in the refugee's life. He or she will guide the refugees through the legal system and try to keep them from being sent back to the fearful situation they escaped. Despite what are usually good intentions on both sides, there may be great barriers to the relationship.

Few lawyers have had any psychological training to help them understand the emotional problems faced by refugees. Without such training, even sensitive people can easily misinterpret the words and actions of traumatized people. In comparison to other, "normal" clients, particularly those from one's own culture, refugees may seem difficult, uncooperative, or unappreciative. Few lawyers would imagine that the normally acceptable attorney behavior described below could be causing strain on their refugee clients.

The initial meeting may be the first time the refugee has ever been to a lawyer's office. Since in many countries lawyers are in league with the powerful forces that persecute people, it may be difficult for the refugee to avoid a natural distrust of lawyers. The formal offices lawyers tend to have may also be alienating to the refugee, who may associate affluence with power and, therefore, fear. Simple country people, like the many Guatemalan Indigenous refugees, for example, may have never been in a high-rise building before. The lawyer often doesn't speak the language, and a translator makes the relationship indirect.

Severely traumatized refugees, those who are recovering from torture, may have left-over fears about their physical safety that would never occur to a lawyer. They may feel more comfortable if they can choose where they sit, so they can watch the door, for instance, rather than sitting in the designated client chairs. Similarly, many refugees feel safer with their family around them as a support system. Isolation is often used as a method of torture. Most lawyers don't know that, and find the huge families of their clients a bit of a nuisance. Since the attorney-client privilege only protects as confidential what is discussed between the lawyer and the client when they are alone, it is only normal for the lawyer to ask the refugee to come into the office alone. The one-on-one interview may be very scary for the refugee.

For the lawyer, the purpose of the initial interview is to evaluate the case, to get the facts, see whether it will be a good asylum case, or whether some other relief will have to be found. There is often limited time for the interview, and that may be further curtailed if a translator is necessary. The lawyer wants to move ahead quickly to the basic facts. What happened to you? Were you persecuted? By whom? This approach may terrify refugees, whose goal for the first interview is more likely to see if this is a person worth trusting with their life and secrets. They may also be baffled by the rapid discussion of the legal process. Rural people, especially if they are illiterate, may not understand the obsession we North Americans have with sequence, and be intimidated by being grilled over dates and times. They may think of time more in terms of phases of the planting, and feel betrayed that their supposed ally seems to be tricking them with these hard questions.

It may take many sessions for the full story to unfold completely, and this invariably proves extremely frustrating to the attorney. There may be memory gaps, or seeming inconsistencies in the details, or dates. The refugee may simply not be able to answer some questions. These problems are common with refugees who suffer emotional problems as a result of their persecution. Traumatized refugees may have forgotten or blocked facts that are very painful to remember. Some people under extreme stress, like torture, take in information in an altered way, as if they are in slow motion. When questioned about such painful experiences, particularly by an attorney brusquely trying to iron out inconsistencies, they may become emotionally overwhelmed and be unable to think clearly. Refugees describe this feeling as a crushing sensation, like drowning in fear. Any answer might be given, just to be out from under that fear.

Lawyers, unaware of these phenomena, don't understand that their questions feel like an inquisition and may be causing their client to relive the painful experience. Instead, the lawyer may feel that the client is deliberately lying, or being uncooperative. One young volunteer lawyer said recently that, at first, this sort of response made him feel the refugee was "jerking me around, and trying to work the system for a green card." He wondered why he should waste his valuable time on an unworthy client. If the refugee didn't appear credible to him, he said, it wasn't likely the judge would believe him, either. These are valid concerns. Certainly, not all aliens have legitimate political asylum claims, and in some cases, people with no real fear of persecution have tried to obtain asylum on false grounds. What is important is that lawyers and judges take into account the effects of trauma upon behavior when forming opinions about refugees' credibility.

These problems can be mitigated by the measures any good counselor would take to build up a trusting relationship: setting aside enough time for interviews, so that everyone can relax; giving the refugee time to tell the whole story without being interrupted; expressing support for what the refugee has gone through, rather than giving a clinical opinion of the chances of a successful asylum claim; and going over the refugee's story as many times as it takes to get ready for court. Building this relationship is important, not just because it is the humane way to treat people, but because not doing it may make it impossible for the refugee to open up and tell the attorney the facts that will prove the case.

A positive experience with an attorney can be very helpful for the refugee. To get support, attention, and reassurance from an attorney can help the refugee regain self-respect. The time during which the case is being prepared may also be a good time for the refugee to get counseling. Many times lawyers will recognize the need for counseling, and make a referral. During the stressful time before trial refugees often manifest somatic symptoms that mask underlying emotional distress. "Sanctuary" workers say the refugees they work with often have migraines, skin ailments, and stomach aches during this time. Refugees may be convinced they have a terminal illness, like cancer or a brain tumor. Other signs of emotional problems may show up in the attitude of the client: constant nervous calling to check on the status of the case; inappropriate anger; or, on the other end of the spectrum, a numb emotionless recounting of past persecution. Their stress may cause increased alcohol abuse, which might in turn aggravate family disputes. This is a very difficult time. Dr. Adrianne Aaron, a psychologist specializing in refugee treatment, tells lawyers to be patient and to expect a lot of missed appointments. The focus of the legal case is the very thing that the refugee has been putting a great deal of energy into trying to avoid.

Despite the need, it is hard for many refugees to get to counseling. They lack funds, there are few counselors who speak their language, and refugees may battle cultural taboos against counseling. Moreover, as Ken Brown, a Tucson counselor who has worked with hundreds of refugees, notes, traumatized people may not recognize that they have a problem. They have survived by adopting a coping strategy that covers up or ignores the trauma, and they believe that this strategy has kept them alive. Regardless of the nightmares, or the migraines, they would rather not delve into the pain they have been holding at bay. In some cases, however, lawyers have been able to urge their clients to go to a counselor by explaining that it would be good for the case to have a psychological evaluation supporting their claim. Once there for the evaluation, the refugee may realize that counseling could be helpful.

Meanwhile, there is no feeling of safety for the refugee. One Guatemalan woman, who waited for several years to have her case adjudicated, said that every minute of the time she was away from her children she was tortured by the fear that the Border Patrol would pick them up and deport them before she could get home and save them. In an egregious case in Tucson last year, a Salvadoran torture victim who suffered from

PTSD was picked up by the police on a routine traffic stop. When the Border Patrol arrived, they put a gun to his head, and ripped up his lawyer's card in front of him. Situations like this are, thankfully, rare, but illustrate the continued feeling of powerlessness refugees have.

Refugees on Trial

Without a doubt, the most stressful step of the asylum process is the trial. Not all asylum cases go to trial, however. If the refugee was never found to be in the country illegally, and applied affirmatively, the case is first heard by a hearing officer, rather than a judge. This hearing is more like an interview with the hearing officer, and there is no attorney representing the INS. If asylum is denied, the refugee will be placed in deportation hearings, and can re-raise the asylum claim as a defense to deportation before the Immigration Judge.

In those cases where the refugee is placed in deportation or exclusion, asylum is decided at a trial, called a "merit hearing." An Immigration Judge hears evidence presented to support the application for asylum. The refugee testifies, describing the persecution he or she suffered, or why he or she has a well-founded fear of persecution. It is an adversarial situation, because a lawyer for the INS, called the Trial Attorney, acts as a prosecutor, cross-examining the refugee and other witnesses for the refugee, and arguing for a denial of the asylum claim. After hearing all the evidence, and the arguments by the lawyers, the Judge makes an oral decision granting or denying asylum.

The trial before the Judge evokes many of the stresses described above–fear of officials, distrust of lawyers, discomfort in formal or institutional settings–and magnifies them. The judge has the refugee's life in his or her hands, and becomes, therefore, a powerful and frightening person for the refugee. In most courts, the judge sits higher than the participants, reinforcing the appearance of power. The tone of the trial is adversarial, and at times the judge may yell at or scold the lawyers or witnesses. The refugee must rely on the court translators, some of whom are not very good, to understand what is happening.

The key to the trial is the refugee's testimony. In the great majority of asylum cases, there is no evidence available other than what the refugee can provide. It is now accepted that refugees often flee their countries with nothing but the clothes on their backs, and have no time to gather documentation of their claims. Moreover, the evidence they need may not be available–death lists, for example, are rarely published. The attorney will offer whatever evidence is available to bolster the testimony, such as country reports, newspaper accounts, letters from family members at home advising the refugee not to come home, etc. For the most part, however, the judge must decide the case based upon what the refugee says, and whether the court finds the testimony to be credible. The judge can deny the case strictly on the ground that the refugee does not appear credible.

The refugee's response to having to testify varies greatly. For many, especially those who have been well-prepared by a supportive lawyer, and who have been over their testimony many times, it can be an important moment of testimonial. Finally, they are able to recount, on the record, the unfair treatment they received, and ask for justice. To be able to stand up before authority and describe the persecution they have suffered is a powerful step toward overcoming the shame and guilt so many refugees feel.

For many others, however, it is a terrible reliving of the traumatic experience itself. The huge stress of the trial, anticipated for months or sometimes years, combined with the anxiety of having to testify and relate the horrors of the past, often causes great emotional turmoil. This is augmented by the judgmental and sometimes sarcastic questions by the Trial Attorney (and often the Judge), implying that the refugee is only here for economic reasons, or that the refugee is exaggerating the danger at home.

The stress causes many emotional reactions. Asylum lawyers always say you just never know what will happen in trial. They are mystified when their clients who have gone over the details of the case several times in preparation for the hearing, testify in court about things they have never mentioned before. Or, worse, forget vital information. One Tucson lawyer described her surprise during the testimony of her client, a man who had been brutally attacked by military police in his country. During the attack, the police said they were looking for the man's brother and sister, who the police believed were subversives. The basis of his asylum claim was that the military had persecuted him, and would do so in the future, because of his relationship with the brother and sister. During his testimony, however, the nervous man forgot to mention that the police had asked about his family members. When his lawyer asked directly, he denied it. After court, when his exasperated lawyer asked him about it, he said he'd just forgotten.

This kind of stress reaction is common. Refugees under stress will resort to the survival strategies that bring them comfort. Unfortunately, the resulting behaviors do not make them look like credible witnesses to the Judge. The edginess, the constant scanning of the room that comes from severe anxiety, may make a person appear untrustworthy, or shady to a relatively affluent North American judge. Witnesses who testify with the flat affect adopted by traumatized people as a way of keeping the fear under control, may appear as if they are making the story up or merely reciting a well rehearsed story someone else has told them. They may minimize the horror, or focus on what seems to the judge to be an inappropriate detail. One Salvadoran refugee, for example, who was imprisoned and severely tortured for over a month, kept coming back to the fact that his torturers had stolen his boots and never gave them back! The rage he could not let himself feel about his torture had been channeled to the less painful theft of his boots.

Many refugees have been denied asylum after presenting their claims to the Judge. To open the wounds enough to divulge the horrible things that have happened to them and then not to be believed by the judge–or worse, to be accused of deception–is devastating. To many, it is further evidence of their own guilt or shame, which many survivors feel. They perceive it as punishment for having left their families behind, or for merely having survived. Logistically, a loss means appealing to a higher court, and more waiting. Emotionally, it means further uncertainty about the future, and continued lack of control over their lives. For those who had hoped to immigrate their families once they received legal status, it means continued separation.

Recent Changes

In 1991, a national class-action lawsuit, *American Baptist Church v. Thornburgh*, 760 F. Supp. 796 (N.D..Cal. 1991), challenged INS discrimination against Central American refugees. In a stunning settlement agreement, the INS agreed to stop all deportations of Salvadorans and Guatemalans in the country at the time of the settlement, and to grant rehearings of their asylum claims before new specially-trained hearing officers, called Asylum Officers. For the estimated 150,000 Central Americans whose cases will be readjudicated, this settlement offers one last hope against deportation.

One of the terms of the agreement benefits non class-member refugees, too. Now, all affirmative asylum applications, regardless of the country of origin of the applicant, will be presented first to the AO's, instead of the INS hearing officers who used to hear the cases. It is hoped that the special training given to the AO's will sensitize them to the situations of refugees from all countries.

How Can Mental Health Practitioners Help?

The first, most obvious, way is to provide the safe, affirming environment lacking in the immigration process. Caring treatment, as explored in the other articles in this collection, offers refugees the help they need to form new, healthy strategies to overcome the traumas they have survived.

Counselors can also take part in the legal process by helping shed light on the psychological effects of the process. A discussion with the refugee's attorney might help him or her understand the situation more clearly. Understanding the symptoms of PTSD or anxiety reaction might help the attorney be more patient, and less inquisitory. One counselor in Tucson suggests a joint session with the lawyer and the refugee.

The most tangible contribution a mental health practitioner can provide to the case is a written evaluation of the refugee's mental condition, to be submitted to the court along with the refugee's asylum application. This evidence is admissible as proof that the refugee has suffered trauma; it corroborates the refugee's story. If the basis of the asylum case is well-founded fear, the psychological evaluation can prove that the refugee is truly fearful of returning home. Since credibility and the moral character of the refugee are issues before the court, the expert opinion of a mental health practitioner, in writing or in live testimony, is also admissible to explain the current behavior of the refugee.

The goal of such a report is to document the symptoms the refugee is suffering, and to explain that these symptoms are normal for someone who has experienced the type of trauma the refugee has endured. Of course, the clinician cannot say whether or not the refugee's story is true. What can be said, and what should be said, is that the symptoms the refugee is suffering are consistent with the story, and are, in fact, proof that something traumatic did occur. If the client suffers from PTSD, the report should explain that the PTSD is a response to a stress outside the normal experience, and that its symptoms form an identifiable cluster which, if not found, precludes the PTSD diagnosis. Since some part of the traumatic experience itself is continually manifested in the PTSD sufferer's present life, in the form of nightmares, or flashbacks, documentation of those manifestations can provide proof to the court that the experience did occur.

Psychological evidence can also mitigate any bad impressions the refugee's testimony might have on the judge, by explaining why the refugee acts as he or she does. Depending upon the symptoms the particular refugee has, the report can explain hyper-vigilance, flattened affect, impaired memory, inconsistent statements, or substance- or spouse-abuse, as part of the emotional problem the refugee is suffering rather than evidence of bad moral character or lack of credibility.

A clearly written report which humanizes the terrible symptoms the refugee is experiencing can provide the judge with a sympathetic lens through which to see the asylum applicant, and can mean the difference between a grant of asylum or deportation. Lawyers and psychologists who have collaborated on asylum cases in this way find they have had great success. Adrianne Aaron has worked with attorneys on many cases around the country, and says asylum has been granted in every case so far in which they have presented evaluations. She and her colleague, Jan Austerlitz at the Moriarty Center in San Francisco, have prepared an excellent manual for use in such cases, including model evaluations for refugees (Committee for Health Rights in Central America, 1987).

CONCLUSION

Refugees seeking asylum in the United States have encountered great obstacles throughout the legal process. Some of the difficulties faced by refugees in the last decade are slowly being changed as a result of lawsuits challenging institutional discrimination. A great deal of the distress, however, is caused by a legal system insensitive to the particular emotional problems suffered by refugees. It is hoped that as lawyers, judges, and asylum officers are informed about these issues, the process can be made less traumatic for the refugees and, therefore, more likely to result in justice.

Collaboration between legal workers and mental health practitioners is essential to this goal. While the primary function of a psychotherapist is helping the refugee patient overcome the trauma he or she has experienced, there is a crucial role for the therapist in the legal process: helping the lawyer understand and present the refugee's mental condition to the court. The therapist playing this dual role will not only better understand the obstacles refugees face, but may also experience the satisfaction of helping them win their asylum cases, and overcome their biggest fear–deportation.

REFERENCES

American Baptist Church v. Thornburgh, 760 F. Supp. 796 (N.D. Cal. 1991). A class action lawsuit filed on behalf of Salvadorans and Guatemalans challenging bias in the asylum adjudication process.

Committee for Health Rights in Central America, & The Father Moriarty Central American Refugee Program. (1987). *Political Asylum, A Handbook for Legal and Mental Health Workers*. San Francisco.

Congressional Record (January 20, 1987). The Report of the General Accounting Office on Asylum Statistics.

Cunningham, M., Silove, D., & Storm, V., (1990). Counseling survivors of torture and refugee trauma, *Australian Family Physician*, 19, 501.

Friedland, J., & Rodriguez y Rodriguez, J., (1987). *Seeking Safe Ground, The Legal Situation of Central American Refugees in Mexico*. San Diego, California: The Mexico-United States Law Institute of the University of San Diego School of Law.

The Immigration Project of the National Lawyers Guild (1990). Immigration Law and Defense (Third ed.). New York: Clark Boardman Company, Ltd.

Matter of Acosta, Int. Dec. No. 2986 (BIA 1985), *modified on other grounds, Matter of Mogharrabi*, Int. Dec. No. 3028 (BIA 1987).

Mejo, S., (1990). Post-Traumatic Stress Disorder: An Overview of Three Etiological Variables, and Psychopharmacologic Treatment, *Nurse Practitioner*, 15(8), 41-45.

Orantes-Hernandez v. Meese, CV 82-1107, (C.D.Cal., filed April 29, 1988), A class action lawsuit filed on behalf of Salvadorans residing in the United States who had been taken into custody by the Immigration and Naturalization Service.

U.S. Committee for Refugees, *Despite a Generous Spirit: Denying Asylum in the United States*, (December 1986).

SECTION IV:
JOURNEYS TO RECOVERY:
THE HEALING PROCESS

Testimonio, a Bridge
Between Psychotherapy and Sociotherapy

Adrianne Aron

SUMMARY. The *Testimonio*, or Testimony, is a therapeutic tool in the treatment of people who have suffered psychological trauma under state terrorism. This article discusses its historical origins and social and clinical applications. The objective realities of the terrorist state are examined in terms of their toxic effects on the community, and the process of Testimony is presented as both a psychotherapeutic clinical method for improving the mental health of the individual, and an act of social and political therapy that makes a significant contribution to community mental health.

Using examples drawn from women who are managing an accommodation to political repression, and their exiled sisters who have

Adrianne Aron, PhD, is a Clinical Psychologist practicing in California. Through her association with CHRICA, the Committee for Health Rights in Central America (347 Dolores Street, San Francisco, CA 94110), she has worked extensively with refugees from El Salvador and Guatemala who have suffered traumatic abuse. Dr. Aron is a founding member of the Centro Ignacio Martín-Baró, a CHRICA project providing Central American refugees with legal and mental health services.

173

had to flee for refuge, the article compares the use of Testimony in a public, social setting with its use in the clinical setting. Through this comparison the interactive psychological and political dimensions of the process are observed as critical for the healing of personal and social wounds, and equally effective in both settings.

THE EMERGENCE OF TESTIMONIO
IN A "LIMIT SITUATION"

The Testimonio, generally recognized as the treatment of choice for people who have suffered psychological trauma under state-sponsored terrorism, was introduced in Chile in the 1970s as a means of reestablishing the personal and political ties severed by political repression. Earlier it had been practiced in Europe with Holocaust survivors. But that it came about independently in Chile during a time of intense political repression is a matter of some interest.

Described as a verbal journey to the past that "allows the individual to transform past experience and personal identity, creating a new present and enhancing the future," (Cienfuegos & Monelli, 1983, p. 46), the testimony is a first-person account of one's life experiences, with attention to the injustices one has suffered and how one has been affected by them. It is based on the belief that to heal, individuals who have been victimized must regain the power to direct the course of their lives.

Elizabeth Lira and Eugenia Weinstein, the principal authors of the technique, published their initial report under pseudonyms (Cienfuegos & Monelli), for in Pinochet's Chile, psychologists assisting survivors of the regime's barbarities could easily have been disappeared,[1] imprisoned, tortured, killed, or expelled from the country for doing such work. Theirs was a Testimonio of sorts, for it declared and declaimed psychology's capacity to resist political repression by defiantly growing in theory and in practice despite–or possibly because of–the risks.

Ignacio Martín-Baró's (1984) concept of a "limit situation" is perhaps the only psychological construct that can explain the emergence of a new therapeutic modality at such a precarious moment. Like the "extreme situation" of the concentration camp (see Bettelheim, 1980), the "limit" appears when life hovers at the abyss, in a world controlled by the forces of destruction. But the emphasis of the "limit situation" is on the potentiating properties of the life-and-death crisis. The existential boundary it marks is not between being and nothingness, but rather between being and being more, and the dialectical process between self and society that it stimulates leads to surpassing prior limitations and effecting change in the world. It is fitting, then, that a therapeutic modality aimed at restoring personal and political efficacy should have been born in the midst of a social catastrophe.

TESTIMONY AS A SOCIALLY THERAPEUTIC ACT

Twenty years of intense political repression in parts of Central and South America have brought forth not only the new therapeutic tool of Testimonio, but the public therapeutic act of Testimonio that takes place outside the clinical context. This process of bearing witness to injustice by public declarations, although not undertaken for relief from psychological symptoms, has distinctively therapeutic features, and like its clinical counterpart finds expression both in the countries where the repression is rife and in those where the victims have fled for refuge.

The public Testimonio, like the clinical process, may be a written account or simply an oral rendering. It may use graphic aids like placards or pictures, and may employ slogans developed by community groups for enunciating their demands. In many areas of Latin America people with little preparation for public expression–most notably, women–have come forward with their testimony to challenge oppressive power structures and to reappropriate for themselves and their communities the moral standards and social order taken away by the repression. The Mothers and Grandmothers of the Plaza de Mayo in Argentina, for example, have inspired the formation of groups like the Co-Madres[2] of El Salvador and the GAM[3] of Guatemala, demanding an accounting for their disappeared children and insisting on punishment for the perpetrators of crimes against humanity. Amid heckling, insults, death threats, kidnappings and bombings that destroy their offices and decimate their membership, they go on bearing witness and demanding restitution, asserting through their testimonies the self-worth and guiltlessness of the whole victimized community. Insisting that their personal histories be understood in the context of massive social destruction, the women who participate in these groups begin to recover pieces of a personal and social identity alienated by the repression.

Because the public testimony is a simple tool requiring nothing more than courage for its application, it is accessible to women when other tools such as the mass media, government office and industrial control are not. But there is another characteristic which helps explain why it is not merely the disenfranchised, but particularly women, who have seized the Testimonio and used it so effectively: it validates personal experience as a basis for truth and knowledge, and personal morality as a standard for public virtue. These are historically feminist principles, invoked now as a truth for the whole community.

The Testimonio promotes a new, accurate understanding of objective conditions, that derives from personal experience yet exceeds the boundaries of the individual psyche. In declaring, for example, that although an act was sanctioned by the government it is nevertheless deviant and criminal, a woman who has been raped or had her children disappeared or been subjected to torture, appeals to her own pre-trauma experience to find a reference point for normality and to establish a standard for judging the perversions of the existing order. In so doing she not only critiques, but also alters, the objective circumstances, by recasting them to fit her own criteria for legitimacy.

The Testimonio cannot, of course, erase the objective reality that brought about its *raison d'etre*. But by re-framing that objective reality, the Testimonio's subjective account of what has occurred contributes significantly to the community's knowledge and mental health. It is a form of *socio*therapy, healing wounds of social trauma inflicted by the terrorist state.

SOCIAL TRAUMA: THE PSYCHOLOGY OF TERROR

Whether the case in point is Chile, with a long history of democratic rule until the CIA-engineered military coup of 1973, or El Salvador, with a long history of oligarchy and oppression, the forms of repression practiced by the terrorist state remain quite consistent (see Amnesty-International, 1984; Chomsky & Herman, 1979). Common tactics include rape, imprisonment, torture, disappearances, forced relocations of people from their homes and communities, verbal and written death threats, and extra-judicial executions by government security forces or para-military death squads.

In El Salvador today, the government's stated purpose in employing these practices is to control subversion; that is, to guarantee the preservation of the existing social order. A citizen's duty, it is said, is to defend that order, i.e., to defend the right of 1.9% of the population to own 57% of the land (Gettleman, Lacefield, Menashe, & Mermelstein, 1986), to allow more than two-thirds of the people to remain unemployed or under-employed (*Diario Latino*, 1990), to support the practice of allocating but one doctor for every 26,000 rural inhabitants (CHRICA, 1985) and of having 38% of its urban families subsist on less than $45 U.S. per month (Martín-Baró, 1987). Those who consider the existing order indefensible, like clergy who have embraced the Option for the Poor, are stigmatized as subversives. In consequence, nuns, priests, church lay workers, even the Archbishop, have been assassinated by the Salvadoran military—subversives all.

The stigma is contagious. It spreads to people identified by kinship or association with the alleged offenders, jeopardizing their mental and physical well-being. It corrupts and distorts the consciousness of those who identify with the oppressed, for the only way to reduce fear is to reduce risk, and this leads to efforts to disassociate from the victims, which in turn leads to confusion. If the Archbishop was a communist, a person might reason, then what happened to him won't happen to me, because unlike him, *I* am a Catholic. The same kind of distortion of consciousness can, and often does, occur in people who have themselves been targeted and victimized, and in the course of the abuse become alienated from their own identities. During torture people come to doubt their own innocence, feeling that they must have done something terribly wrong if the government has singled them out for such prolonged and excruciating pain.

Because the whole community is at risk, each individual must seek ways to survive in the environment of terror. Those who belong to groups that have been specifically targeted (e.g., labor and student organizations, health care providers, teachers, human rights workers, clergy) often can find no way, and flee for their lives. This flight response, enacted by more than a million Salvadorans and Guatemalans in exile, is not without its own psychological costs, for it forcibly separates families and dooms people to live as strangers in strange lands. Another response, common among people who feel at risk but not in imminent danger, is to stay home and play dead—hear nothing, see nothing, and above all, say nothing. Salvadoran children's drawings of human figures without mouths offer a graphic example of the psychological costs of this response (see Aron, 1990; Roe, 1986, 1989). The only remaining option for those who are at risk, apart from doing nothing and awaiting the footsteps at the door, is to fight—either physically by joining the armed resistance, or psychologically by bearing witness to what is going on and speaking out.

SOCIAL RECOVERY:
THE PSYCHOLOGY OF TESTIMONIO

Testimonio and Community

Within the community the Testimonio, as a voice for those afraid to speak, becomes the courageous deed that enables others to come forth in solidarity. That is, it becomes the catalyst for its own support network which, until its utterance existed only in fragmented form, as unrealized potential. For stigmatized victim and supporters alike, the question of responsibility becomes clear: the government is identified unequivocally as the agent of injustice. The government lays the blame for the nation's social convulsions on the people themselves; and only when the people have formally contested this accusation does the locus of culpability move to where it properly belongs. With this knowledge formalized, the community is liberated from an ideologized reality that has become internalized, much in the way that communities are freed through women's protests, of believing that victims of sexual assault are to blame for the crimes committed against them.

Broadly speaking, the Testimonio's therapeutic value consists in its affirmation of critical, ego-sustaining principles that have been compromised as a result of the traumatic experiences to which individuals and their communities have been exposed. Among these principles are the right to free expression, especially as regards the injustice of what has occurred; a belief in the human capacity to vanquish, through solidarity, the negative human capacity to destroy life; and a belief in one's own value as a human being and a member of a community. Because personal and social identity are necessarily interdependent, individual affirmation generally carries meaning for the community at large, as can be seen in an incident that occurred in El Salvador in 1989.

In January of that year, a 23 year-old catechist from the village of J___[4] was en route to San Salvador to visit a priest. At a town along the way, where she got off the bus to inquire about a job at the local factory, government soldiers spotted her and forced her into their van, saying her documents were not in order. She screamed at them, "You have no right!" She banged on the window and demanded to be let go. They stuffed a dirty rag in her mouth.

The soldiers kept the woman gagged until they reached their headquarters, where they were joined by their superior officer who ordered her to undress. When she refused, they ripped her clothes from her body. Accountable to no one except their commanders (see Aron, Corne, Fursland & Zelwer, 1991), they gang-raped her while laughing at her vows to denounce them in public. The following day they raped her again and then, finished with her, dumped her on a country road.

The young woman, with the help of church and human rights workers, went to the nation's capital and appeared on national television, telling her harrowing tale and demanding that the five soldiers, whom she identified by name, be brought to trial. In retaliation, the military went to her village to threaten her relatives and friends. But her valor won strong approval from her fellow villagers, who remained undaunted. In a special Mass said in her honor people came forth to express their admiration for her courage. Among them was an old man who felt moved to correct the mistaken Salvadoran stereotype of women as weak, and to remind the community of how much they could learn from their women, who, though targeted for sexual abuse, dared to resist the repression by denouncing it (CDHES, 1989).

As Martín-Baró (1990) has pointed out, under conditions of state terrorism the victimization of an individual has a toxic effect on the whole community, and what needs to be healed, therefore, is not only the many individuals who have suffered abuse but the social structures undermined and corrupted by the violence. As well as formal institutions such as the family, the educational system, the church, the courts, etc., the emotional foundations that support the social structures–trust, compassion, attachment, and a feeling for civic virtue–are also damaged and require repair. The young woman's act of telling her story in public was an example of a healing process taking place both within individuals and within the social structures and their supports.

The woman's Testimonio was self-empowering, affirming her own knowledge of the injustice she had suffered. It inspired not only the solidarity that would assist in her personal recovery, but also the rehabilitation of a community that might have remained paralyzed by fear. Her decisive accusations of the military also left no doubt about who was responsible for these abuses–a clarification that increased the community's understanding of its subjugation, but also helped men in the community to reflect meaningfully on certain aspects of women's realities. And this latter reflection represented more than a breakthrough in sexual stereotyping and a recognition of the compounded oppression experienced by women under conditions of state terrorism; it signified also an affirmation of the community's emotional commitments to one another, more poignant perhaps for having been articulated by a man, in a culture where emotional nurturance is generally considered a female responsibility.

The personal healing of the young catechist from J___ will require more than her own act of testimony and the solidarity it engendered, just as the community will need more than affirmations and courage to repair the damage to its social structure. But the Testimonio has altered the conditions for recovery, making them more favorable for both the individual victim and the community at large.

Testimonio in Exile

For women who have sought refuge abroad, the physical risks attendant to the act of Testimonio are considerably diminished. But, separated from the community of potential commiserators and allies, the refugee woman who practices the Testimonio in a clinical setting faces other difficulties. Telling her story in a foreign country, she cannot benefit from the liberating interactive process which is possible only within the community, and this may tap a despair that itself must be addressed in therapy. Most likely she tells her story to a clinician of the host culture who has no direct personal experience of severe repression, and who may not only lack insight into the damage to a life course caused by such stressors as chronic fear, torture and forced exile, but may lack the capacity even to handle, let alone repair, such wreckage. The refugee fears with good reason that if she turns over the shattered pieces of her violent biography, the listener too may break. A Chilean refugee, for instance, lost her English translator during a gynecological exam in California, when the doctor gently inquired about the patient's vaginal scars. Upon hearing that live rats had been pushed into the woman's vagina during torture, the translator fainted.

Generally, though, in the United States the most serious impediment to communication is the refugee's fear of revealing her ambiguous immigration status–a disclosure that could lead to deportation. Because this fear is so pervasive it is rare for Central American women to seek interaction with other refugees or to trust strangers of any stripe or nationality. The majority are living as housekeepers in isolated homes, and in a great many cases, communicating with no one.

Testimony for Political Asylum

Some come forward to seek political asylum, but must then submit a declaration to explain why they fear returning to their countries. This process is made easier when psychotherapists assist by preparing psychological evaluations to accompany the asylum applications. The clinical interview on which the report is based can constitute a form of Testimonio, for when the refugee's story is told in a therapeutic setting, it unfolds within the safety of a "bond of commitment," becoming clearly differentiated from the legal testimony that must be given before the Immigration Officer.

The bond of commitment. The bond of commitment is one in which the therapist takes an ethically *non-neutral* attitude toward the client's suffering (Becker, Lira, Castillo, Gomez, & Kovalskys, 1990). It involves discarding the principles of professional distance and detachment, in order to stand with the client against the structures that support human rights violations, and thus prove one's worthiness as a safe container for the toxic information of the victim's life. The Immigration Officer, to whom the refugee is required to tell the story of abuse (for this is what consititues the case for asylum) receives the information but may disbelieve or discount it, and may have no appreciation for its relationship to the victim's agitation, depression, fear and overall behavior. The relating of the traumatic story is painful under the best of circumstances, but before a powerful judge who may be totally unsympathetic, politically biased, and unwilling to accept its veracity, the experience is for many people nearly unendurable.

The therapist must be all the judge is not: someone who can be counted on to believe what has happened, and to deplore it; who can understand one's feelings and behaviors in relationship to the traumatic events, and who one can trust as an ally on the side of life. To be able to help, the therapist must be alert to the difference between the origins and meanings of the psychiatric symptoms presented by persons who have been subjected to the abuses of state terrorism, and similar symptoms in others. Here, as the Chileans who coined the term "bond of commitment" explain, "it is taken for granted that the patient's disturbance is the result of a traumatic experience inflicted purposefully and criminally for political reasons" (Becker et al., 1990, p. 142). When a clinician is able to explain to an immigration official that that is the case, the veracity of the refugee's story becomes much harder to deny (CHRICA, 1987). Even before the settlement of *American Baptist Churches v. Thornburgh* (1990), when the United States was systematically denying political asylum to virtually all Salvadorans and Guatemalans who applied, more than 85% of the cases in which psychological evaluations were presented, were granted.

Effects on the host culture. When the Testimonio contributes to a favorable political asylum outcome, it may be said to have a social dimension with respect to the *North* American community. An admission by the United States courts that people are abused by their governments in El Salvador and Guatemala, belies the U.S. State Department's contention that to qualify as free and democratic a state need only hold elections. It validates the refugee's claim that these "friendly democracies" are not always so friendly to their own citizens.

RECOVERING SPEECH, TRUST AND VALUE

Affirming the Right to Free Expression

"If you talk, they kill you, and if you don't, they kill you anyway,"
Celia D., a 35 year-old Salvadoran woman told the psychologist in California. Being able to say that was worth a great deal, and may bring her
in time to an ability to tell her story–of a sudden flight into exile, of leaving her 6 year-old son and 3 year-old daughter with their father ("I
wished I could become a bird, to fly away to see my children in El Salvador"), of her panic when the letters stopped coming, of her clandestine
return to her country to look for her children, of finding out from the
neighbor who took them in that her husband had been disappeared, of
fleeing again with her children, sneaking them across the U.S. border.
While she can prize her present right to speak, the pain of the past inhib-
its all desire to talk about it.

The skeletal account is a beginning. It represents a penetration through
the wall of silence erected by fear–no small feat when one has already
had to flee for her life and is the wife (or is it widow?) of a disappeared
husband who was taken away and never heard from again. If she talks in
exile, who will be privy to her testimony (the authorities at home?) and
what might happen as a consequence to other members of the family? The
therapist cannot hurry her. Before she can confront the pain of the past,
she needs time to acclimatize to the unusual safety of the present. In this
warm-up period where she learns to trust, the therapist is guide, trainer,
and above all, barometer.

When Celia D. feels ready to continue she will tell more about the
main events she has sketched, filling in the background and including
minor events that provide context. In ways that are sometimes quite unexpected, she will elaborate details surrounding the traumatic experiences.
Oriana M. needed to tell all the ingredients of the chicken soup she sold
to the soldiers before the Salvadoran guerrillas threatened to kill her for
lending support to government troops. With the same precision, and in the
same sentence, she recounted to the therapist the exact words of the death
threat she received and the recipe for the soup she cooked–carrots, onions,
fresh beans. . . . The details surrounding trauma are furnished by circumstance, not logic. Elsa Esquivel Rojo, in recounting her unsuccessful but
unending search for her disappeared son in Chile, recalls the homemade
bread and hardboiled eggs she prepared for him 17 years before, when
there seemed to be a lead to his whereabouts (Politzer, 1989).

Testimonio invites attention to detail, an essential response to the macabre meticulousness that often characterizes the atrocities being recounted. Rigoberta Menchú must not gloss over in a paragraph or two the agony of her brother as she watched him being first taunted, then forced to walk on his flensed feet, then dragged because his tortured body was too swollen and lacerated to stand erect, and finally burned alive by the Guatemalan army. Seven pages of *I, Rigoberta Menchú* (Burgos-Debray, 1984, pp. 173-180) are devoted to this monstrous scene–not to horrify as she was horrified, but to explain so that others can believe the unbelievable, accept the reality of the really unacceptable. It was precisely to accomplish this that she learned Spanish, a language that would give her access to people beyond the few remaining survivors of her Quiché-speaking community and permit her to publicize her grief, her rage, her determination to struggle.

Vanquishing Through Solidarity the Human Destructive Capacity

In the Testimonio she gives to delegations of North Americans who come to her refugee camp on the outskirts of San Salvador, Tonita, too, spares no details. She describes to the people whose government trains the soldiers, the day she returned home to find the decapitated corpses of her mother, sister and three children propped up at the table, their hands resting on their severed heads. The 18 month-old's arms were evidently too short to reach; the soldiers had nailed the baby's hands to her head.

"With so many tellings, Tonita's testimony has acquired a repetition quality," observes a priest who has heard it at least a dozen times (Santiago, 1990, p. 292). He describes a terror in her eyes, but a truth and strength in her achievement, which is to deliver to the North American government through the visiting emissaries the words that the terrorist state has tried to silence: "*No más,*" she says, "No more money for this war." By transforming a passive experience into an active response, the Testimonio "allows us," as a refugee in California put it, "to commit a violent act, in speech, against the repression."

Whether in a therapy session in exile or in a church at home, the need is for contextualizing the suffering, which requires externalizing the pain–locating its causes, identifying its origins; that is to say, seeing, as Tonita does, the connection between the traumatic event and the structures which order social life. When there is an audience for this critical pronouncement, and the audience can reflect back to one the wisdom it contains, the victim can see some hope for restructuring social life. Thus, through the sense that solidarity exists, trust can be re-established and hope restored.

Reclamation of One's Personal and Social Value

The individual who has been damaged by state violence must reclaim more than a voice and a sense that it is possible to have allies in this world; also needed is a belief in one's own value as a human being and a member of a community. The Testimonio, by retracing the thread of a life course until it was broken by the repression, and the survival skills that promoted life after the traumatic events, facilitates a recovery of personal and social identity, a mending of the life line.

María Eugenia, a refugee in Mexico who was a university professor until the repression drove her out of Guatemala, was able to recount her academic development, from her rural elementary school, to the nuns' school in the city, and on to her first job as a grade school teacher. As she continued to grow intellectually and politically, she taught at all academic levels, and as the strength and arbitrary acts of the Guatemalan military grew, so did María Eugenia's political militancy. Then one day the thread was cut by a piercing death note from the Secret Anti-Communist Army. They gave her 48 hours to get out of the country.

Reflecting back on her second year of exile, she wrote in her Testimonio while in therapy in Mexico:[5]

> I suddenly had to realize that I had lost my country, my family, my compañeros, my friends, my work; this caused me unbearable pain . . . On a professional level, I'm nobody here . . . professionally I feel like a devalued coin.

The therapist, with an ear for feminist concerns, reflects on how María is "forced by exile to 'regress' to a condition that she never lived, of economic dependence," supported by a man and miserable with her lack of independent means (Aresti, 1988, p. 74). María's Testimonio finds the connection between the responsible parties and her diminished condition. She asks,

> Who has given a social minority the power to expel from their country people whose only crime is to question an unjust system? With what right do they isolate a person from her country and emotional world, from the social and work relationships that gave meaning to life? . . . for me this has been terrible. I do everything in my power to justify the bread which I eat, the roof that covers me. Nevertheless, I feel kind of incapacitated, like a "political retiree."

María makes her bold denunciations in the therapist's office, frustrated by her lack of access to her tormentors:

> To whom can I address my protest for this injustice if those who threw me out are the ones who control justice? Where do I go to complain and shout in rage that exile is unnatural and inhuman?

Yet, safe in the bond of commitment, she can also own the ways in which she feels defeated:

> To force one into exile is not an act of torture or murder, but an act of orphanage, leaving the victim with the yearning, the memory, the impotence, the affection for what is left behind. The thirst of the exile is not physical; it is a thirst for affections, for beloved landscapes, family traditions, local customs. While prisoners are kept in a jail with walls, the exiles' cell is the space beyond their country's borders.

She can also replenish the worth of the coin that became devalued, and put it back in circulation in the community. Toward the end of her Testimonio she explains,

> I agreed to write this because I thought that all the pain that we experience cannot paralyze us, cannot destroy us physically and emotionally. We need to sort of process it, purify it and put it in the service of others. I wrote my humble but authentic experience so that others who are ignorant of our Calvary might learn, and think about what it might mean for a human being to be brutally uprooted from his or her ground and sent like a felled tree, to places far away from where it belongs, without compassion.

When her Testimonio ended, María Eugenia was ready for deeper therapeutic work, and to return to teaching. She began seeing students as a private tutor. In her first tutorial, her therapist reports, "after eight years of not working, she began her class with the famous words of Fray Luis de Leon,[6] 'As we were saying yesterday . . . '" (Aresti, 1988, p. 75).

With yesterday back in her possession, rescued from the hands of her oppressors, María can move forward to tomorrow, confident that her personal and social existence have meaning.

A BRIEF CRITIQUE

The Testimonio is far from a final solution to the psychological damage wrought by political repression. It holds open wounds that, if not properly cared for, may continue causing pain. Vigorous discussion sometimes ensues in the Central American refugee community concerning the practice advocated by some groups, of members going around to gatherings of people of the host culture, to relate their personal stories of extreme persecution. Defending the practice are those who feel this is an essential form of political education, without which the people of the host culture will never grasp the horror of what the refugees have experienced. Opposing it are those who feel that the duty to bear witness in this way constitutes yet another imposition on the refugee, forcing the victim to comply with somebody else's agenda, somebody else's idea of what needs to be done.

It seems to me that the question turns on whether the subjective experience for the refugee is or is not therapeutic.

There is no doubt that the telling of one's story before a group of sympathetic listeners with a potential for becoming active in the struggle against injustice, is of benefit to the audience. This does not make it, by some mechanical or automatic process, beneficial to the victim. To benefit from the painful re-telling, the victim must feel less *victim* and more *survivor*. Repeated tellings of one's story, by keeping the wound open and clean, and preventing it from festering, provides a good medium for this transformation to occur, but if it fails to occur spontaneously, additional assistance in the form of therapy should be secured to help bring it about.

With regard to the exercise of free expression, it is certainly therapeutic to reclaim the right to speak, but to be *free*, speech must be voluntary; it must be motivated by a desire to communicate one's story to others, in the hope that those others will in turn be motivated to do something to change the conditions that produced the terrible experience. People who believe they can be effective in motivating others to act are, by virtue of that belief, being transformed from victims into survivors. They may not know *why* they have survived, but they know there is work to be done to make their own survival meaningful and to honor the memories of those whose voices have been silenced. Their reclamation of the right to free expression is a therapeutic act made possible by, but also contributing to, the second affirmation of the Testimonio–that human beings can come together to vanquish the forces of destruction.

Among refugee groups who present public testimonies, this affirmation of solidarity is perceived as the redeeming benefit of the practice, the good that justifies the pain attendant to each and every re-telling of the abominations of one's story–a pain so severe that in many cases it has shut down the equipment for expressing anguish, causing the person to present the same blunted affect in the *Nth* telling as in the first. How, one might ask, can this be therapeutic? Is not the persistence of the flattened affect, a symptom of Post-traumatic Stress Disorder, proof that this act is counter-therapeutic? Here, although it may seem strange, I believe a therapeutic activity is in progress. When the individual has reclaimed enough faith in humanity to believe in the abstract that others will want to come forward to fight against injustice, that individual will in time be able to feel the concrete effects of human solidarity. But to regain the kind of trust that is necessary to affirm the possibility of such solidarity, one has to test the mettle of those who would be counted on to come forward, and what better gauge does the refugee have than her or his own story?

When the refugee stands before an audience made up of people who have no personal stake in repudiating the things that have happened, apart from their outrage as decent human beings, this is a powerful indication that not just *I*, but *We*, understand that such things must not be allowed to happen. The refugee who is able to discover human solidarity with his or her own personal experience, will be able in time to feel and react emotionally to this solidarity. For this reason, the personal testimony–provided that it is believed and responded to with compassion–is therapeutic, and is worth trying even when the individual does not feel motivated to make the effort, and even though the effort entails a great deal of pain.

Finally, there is the question of whether a testimony given in compliance with someone else's request, but without strong personal motivation, can have the therapeutic effect of restoring one's sense of value as a human being and a member of a community. To be sure, there are certain objective conditions promoting such restoration. When a group urges a refugee to act as part of a community of victims in diaspora, the individual's cultural identity receives validation, as does his or her personal story. And through the group interaction the refugee also participates in reconstructing the emotional foundations undermined by the repression, thereby contributing *in absentia* to social recovery in the homeland. Furthermore, support from other refugees in the group means that the Testimonio, though an account of loss, is delivered from within a context of solidarity, signifying a degree of gain and recovery. Still, it cannot be said to have the therapeutic effects of restoring self-worth and a sense of membership unless it is *experienced* that way.

So long as the Testimonio is given principally for others, without a sense of benefit to the self, one necessarily remains separated, existing as a resource for those others to exploit, or an exhibit for their edification.

The person who has been the victim of state-sponsored violence has done enough to serve the needs of others. The time of recovery is a time for acting *with* people, not *for* them, and being their partner, not their instrument. If the Testimonio is experienced not as a joint venture, but rather as capitulation to pressure, it will come to represent separation instead of linkage, and is likely also to shut down receptivity to the therapeutic solidarity it brings forth.

Thus, in order for the Testimonio to serve its therapeutic purpose of helping one feel value as a human being and member of a community, it must be undertaken as a voluntary act. It must be appreciated by others and reflected back in life-affirming ways. It must lead to a discovery of the interdependence of speaker and audience as members of a human community who can work together on the side of life and justice. When those characteristics are in place it will, as the Chilean psychologists promised, "transform past experience and personal identity, creating a new present and enhancing the future."

NOTES

1. "To be disappeared," a new verb form originating in Guatemala in the 1950s, refers to the act of being taken away by representatives of the government, who later claim that they never saw you, have no knowledge of your whereabouts, and no record of any arrest or detention. Those who have suffered this fate are "disappeared ones," *desaparecidos*. The families of the disappeared live in a tragic limbo, without confirmation that their loved one are either dead or alive.

2. Committee of the Mothers and Relatives of the Disappeared, Political Prisoners and Assassinated of El Salvador.

3. Grupo de Apoyo Mutuo, Mutual Support Group.

4. Although the young woman gave public testimony, her name is withheld here lest publicity abroad become a stimulus for renewed violence.

5. Quotations are from Maria Eugenia's Testimonio, as given to Dr. Lore Aresti and published in Aresti (1988).

6. Forced by the Inquisition to abandon his post at the University of Salamanca, this Spanish religious and literary figure of the 16th Century returned to teaching after a five year hiatus, resuming with the famous phrase.

REFERENCES

American Baptist Churches v. Thornburgh (1990). c-85-3255-RFP.

Amnesty International (1984). *Torture in the eighties*. London: Amnesty International.

Aresti, L. (1988). Political reality and psychological damage. In Aron, A. (Ed.), *Flight, exile and return: Mental health and the refugee* (pp. 54-76). San Francisco: Committee for Health Rights in Central America.

Aron, A. (1990). Testimony before U.S. Senate sub-committee hearings on Children of War. *Congressional Record*, April 3.

Aron, A., Corne, S., Fursland, A., & Zelwer, B. (1991). The gender-specific terror of El Salvador and Guatemala. *Women's Studies International Forum, 14 (1/2)*, 37-47.

Becker, D., Lira, E., Castillo, M.I., Gomez, E., & Kovalskys, J. (1990). Therapy with victims of political repression in Chile: The challenge of social reparation. *Journal of Social Issues, 46(3)*, 3, 133-149.

Bettelheim, B. (1980). Individual and mass behavior in extreme situations. *Surviving*. New York: Vintage.

Burgos-Debray, E. (Ed.). (1984). *I, Rigoberta Menchú: An Indian woman in Guatemala*. London: Verso.

CDHES (1989, January). Testimony taken by Comisión de Derechos Humanos de El Salvador (Non-Governmental Human Rights Commission of El Salvador).

Chomsky, N. & Herman, E.S. (1979). *The Washington connection and third world fascism*. Boston: South End Press.

CHRICA (1985). *El Salvador 1985: Health, human rights, and the war*. San Francisco: Committee for Health Rights in Central America.

CHRICA (1987). *Political asylum: a handbook for legal and mental health workers*. San Francisco: Committee for Health Rights in Central America.

Cienfuegos, A.J. & Monelli, C. (1983). The testimony of political repression as a therapeutic instrument. *American Journal of Orthopsychiatry, 53*(1), 43-51.

Diario Latino (1990). February 2. Cited in *El Salvador: A decade of war*. Los Angeles: El Rescate Human Rights Department.

Gettleman, M. E., Lacefield, P., Menashe, L. & Mermelstein, D. (1986). *El Salvador: Central America in the new cold war*. New York: Grove Press.

Martín-Baró, I. (1984). Guerra y salud mental. *Estudios Centroamericanos (ECA)*, *39*, 503-514.

Martín-Baró, I. (1987). *Asi piensan los salvadoreños urbanos (1986-1987)*. San Salvador, El Salvador: UCA Editores.

Martín-Baró, I. (1990). Reparations: Attention must be paid. *Commonweal*, March 23, pp. 184-186.

Politzer, P. (1989). *Fear in Chile*. New York: Pantheon.

Roe, M.D. (1986, October). *Personality development among refugee children in Central America: Drawings of self and family as windows*. Paper presented at Annual Conference of the Minnesota Association for the Education of Young Children, October 11.

Roe, M.D. (1989). Drawing on the future. *Links: Central America Health Report*, *6 (1)*, 6-7.

Santiago, D. (1990). The aesthetics of terror, the hermeneutics of death. *America*, March 24, 292-295.

Healing the Wounds of the *Mahantdori*

Theanvy Kuoch
Richard A. Miller
Mary F. Scully

SUMMARY. The magnitude of the *Mahantdori*, or Cambodian holocaust, must be understood by therapists who are trying to help the survivors deal with the illness and injuries that are a product of this destruction. This paper presents an overview of the events that have come to be known as the *Mahantdori* and a model for treating the multiple levels of trauma with which the Cambodian family must deal. The Contextual Model of Family Therapy, as described by Ivan Borzormenyi-Nagy, is used as the structure for helping to rebuild trust within the family while at the same time treating the injuries of the individual family members. The changing role of Cambodian women and their need to form new support groups because of their devastating loss of family are described.

The Cambodian people call the period between 1970 and 1980 the *Mahantdori*, meaning the time of great destruction. The word has no

Theanvy Kuoch, MA, is a Cambodian survivor of the Pol Pot Regime. She has a Master's degree in Family Therapy and is Executive Director of Khmer Health Advocates, Inc. in West Hartford, CT. She was recently reunited with her only son after an 11 year separation.

Richard A. Miller, MD, is a Psychiatrist and Family Therapist who has been working with Khmer Health Advocates, Inc. since 1983. He has travelled to the refugee camps in Thailand and is presently struggling with the complexities of the Khmer language.

Mary F. Scully, RN, MA, is a Psychiatric Nurse and Family Therapist who worked in a refugee camp in Thailand in 1980, and has been working with Cambodian families ever since. She is Assistant Director of Khmer Health Advocates.

The authors gratefully acknowledge Carol Berto and Francie Mantak for their important contributions to this paper.

191

political connotations and implies no blame. It simply describes what
many people believe to be the fulfillment of a prophecy. And the prophecy reads:

> A darkness will settle on the people of Cambodia
> There will be houses but no people in them
> Roads but no travellers upon them
> The land will be ruled by Barbarians with no religion.
> The blood will be so high as to touch the belly of the elephant
> And only the deaf and the mute will survive. (Bruno, 1986)

The reality of the *Mahantdori* challenges human understanding since
the destruction of Cambodia was far greater than the loss of institutions
and material possessions. For most Cambodians, the *Mahantdori* meant
a complete loss of reality as they knew it. The target of this great destruction was the Cambodian family, the prize of Cambodian life, the institution that has remained stable since the fall of the ancient civilization of
Angkor Wat in the 14th century.

The *Mahantdori* has changed the face of the Cambodian family forever.
Today, it is believed that between 60% to 65% of adult Cambodians are
women. Women inside Cambodia and abroad must deal with the hardships
of being the head of the family, the primary provider and primary homemaker, starting a new life for their family with little more than the clothing on their backs.

Despite their burdens, the strength of Cambodian women is a source
of hope for all who work with them. As with other cultures, Cambodian
women are the first to seek treatment. They do so not because they are
weaker or more symptomatic, but because they are more likely to face the
reality of their experiences and seek solutions for themselves and their
families.

In these pages we will describe a process for healing through historical
and cultural understandings and the use of Contextual Family Therapy.
We focus on the Cambodian women's story, as the *Mahantdori* has
changed their traditional role and made them the leaders in the healing the
wounds of their family and perhaps their nation.

BACKGROUND

My sister and 1 tried to escape from the Khmer Rouge but they
caught us and took us to a small house in the forest. My sister had

been shot in the side and I could see all of the blood, but they chained her to the wall and I could not reach her. We were chained there for many days when they brought in the young man who was helping us to escape. They made him dig a big hole in the ground and then they buried him so we could only see his head. He did not die for a long time and he did not beg or scream. His tears just fell and he asked them why they had to do this to him.

As in many Asian cultures, the role of the family is central to the survival of the individual. One's sense of wholeness comes from belonging to a family. Buddhism and Brahmanism reinforce the importance of family with age-old customs and rituals which provide meaning and comfort in times of change or distress. For the Cambodian family, the *Mahantdori* was a time of continuous betrayal. The Khmer Rouge, understanding the power of the Cambodian family, systematically worked to destroy trust between family members.

Therapists who wish to understand the layers of trauma that Cambodians have suffered must first understand that the Cambodian nation has traditionally viewed itself as one big family. Familial terms such as brother and sister, aunt and uncle, and niece and nephew are commonly used as titles for addressing members of the community, neighbors, and friends. The familial concept of community relationships is built to some degree on a reality. The practice of keeping concubines by feudal warlords ensured regional loyalties by establishing blood relationships. The children of these unions created alliances that were often tense but nonetheless unified a great number of people along family lines (Ebihara, 1986).

Prince Sihanouk, the former ruler of Cambodia who some people still consider to be a god, specifically refers to the people of Cambodia as "my children." As a leader, he chose to keep them uninformed about the Viet Cong sanctuaries and the "secret" American bombings which ultimately cost almost 100,000 Cambodians their lives. In an attempt to regain his power after a coup in 1969, Sihanouk became the nominal head of the Khmer Rouge, giving legitimacy to a group that was already well known for its atrocities (Etcheson, 1984).

The bloody civil war which raged between 1970 and 1975 split family loyalties and created a nation of refugees as people moved endlessly in search of safety and food. The city of Phnom Penh grew from 200,000 to over 2 million in a few short years. The Lon Nol government, infused with millions of American dollars, became a model of corruption. The middle class, stunned by their new-found affluence, rushed off to buy TVs and new cars while thousands of refugees, living on the outskirts of the city, starved to death.

Instead of peace, Pol Pot's victorious Khmer Rouge brought genocide when they came to power in 1975. They brutally and systematically began destroying all elements of the Cambodian family which they felt were undesirable. These included the "upper class," professionals, people who wore glasses, ethnic Chinese, Muslim Chams, and numerous other group (Kiernan, 1990).

The use of terror and betrayal was vital to the Khmer Rouge method of control, but as trust broke down among the people, it also broke down within the Khmer Rouge leadership. By the time the Vietnamese invaded in early 1979, mass graves were being dug around villages, and no one was safe from genocide.

When the Vietnamese invaded Cambodia, there was relief that the Khmer Rouge had been pushed out, but there was also a fear that Vietnamese Communism meant more of the same brutality. Thousands poured across the border into Thailand, seeking shelter and safety. The international community, which was well aware of the policies of the Khmer Rouge, chose to look away as Thailand pushed thousands of people to their death over the Dang Rek mountains. Ten thousand are known to have died in that one incident, and many believe that thousands and thousands more died in similar incidents along the border (Lawyers Committee for Human Rights, 1989).

The faces of Cambodia's starving masses hit the airwaves in November of 1979, and the greatest humanitarian relief effort in the history of the world was launched (Shawcross, 1984). But as the media tired of refugees, camps became a place of terror. In the day time, the presence of international relief workers created an air of order. At night, people were robbed, beaten and murdered. Rape was (and is) so common that many women married only because it was too dangerous for a woman to be alone.

For over a decade, hundreds of thousands of people have lived in concentration camps that barely meet the United Nations minimum requirement for space for short-term shelter. Living on subsistence diets of rice and canned fish, they often survive on only four gallons of water per person per day (Reynell, 1989). A policy of "humane deterrence" was established to create harsh conditions which would discourage people from coming to the border (Shawcross, 1984).

The civil war, the American bombing, and the disruption of the Cambodian economy were responsible for separating millions of people from their families and homes and in part laid the ground work for the *Mahant-*

dori. The Khmer Rouge systematically planned the destruction of the Cambodian family as part of their policy of genocide. They sought to purify the country of Western as well as traditional Cambodian authority figures, such as monks, politicians, and soldiers, and impose a state based on radical communist philosophy. The Vietnamese-backed government which took control of the country in 1979, though less harsh than the Khmer Rouge, is also known for its human rights violations.

TREATING THE CAMBODIAN FAMILY

> I saw the baby lying next to his dead mother. His head was so big and he looked like an old man. His arms and legs had no muscle and he looked like a skeleton. I did not want to pick him up because no matter how I touched him, I was going to hurt him. (an American relief worker, 1979)

The Contextual family therapy model was developed by Dr. Ivan Borzormenyi-Nagy, a pioneer in family therapy and himself a refugee from Hungary. We have chosen Dr. Nagy's model because it offers a framework for treating a family which is respectful of cultural differences as well as attentive to the complexities of a traumatized family. Contextual therapy is based on a belief that the family is the greatest resource available to the individual, and its primary goal is rebuilding trust among family members.

The basic framework for this model comes from a four-dimensional view of the family (Ulrich, 1983):

1. The factual dimension refers to what has happened to this family. What were the events that affected their lives as individuals, and as a family?
2. The psychological/physical dimension refers to the physical condition of each family member. How do they deal with their personal traumas? What defense mechanisms do they use? What are their needs for treatment?
3. The transactional dimension refers to how the family behaves together. It includes ideas such as distancing and pursuing, coalitions, and scapegoating.
4. The ethical dimension refers to the therapist's need to give therapeutic consideration to all family members who will be affected by therapy. It likewise means a commitment to deal with the issues of fairness and give-and-take between family members.

While the contextual model warrants greater discussion, we will use the framework of these four dimensions for describing our work with Cambodian families over the past decade. We will focus particularly on the issues which pertain to Cambodian women, who offer access to the family.

WHAT ARE THE FACTS?

The man from immigration began to scream at her. He called her a liar and he threw her file at her and told her her family would never go to the United States. This happened because she could not remember the names and ages of her children. When she got home, she took a knife and cut out her tongue. (Chonburi Refugee Camp, Thailand, 1981)

Perhaps the most important fact to understand in dealing with Cambodian families is that it is very dangerous for them to tell the truth. "Telling your story" was part of the Khmer Rouge process for controlling the population. In the first months after the fall of Phnom Penh, people were forced out of the cities and made to give written biographical statements to the Khmer Rouge leaders. People learned very quickly that to tell them that you could read and write or that you spoke a foreign language, meant death. The questioning process was repeated many times to catch people in lies.

Once in the refugee camps, people were again asked to tell their stories. Immigration officials used a very similar process to catch people in lies. Anxiety and the inability to remember concrete facts were taken as proof that the person was lying rather than an indication that the interrogator had tapped into a traumatic memory.

In the therapeutic process, the collection of facts is a painful and anxiety-provoking experience. We nonetheless pursue this early in therapy as a means of helping a family re-create an image of themselves. The genogram is the most useful tool as it allows the family to see their family information and to explain the sometimes complex relationships within the family, such as in families where the father had two wives.

We let the family know that this information belongs to them and we will give them copies. The majority of Cambodians here in the United States are struggling to help bring close relatives in the camps to the U.S. Their efforts on behalf of the family are part of the active healing process.

The search for the objective truth is a frustrating process. It is not part of our agenda to pursue the truth to the core, even when doing an evaluation for other agencies such as schools or courts, because for many people, access to the facts is simply not psychically available, or the truth continues to be perceived as dangerous. *The hard and cold reality remains that Cambodians are still being threatened and their families are persecuted inside Cambodia and at the border.* People often feel they must lie about where family members are or what they did before the Khmer Rouge so they will not be extorted by one faction or another. Families will also leave out the names of members who died or are missing because it is too painful to talk about them.

For many the prophecy continues to control life powerfully. And the line, "only the deaf and the mute will survive" has meaning for people who continue to be terrorized by being labelled as "traitor" for talking about the atrocities of the Khmer Rouge.

The therapy team's understanding of the available facts is vital to helping people create their new family story. An understanding of what is going on inside Cambodia, at the border, and in the community is helpful in building a relationship with the family. It is heartbreaking to see the pattern of traumatic events and how people are victimized again and again.

PSYCHOLOGICAL DIMENSION

They took my daughter and made her kneel on the ground in front of the whole village. "Tell them you are a traitor and an enemy of the people."

"No, I am not," she said. Then the soldier pointed his gun at her head and pulled the trigger. But he made the bullet miss her. Then they took her to the well and said, "tell us how you betrayed Cambodia or we will put you down the well." "I did not betray my country," she said, and they tied her by the feet and put her down the well for a long time. "Tell them you are a traitor or we will beat you." This time she was too tired and said, "Yes, I am a traitor and I want you to kill me."

But instead, they beat her and beat her until her whole body was broken, and I did not even know how to pick her up. That was the time my daughter decided she did not want to speak anymore. Now it is three years, and we have not heard her voice. They did this because she could speak English and French. (K. H. 1980)

Evaluation of the individual's physical and psychological state is where we as a therapy team build our initial relationship with a family. In a recent study Mollica, Wyshak, and Lavelle (1987) found that each Cambodian had experienced an average of 16 trauma events, including three torture events. Allodi (1991) in his work with torture victims defines torture as a major trauma, not expected to occur in anyone's lifetime, that is intentionally inflicted for the purpose of punishing or controlling the victim. He also points out that the severity of the trauma and one's fear of persecution are significantly related to the level of post-trauma symptomotology. Cognitive deficits are often a part of the post-trauma picture.

Because 95% of Cambodians over the age of 12 are refugees and victims of the Pol Pot Regime, psychological and physical evaluation must focus on trauma as the central issue. We use the Khmer version of the Hopkins Symptoms Checklist in our evaluation as well as our own Post-Traumatic Stress Disorder (PTSD) questionnaire. Likewise, we give great attention to the person's history of injuries and illnesses (Mollica, 1988).

Memories of events that occurred in conjunction with an illness are often as traumatizing as a torture event. Our own therapist, Theanvy Kuoch, who is also a survivor of the Pol Pot Regime, recalls almost dying from an infected hand. She has vivid memories of waking nightly to see her arm swarming with ants and being too weak to push them off.

Khmer Health Advocates unfortunately does not have the facilities to do physical evaluations, nor do we have the personnel to adequately coordinate health evaluations. Cambodians in Connecticut are rarely on welfare and often are working with little or no medical benefits. This makes it difficult, if not impossible, for them to get specialty examinations, such as neurological exams, without insurance. When a person's physical problems are coupled with language problems, the system is nearly impossible to negotiate.

Even when they finally do get to see a doctor, the experience is often disappointing for Cambodians. We recall reviewing the medical records of a 60 year-old woman whose family had applied for disability. Her major complaint was high blood pressure and even though three doctors had done a "complete physical," no one had asked her if she knew her name or where she lived. She had been turned down for disability twice, despite the fact that she was completely disoriented and her family could not leave her alone at all. In many cases, American doctors have declared their Cambodian patients' ability to understand and speak English as adequate when this was clearly not the case.

By the time we get to see the patient, they have exhausted "Chinatown medicine," as well as the limited traditional medicine available in the area. They also feel hopeless about dealing with Western medical systems. For this reason, we try to complete the evaluation process quickly and begin to treat depression and post-traumatic stress disorder vigorously.

MEDICATION

Kinzie, Leung, Boehnlein, and Fleck (1987) have shown that Cambodian refugees are more likely to follow through and take traditional, side effect prone antidepressants than are Vietnamese or Laotian refugees. They hypothesized that due to the more severe and prolonged trauma that Cambodians have lived through, and thus their further subjective suffering, the medication gives them more symptom relief. In our practice, we have come to rely frequently on fluoxetine (better known by its trade name, Prozac), a new antidepressant affecting the serotonin neurons, which has an extremely low incidence of side effects and can be given once a day. Our Cambodian patients feel much more comfortable with fluoxetine than with traditional antidepressants, with their numerous side effects, or with alprazolam (Xanax), which they fear might be addictive. The high level of compliance among our patients may also flow from the resemblance of fluoxetine capsules to antibiotics, true miracle drugs, which, when introduced to Cambodia in the 1960s, had a profound effect on decreasing infant mortality.

In our experience, fluoxetine has not only had the expected and well-documented antidepressant effect (Chouinard, 1985; Feighner, 1985; Stark and Hardison, 1985), but has also had dramatic effects on many PTSD symptoms. We have observed a great decrease in obsessive and intrusive thinking that can be such a disabling part of PTSD. Many patients tell us that they feel more themselves, find it easier to concentrate, are less distrustful of others, and can access their trauma experiences without either denial or feeling overwhelmed. For example, one patient reported that she still had nightmares, but instead of waking up in the middle of the night reliving the original trauma for hours at a time, she would realize that she was having a dream about something that had happened in the past and go back to sleep.

Finally, while we do not have hard data, we also suspect that fluoxetine helps with addictive behaviors such as gambling, drinking alcohol, and obsessive shopping, which are a source of much trouble in some of our families.

In addition to depression and PTSD symptoms, many of our patients also have considerable anxiety, while some have outright panic attacks. We often see anxiety disorders in our younger patients, and these can be at the root of many physical complaints, greatly limiting their involvement and success in school and the community. With these patients, we have had some success with small doses of alprazolam (Xanax) or trazodone (Desyrel), either alone or in combination with fluoxetine.

Mollica, Wyshak, and Lavelle noted that all of 21 Cambodian patients with a diagnosis of PTSD had at least one other psychiatric diagnosis, usually major depression (1987). And Kinzie, who first described PTSD and the concentration camp syndrome in Cambodians in 1984, along with Boehlein, Leung, Moore, Riley, and Smith noted that 92% of 110 clinic Cambodian patients had PTSD, although they had been previously labelled otherwise (Kinzie et al., 1990).

Although PTSD, Depressive Disorders, and Panic Attacks are useful and well-defined diagnoses which have been cross-culturally validated, they do not do justice to the full range of physical, social, and psychological outcomes in the individual and family of *Mahantdori* survivors. Other known outcomes of early childhood traumas include borderline personality, multiple personality disorder, victim sequelae disorder, conduct disorder, organicity, and substance abuse. Terr (1991) and Herman (Hawkins, 1991) have independently pointed out that childhood traumatic experiences can underlie and unify such diverse diagnoses and symptoms. What is important, and what must be addressed in psychotherapy, is less the diagnoses themselves than the centrality of the initial traumatizing experience.

We find with our patients, whether they are in the emotionally numbed phase or the overwhelmed intrusive phase of PTSD, that at some point there is a need for each of them to tell their story both to achieve some measure of peace and as part of the process of rebuilding the family. In this process, over-emphasis on individual diagnoses may obscure broader family issues and the obvious point that one or several diagnoses can usually be made in all family members of any "identified patient."

It is a central tenet of both Contextual Therapy and our own beliefs that the major healing power lies within the family itself. In this regard, Kinzie, Sack, Angell, Manson, and Rath (1986) have shown that for Cambodian child survivors, the presence of even one close family member in the household greatly decreases both the likelihood of psychiatric diagnoses and the globally perceived dysfunction that others observed. Thus while 13 of 14 children living in foster families had a psychiatric diagnosis, only 14 of 26 living with a family member had such a diagnosis.

TRANSACTIONAL DIMENSION

My brother was always in trouble. He never listened to my parents and would not study even though he was very intelligent. My parents cried about him all the time and I always had to try to keep him out of trouble or hide it from my mother and father. During the Khmer Rouge we were all starving, so my brother went to steal honey for us. But the Khmer Rouge caught him and cut his throat. Every night I see his face. I should have stopped him.

Sometimes it is difficult to remember that family life began before the Pol Pot Regime and that the family's story prior to the civil war and fall of the country is as important as during the trauma years of 1975 to 1979. What is clear is that family patterns of behavior are woven into the interpretation of every trauma story, and family members view the awful things that happened to them on a very personal basis rather than part of a collective national experience.

Children in particular readily take blame for events over which they have no control. For example, a 24 year-old man who was only 8 when his father was taken away by the Khmer Rouge believes that he is responsible for his father's death. He describes an incident where he caught his father stealing food from the family reserve. "I looked at him with such anger that he decided to run away, and that's when the Khmer Rouge caught him and killed him." As the "perfect child" in the family, he felt that he was not allowed to have negative feelings. To a certain extent, this continues to be true; even today, his siblings respond dramatically when he is angry or critical of them.

As Cambodian families attempt to adjust in their new country, they often focus on family behavior patterns rather than the trauma experience. Behavior prior to the *Mahantdori* often is considered much more important than anything that happened during the period of trauma. "You always ran away when you had a problem." "You always wanted to be the boss." "Father loved you best." While it often seems that family members are acting out old conflicts, these statements often conceal underlying accusations about trauma events. Having never heard, as a family, each others account of what happened throughout during the *Mahantdori*, family members hold unfounded ideas about who helped and who didn't. For example, during recent session, a woman who consistently attacks her husband's passivity during family sessions, began to scream, "you always abandon us just like you did during Pol Pot." The surprised husband, said, "I ran away because they were coming to take me. I sent a message to you to meet me, but you never came."

ETHICAL DIMENSION

The Khmer Rouge came into the city and began going from house to house. My sister and I and her 2 year-old son were in the living room. The Khmer Rouge soldier said to my sister, "You are the wife of a government official." Then he took his gun and shot my sister in the head. I am not a human being anymore. I never cried for my sister.

The ethical dimension refers to issues of fairness within a family. The rules for fairness are not defined by the therapist, but by the family itself. Family legacies and loyalties, religious beliefs and cultural values are part of this dimension, and their interpretation becomes a central part of rebuilding trust in the family.

Sophia, the woman who never cried for her sister, had betrayed her own sense of duty. Without tears, she told her story to countless people and could not be comforted by rational assurances that she could not act any differently under the circumstances or that she could not be responsible for the actions of the Khmer Rouge.

Her sorrow broke when the therapist asked her how she had helped her sister before the Khmer Rouge came. She told the story of how she was the youngest in the family and her sister had loved her like she was her own child. When the sister had given birth to the baby who was killed, she had been very ill and Sophia left school to take care of her. The sister always recalled Sophia's kindness to her. With these memories came the tears she had held for almost seven years.

Sophia clearly experienced her psychic numbing as an abandonment of her family. Her emotional reconnection with her sister opened the way for her to deal with other members of the family. She began searching for a lost brother and felt closer to her siblings who were living nearby. This experience did not change her symptoms of PTSD, but for the first time, she could think about what had happened to her and her family without being immobilized by guilt.

Survival guilt is a core symptom of PTSD. It is the single most immobilizing force in Cambodian family relationships. It is better not to speak than to talk about experiences that come from a separate reality, a reality for which there is no frame of reference in family life prior to 1970.

The question, "why didn't you help?" is heard over and over again in family conflicts. They are directed at everyday family issues and rarely if ever toward the events of the *Mahantdori*. However, the effect is so powerful and heartbreaking that it clearly belongs to the trauma.

The dilemma for the family therapist is how to help a family deal with guilt and issues of fairness when it is clear that not all the family members can tolerate a discussion of trauma events. Dr. Nagy, a survivor of war and displacement, has dealt with this complex issue with a simple question: "How did you help your family?" (Boszormenyi-Nagy and Spark, 1973).

The power of the question is seen when each family member is given the opportunity to describe what happened to them from their own perspective. Often it is the pain of confession of helplessness that mobilizes the family to help a member talk about his or her personal trauma.

A family we have seen for years called an emergency meeting because the mother wanted to move away from her daughter's house because the family was always fighting. There was an angry exchange between the siblings about who started the fights and who helped around the house and who didn't. Through the discussion, it became clear that the second daughter was the most helpful. She was then attacked by her siblings for being controlling and manipulative in her motivation.

At that point we asked her how she helped her family during the Pol Pot regime. She immediately said that she knew her brother and sister blamed her for the death of their father because they were always talking about how he had been captured by the Khmer Rouge when he went to look for her.

"You don't know what happened to me," she said. "You stayed with our parents, but the Khmer Rouge took me away. You'll never understand, but I did try to help. I tried to run away and go home, but they brought me back and punished me." After that she did not want to talk anymore.

The family decided to separate. The mother and two children went to live in their own apartment. The mother said, "This is better. I need to talk about what happened and I know that hurts my daughter. Anyway she needs time alone with her husband." The separation was painful but soon improved, and the family now gets together regularly.

The therapist helps the family focus its story around the theme of helping. How did you try to help? and how can you help now? are questions that relieve anxiety and the sense of helplessness and hopelessness which overwhelm survivors.

The Cambodian term for depression is *thlek tuk chet* which means the heart and mind are no longer connected (Kuoch and Scully, 1984). Telling stories which re-connect the hearts and minds of survivors has a powerful effect on mobilizing them to help find solutions for today's problems.

THE IMPACT OF THE MAHANTDORI
ON CAMBODIAN WOMEN

"Where is your baby's father?" the relief worker asked.
"In Khao-I-Dang camp with his other wife," she replied.
"When were you married?"

"My husband was travelling to the border and stopped at my house and asked my mother if he could stay for the night. I never knew him before that time. During the night he came to my bed and forced himself on me. I fought with him, but he was too strong. From that time he was my husband."

Traditional Cambodian society has very strict rules for a woman's conduct. Her adherence to these rules brings the family honor; deviance brings great shame. Many Cambodian women, like the woman above, attempt to recapture that honor by denying trauma, by renaming their rapists as their husbands. During the *Mahantdori*, women lost the ability to be good Cambodian women. They were raped and forced into marriages, and all the protective controls of the past were gone.

Today, twelve years after the *Mahantdori*, Cambodia is a country of women and children. It is believed that at least 60-65% of the adult population are women and over 50% of the population are children. Women are the primary providers and caretakers for the Cambodian family. Cambodian women who have settled in the United States not only must survive without the support system they had in Cambodia, but they must also deal with the complexities of raising their children in a new culture while still supporting family members who remain inside Cambodia.

These pressures, combined with the trauma, have produced a backlash among Cambodian men and women who want to cling to the old traditions as a way of ordering the chaos of their lives. All of these factors produce tremendous pressure for women who are struggling to find a way to survive and a way to understand their new roles.

An old Cambodian proverb compares a man to a diamond and a woman to a piece of white cotton. When they fall in the mud, the diamond can be washed clean, but the cotton remains dirty forever.

The role of Cambodian women has traditionally been very important. The daughter who behaves properly brings great honor to the family, and the daughter who marries well can bring her family wealth and security.

Ideal women's roles come from a long tradition, dating back to early Cambodian history. Every school girl learns the "Women's Rules" which describe the correct behavior for a Cambodian wife. While Cambodian women may laugh at the idea of this "perfect woman," they nonetheless pass on the belief that it is the Cambodian woman who preserves the good name of the family.

The anguish of Cambodian women when they "lose face" or make a public error is testimony to their loyalty to the legacies of their culture. A woman who divorced her husband after years of being beaten and abused did not want to attend any community actitivies because she felt she had lost honor for her family. And, in fact, members of the community told her that she should not continue her volunteer work with Cambodian children as she was no longer a good role model.

The reality of the *Mahantdori* creates a powerful conflict for Cambodian women. Like the men, they have a loyalty to the "Cambodian Way." The need to preserve the Cambodian culture is based in large part on the need to believe that somewhere the old Cambodia still exists and is waiting for them to return.

To give up this belief is to look into the face of the Cambodian holocaust and accept the loss and the cruelty of that experience. Again the prophecy comes to mind and the closing line, "only the deaf and the mute will survive."

BREAKING THE SILENCE

The woman went to the leader of the Khmer Rouge. Her clothes were ragged and her hair untouched. She began screaming, "Give me back my children or kill me." The Khmer Rouge leader knew that he had sent ten of her children to work on the youth mobile team. She continued to scream and scream and now he became afraid. Her eyes looked so strange that he was sure she had a powerful spirit in her. He ordered his men to find her children and bring them home.

Cambodian women have made great sacrifices to keep their families alive. The other side of their trauma is the great strength which they have earned through these experiences. Without the extended family as a source of support, they must now rely on each other and build a community. The familial words are still used. Sisters and aunts pull together to share information and help each other in times of need.

As therapists dealing with people who often are distressed and have no family to support them, we have frequently called on members of the community for help. A group of women has formed to offer each other practical help as well as to encourage one another to speak out about their experiences. They gain strength from each other knowing that they are not alone, and that other women share their nightmares of the past and burdens of the future.

The *Mahantdori* changed the role of Cambodian women forever. They can never return to the days of the "Women's Rules." Our hope is that the terror that erased the old ideal of Cambodian womanhood will bring a new perspective on the strength and capabilities of women. Our hope is that one day these women will find the strength to rebuild the Cambodian nation, wary of the past but still hopeful for the future. Our hope is that they will not fulfill the last line of the prophecy, but find their voice for Cambodia.

REFERENCES

Allodi, F. (1991). Assessment and treatment of torture victims: A critical review. *Journal of Nervous Mental Disorders*, 179, 4-11.

Boszormenyi-Nagy, I. & Spark, G. (1973). *Invisible loyalties: Reciprocity in intergenerational family therapy.* Hagerstown, MD: Harper & Row.

Bruno, E. (Producer). (1986). *Samsara*, [Film]. San Francisco: Bruno.

Chouinard, G. (1985). A double-blind controlled clinical trial of fluoxetine and amitriptyline in the treatment of outpatients with major depressive disorder. *Journal of Clinical Psychiatry*, 46, 32-37.

Ebihara, M. (1986). Svay, a Khmer village in Cambodia. *UMI Dissertation Information Service.*

Etcheson, C. (1984). *The rise and demise of Democratic Kampuchea.* Boulder, CO: Westview Press.

Feighner, J. (1985). A comparative trial of fluoxetine and amitriptyline in patients with major depressive disorder. *Journal of Clinical Psychiatry*, 46, 369-372.

Hawkins, J. (1991). Rowers on the River Styx. *Harvard Magazine*, March-April, 43-52.

Kiernan, B. (1990). The genocide in Cambodia, 1975-79. *Bulletin of Concerned Asian Scholars*, 22, 35-40.

Kinzie, J., Boehnlein, J., Leung, P., Moore, L., Riley, C., & Smith, D. (1990). The prevalence of posttraumatic stress disorder and its clinical significance among Southeast Asian refugees. *American Journal of Psychiatry*, 147, 913-917.

Kinzie, J., Leung, P., Boehnlein, J., & Fleck, J. (1987). Antidepressant blood levels in Southeast Asians: Clinical and cultural implications. Unpublished manuscript.

Kinzie, J., Sack, W., Angell, R., Manson, S., & Rath, B. (1986). The psychiatric effects of massive trauma on Cambodian children: The children. *Journal of the American Academy of Child Psychiatry*, 25(3), 370-376.

Kuoch, T., & Scully, M. (1984). Cambodian voices and perceptions: A collection of materials, experiences and cross-cultural understandings. Unpublished manuscript.

Lawyers Committee for Human Rights (1989). *Refuge denied: Problems in the protection of Vietnamese and Cambodians in Thailand and the admission of Indochinese refugees into the United States.* New York: Lawyers Committee for Human Rights.

Mollica, R. (1988). The trauma story: The psychiatric care of refugee survivors of violence and torture. In F. Ochberg (Ed.). *Post Traumatic Therapy and Victims of Violence* (pp. 295-314). New York: Brunner/Mazel.

Mollica, R., Wyshak, G., & Lavelle, J. (1987). The psychosocial impact of war, trauma and torture on Southeast Asian refugees. *American Journal of Psychiatry*, 144, 1567-1572.

Reynell, J. (1989). *Political pawns: Refugees on the Thai-Kampuchean border*. Oxford: Refugee Studies Programme.

Shawcross, W. (1984). *The quality of mercy: Cambodia. holocaust and modern conscience*. New York: Simon & Schuster.

Stark, P., & Hardison, D. (1985). A review of multicenter controlled studies of fluoxetine vs. imipramine and placebo in outpatients with major depressive disorder. *Journal of Clinical Psychiatry*. 46, 53-58.

Terr, L. (1991). Childhood traumas: An outline and overview. *American Journal of Psychiatry*, 148, 10-20.

Ulrich, D. (1983). Contextual family and marital therapy. In B. Wolman, & G. Stricker, Eds. *Handbook of family and marital therapy* (pp. 187-211). New York: Plenum.

Women and Political Torture:
Work with Refugee Survivors in Exile

Barbara Chester

SUMMARY. Although women and children represent 80% of persons who flee their countries for reasons of persecution as refugees, scant attention has been given women in the literature describing severe human rights abuses, including torture. Torture is an extreme form of trauma that involves the strategic destruction of the human being. The torturer uses every aspect of the person's being. In the case of women, their own femaleness is used as a weapon. This paper focuses on special issues faced by women who are survivors of torture. The author directed the first center in the United States providing multidisciplinary care for survivors of political torture.

I wish I could have my family living together.
The devil takes lives one by one.
Satan has no mercy on children who don't have parents
to live with. No laughing could I have–only sadness inside.
My mind wept harder when it reminded me.
This happens in the world.
(Vannak Pok, 18 year-old Cambodian woman)

Barbara Chester received her Doctorate in Psychology from the University of Minnesota in 1976. After teaching at the University level both in the United States and abroad, she returned to Minnesota and established a number of private, non-profit agencies that work with severe emotional trauma. These include the Center for Victims of Torture, the first agency of its kind in this country to provide multidisciplinary health and mental health care to survivors of political torture by foreign governments. Currently, Dr. Chester is a Consultant in private practice in Flagstaff, AZ, working with several Native American groups including the Hopi and Havasupai Tribes.

During the past ten years, unprecedented numbers of people have sought refuge within the United States. These people chose to flee their homelands for many reasons, including war, arbitrary and illegal detention, political imprisonment, "disappearance," extra-judicial executions, and civil strife. Although women represent the majority of adults who flee their countries for these reasons (Amnesty International, 1990), very little attention has been given them in the literature describing torture and persecution.

Research on the rehabilitation of political torture victims is fairly new. The research itself has been very basic in both scope and design, and in some cases has been complicated by the need for security and protection of both the clients and researchers. In addition, wide networks for the coordination and sharing of information are just now in the process of being formed.

The literature on recent (post-Holocaust) survivors is itself reflective of the two parallel routes that are evident in the evolution of torture treatment. The first route is evidenced by the medical and psychiatric literature that focuses on documenting the types of torture experienced by victims, and the short-term, mostly physical symptoms exhibited by survivors. The second approach is demonstrated by groups working under conditions of repression. For obvious reasons, these studies are generally not well documented, and tend to be politically oriented (Chester, 1990). The scant literature on women survivors of torture is also reflective of these biases, and suffers from the shortcomings inherent in these approaches. Due to their size and scope, these studies generally overlook the cultural diversity of torture victims.

A Canadian study, for example, compared 28 female and male victims of torture from Latin America. On the basis of this sample, a majority of whom were well-educated Chileans, and the reliance in large part on self-report, the authors concluded that women were tortured less frequently and severely, and that there was a clear association between the degree of political participation and severity of torture. Women also reported rape more frequently, as part of the torture experience (Allodi & Stiasny, 1990).

At at the Center for Victims of Torture in Minneapolis, the clinical work experienced in both the planning and providing of services indicates two ends of a possible continuum of survivors. At one end of this continuum are people from countries such as Cambodia which suffered massive trauma involving large segments of the population. Typically, survivors have few shared words to describe the experience. Because of tremendous cultural shame, they suffer from a lack of community support for speaking out. In addition, because they tend not to politicize their own situation, they often do not define themselves as survivors of political torture, neither needing nor deserving of specialized care.

At the other end of this continuum are people whose action on behalf of a well conceptualized and articulated set of values and beliefs led to arrest and persecution. These values, whether humanitarian, political, or religious, have been politicized by the individual, community and/or state. Amnesty International prisoners of conscience tend to fit this mold, as do clients from South Africa, Eastern Europe, and the Southern Cone (Argentina, Chile, Uruguay, Paraguay, and Bolivia). These individuals often receive the support of both local and international communities, and will accept care if it is defined and conceptualized correctly. For example, the International Rehabilitation Center (RCT) in Denmark makes clear in their mission statement that torture victims are normal people who have undergone an abnormal experience (Genefke & Aalund, 1983).

These distinctive extremes have been noted specifically for women in Latin America: "In the first cluster of countries, those forming part of Central America, political torture reaches women as daily terror. Women are most often injured or killed in contexts of generalized violence: in massacres, attacks on churches during mass, and the burning of villages. . . . By contrast, in the countries of the Southern Cone, where a military government or succession of military governments have been entrenched for decades, women are systematically identified . . . as 'enemies' of the government. They are methodically tracked down and incarcerated" (Bunster-Burotto, 1986, pp.297-298).

Due to the scarcity of data, it is perhaps best to take a broad overview and combination of approaches in order to look at treatment implications for the culturally diverse group of women who are survivors in exile.

THE CENTER FOR VICTIMS OF TORTURE

During the past ten years, more than thirty clinics and centers have emerged around the world as a response to the practical and ethical need to provide care to survivors of torture. Due to their geo-political locations, these agencies address vastly different treatment issues and populations (Chester, 1990).

The Center for Victims of Torture (CVT) in Minneapolis was the first agency in the United States to provide multidisciplinary and specific treatment for survivors of politically motivated torture by foreign governments. The mission of CVT is to provide rehabilitative treatment for survivors and their families, to conduct research regarding effective treatment approaches, and to provide information, education and training toward the prevention of torture. It was my task to plan strategies to implement this mission, and to serve as director and then clinical director from the program's inception.

From May of 1987 through May of 1990, the Center received calls from 391 potential clients. Of the 90 survivors who received extensive assessment, evaluation, and intervention, approximately one-fifth were women.

These women came from the African continent (33%), the Middle East (22%), Latin America (11%), and Southeast Asia (17%). The remaining 17% were survivors of the Nazi Holocaust or U.S citizens tortured abroad. They range from 20 to over 50 years of age. Almost one-quarter were tortured prior to age 18. Thirty percent are refugees, 16% are U.S. citizens, and the remaining women have received or are in the process of applying for political asylum. All but one suffered physical torture including beatings, burning, use of electricity, and/or falanga (blows to the soles of the feet). Other forms of torture included threats of death to self or loved ones, humiliation, being forced to watch the torture of others, and mock executions.

It is from these women, as well as from other women survivors in the community, that all unreferenced comments are provided.

TORTURE

Torture is an extreme form of trauma. Of countries surveyed by Amnesty International almost half reserved the right to torture their own populations (Amnesty International, 1984). Torture is an institutionalized form of violence from which there is no escape, safety, or redress.

> Torture is cheap and contagious. It is also exportable and standardized. It has its own language and rituals. (Maria Socorro Diokno, the Philippines)

Torture has been defined in a number of ways. In Western countries, the primary emphasis is upon legal definitions that were formulated for purposes of treaties and conventions. According to these, torture is defined by the elements of severe pain and suffering, inflicted by one or more people who are agents of the state, for the purposes of interrogation, punishment, or for any other reason. Torture is a purposeful and systematic activity (World Medical Association, 1975). Survivors describe torture in their own ways:

> They took away my power. They returned me, impotent, to my community.

> They crushed my soul. I feel like a bird without wings.

The methods of torture are designed to break the person' s will and to cause the individual to "lose" or "betray" him or herself. These methods are manipulated and combined in an effort to crush people physically and psychologically, to force them into dependency (helplessness), and to instill fear. The intended result is to destroy people's capacity for self-defense, identity, and control over their own lives, so that they are released, broken, into the community as a warning to others. "The suffering of the individual is thus the torturer's access to the community" (Schlapobersky, 1990).

The purpose of torture is thus to control the population and to eliminate all actual, potential or perceived dissent. It accomplishes its purpose by exploiting and perverting all aspects of human life. Torture is therefore the strategic destruction of the human being: the physical, emotional, social and spiritual self. The torturer, as agent of the state, uses every aspect, every value, and every relationship as a weapon.

In the case of women, their own femaleness is used against them.

SEXISM

Like other forms of violence, torture can be viewed as a process, often a life-long process that has its roots in the historical and societal antecedents of a country. This process involves the normalization of violence, the politization of all systems, and the exaggeration and institutionalization of existing hatreds and tensions. In Iran, for example, wearing of western dress, having full-time employment, and wearing lipstick or nail polish have become political acts with severe consequences. One client reports that female members of the Revolutionary Guard would approach offenders with handkerchiefs saying "Here sister, let me help you." They would then remove the make-up with these handkerchiefs which hid razor blades and were soaked with acid. Another woman was tortured and sentenced to death by stoning for adultery. Her crime was her profession; as a professional dancer, she performed in public with male dancers.

In Latin America, the relationship between a patriarchal military dictatorship and the enforcement of secondary status for women through discrimination and violence has been well articulated: "With the onset of the military dictatorship, the already existing sexual discrimination was exacerbated. Being a woman meant being a second class citizen. [Now women faced] double exploitation; [the junta as well as] domestic violence, prostitution, the use of women as objects for publicity, the devaluation of older women, etc." According to these authors, sexism has been exacerbated by new laws that seriously impact women economically, and the imposition of "an ideal feminine model, headed by the first lady of the nation" (Huneeus & Busto, 1989, p.3).

And again, "One of the essential ideas behind the sexual slavery of a woman in torture is to teach her that she must retreat into the home and fulfill the traditional (and secondary) role of wife and mother" (Bunster-Burotto, 1986, p.307).

MOTHERHOOD AND PREGNANCY

One client reports that in her country, women are often abducted with their children because the prison authorities find the presence of children "useful for gaining confessions." Other women report that when pregnant women are abducted, they face several terrible prospects including electrical torture of the fetus in the womb by inserting live wires through the uterus of the mother (de Mariani, 1987).

Chilean psychologist Teresa Huneeus (1989), describes her own ordeal under the Pinochet regime:

> I became a Mother before becoming a professional, and it was as a Mother that I have suffered the greatest violence . . . the violence of . . . receiving an urgent call 'mother, come I need you, Antonio has disappeared' . . . Suddenly becoming aware that this incomprehensible phenomenon 'disappearance' was happening to us . . . The violence of feeling my daughter's pain when she handed her child over to me saying 'they are too close . . . I cannot risk being taken with him, take care of my child' . . . The violence of receiving the feared news; 'they got her' . . .

SEXUAL VIOLENCE

It is not surprising to discover that both survivors and health practitioners report the extensive use of sexual violence against women torture victims. Reports indicate a high prevalence of sexual violence among tortured women and female adolescents from Southeast Asia (Mollica, 1990). A similar pattern was found in a sample of 28 persecuted or tortured women from Latin America, now living in Canada. Investigators found that 64% had been sexually abused, and that 44% reported violent rape as part of the torture experience (Allodi & Stiasny, 1990). In a Danish survey of 200 persons, one-third of the 39 women torture victims reported incidents of sexual violation. A majority of these women (54%) were from the Southern Cone and the remainder were from Greece and Spain (Christiansen & Juhl, 1990). Of the 18 women survivors receiving extensive assessment, evaluation, or long-term therapy at the Center For Victims of Torture in Minneapolis through May of 1990, 60% disclosed incidents of sexual violence.

Torture makes patently clear the fact that rape is both an act of violence and a form of social control. In Lawrence Weschler's (1990) superb analysis of torture and impunity, he describes various factors that brought an end to the military dictatorship in Brazil. In an interview with General Golbery do Couto e Silver, he cites the General's opinion that there were two cases that "galvanized a change in military opinion." One case involved a security agent who was prosecuted for having sex with a female relative of a prisoner as a bribe to secure intervention on the prisoner's behalf: "It's very strange. Rape as a part of torture was perfectly ok: that was an effective method of investigation, a way of sparking fear which would provoke confession and elicit information–all very professional. But rape for pleasure–the very thought that the torturer could be doing anything for his own pleasure–that really shook them up" (pp. 67-68).

Women from Iran report that the execution of virgins is prohibited by Muslim law. Women political prisoners were, therefore, routinely raped so their possible eventual execution could be accomplished within the tenets of proscribed religious practice. A South American woman reports the extensive use of insertion of objects, animals, and insects into the vagina as a form of sexual torture. An African woman describes the death by infection of a cell mate, a young adolescent, caused by extensive sexual misuse. This woman herself experienced gang-rape by security officers, and was terrified, even years later, that this event would cause her own death.

The re-victimization or "second wound" is also apparent in women who suffer from rape during torture. One client from Africa was severely violated and humiliated during her two years as a political prisoner. After her release, she continued to suffer from persecution as a single, female, refugee. Against great odds, she was able to migrate to the United States with her three young children. At her political asylum hearing, the government Immigration and Naturalization Service (INS) attorney remarked that it was a well known fact that women exiles from her country often practiced prostitution to survive. He made the point to the court that this woman was, in fact, confusing rape with prostitution. The severely traumatic experience suffered by this distinguished and courageous young woman was discounted by, in essence, calling her a whore.

The fact that rape of tortured women is so prevalent, and so humiliating, creates a barrier to many female survivors. They will not disclose the fact of their imprisonment, or seek treatment, because they fear that if others know that they were tortured, their communities will assume that they have therefore also been raped. The stigma of rape thus prevents these traumatized women from seeking aid for the sequelae of torture. Said one Cambodian woman, "The shame is not being raped . . . the shame is that others know about it."

AMNESTY, IMPUNITY, AND, SILENCE

Both historically and at the present time, the issues of amnesty and impunity emerge as dictatorships and military governments end. Ostensibly, to serve the ends of social peace and stability, governments invoke "Due Obedience" laws which are, in essence, an amnesty for torturers that promotes "forgetting" on a social level.

Torture, like other forms of violence, thrives in secrecy. The privatization of what is essentially a widespread, public event, "imposes silence upon a world of pain" (Lira, Becker, & Castillo, 1988, p.13). Nevertheless, it is important to note that silence on the part of victims is part of the phasic nature of the trauma response. In essence, after torture, a person's life becomes a continual conflict between the need to avoid and forget, and the need to remember and bear witness. After torture, "Something silences oneself within . . . Even if one speaks, there remains that which cannot be said . . . Perhaps the dimension of physical and psychic suffering, the humiliation, shame, and guilt reach such level of horror that it cannot be discussed because of the risk that it be repeated" (Lenhardtson, 1990, p.94).

For women, the societal need to forget imposes additional consequences: "Sadly enough, as democracy is being reestablished in our country, a new conflict has arisen for us. We are torn between this consciousness of our role as women in society, and the social pressure to return to our old roles. The crisis is over, and once again we are being relegated to fulfill our traditional feminine roles" (Huneeus & Busto 1989, p.1).

THERAPEUTIC RESPONSES

Because the methods of torture are strategic, the healing process for both the community and individual must be equally strategic (Chester, 1990). Into the treatment setting, the woman survivor brings not only her history of trauma, but the strengths of her femaleness, her culture, beliefs, and values.

At a special working conference for North American medical, mental health, and social work practitioners held in Minneapolis in June of 1989, participants agreed that "a crucial issue in dealing with trauma is the capacity to take action," especially action at the level of community groups. Women, they agreed, are especially good at this because they have had to do it traditionally in response to oppression (Garcia-Peltoniemi, 1989).

"I realized that I knew how to act, what to do, with the judges, lawyers, police, military, guards . . . I knew how to exert pressure without importunating. Obtaining, bit by bit, some information, acting as if I was patient and even trusting, when necessary, smiling at the right moment, being quiet when I had to be. I knew how to efface myself, my husband instead was paralyzed. Later, I found out mine was the same as many other women's experience" (Huneeus & Busto, 1989, p.3).

Self-help and support groups are a natural mechanism for many women. In Argentina, for example, during the years 1976-1983, more than ten thousand political prisoners were taken, and thirty thousand people (including 400 children) were "disappeared" (Bozzolo, 1989). The Abuelas De Plaza De Mayo (Association of the Grandmothers of the Plaza De Mayo) was formed during this time by a group of women, grandmothers, whose children and grandchildren were "disappeared" during this so-called "dirty war." From isolated individuals petitioning large and terrifying security organisms, they began to march together in the Plaza with placards depicting their loved ones. Today, they are a formidable political force not only in their own country, but throughout the world, with an associated technical team of 18 professionals including lawyers, doctors, and psychologists. "We did not intend to start a movement, we only wanted to find our grandchildren"(de Mariani, 1987).

Although women from various groups in Ethiopia and Southeast Asia state that disclosing information pertaining to personal trauma is unusual and not traditionally sanctioned, the wrenching experience of exile and massive death of family members may serve to enhance the use of groups as a singular means of support in exile.

For example, among patients receiving treatment at the Indochinese Psychiatry Clinic in Brighton, Massachusetts, it was determined that the group with the most debilitating psychiatric disorders were Cambodian widows, who had not only been traumatized, but "marginalized" as well. As a response to this, several Cambodian women's self-help groups were established. Later results showed that of all groups surveyed in an outcome study, the Cambodian widows showed the greatest improvement after six months (Mollica, 1990).

In 1989, the Center For Victims of Torture in Minneapolis formed an international women's support group, composed of five women from various countries in Africa, Asia, and the Middle East. The group was small, very time limited, and composed of women with varying educational levels and ability to speak English. Still, they managed to communicate feelings about their experiences of torture, trauma, and exile. The last session ended with the women bringing songs or poems to each other from their countries of origin. They were stories of love and sadness, power and healing.

Each woman spoke of the vast richness of experience represented in the group, the similarities and differences of their responses to extreme trauma and exile. A Southeast Asian woman, debilitated for ten years with crippling depression, headaches, and nightmares, connected with her strength and anger after hearing a South African woman share her reactions to apartheid. "I used to have a heart like a tiger, but now I feel faint. I will learn again from you." Similarly, women from the dominant cultures of their society were able to name and confront their confusing experiences with racism in this country (the United States).

CONCLUSION

Women in countries of repression have demonstrated great fortitude in organizing groups for political and social action. This strength has been exploited successfully for therapeutic purposes in some instances by medical and mental health practitioners working with women survivors of torture. Support groups composed of women from homogeneous populations, such as the Cambodian women's group in Massachusetts, and heterogeneous populations, such as the international women's group in Minneapolis, show promise as a technique for empowering women to connect with their own inner strength, and the strength of other women who have undergone similar experiences. This is particularly promising in countries of exile, where traditional sources of support are often unavailable.

In addition, it must be kept in mind that although women share common experiences because of their gender, they are still culturally diverse. This cultural context provides alternative explanations of both the cause of the trauma, as well as for appropriate intervention. The South African woman, for example, viewed the basis of her trauma as essentially political. Exploring options for political action, even in exile, was essential to both her acceptance of treatment and to her recovery. The Southeast Asian woman, on the other hand, viewed her misfortunes as a result of both karma, and experiences with witchcraft in her country of origin. Working within her world view was necessary for both therapeutic rapport and meaningful intervention.

If we are to provide vital healing strategies and facilitate the "re-making" of the tortured women's world, we must make a concerted effort to understand and utilize the strengths of both their gender and cultural contexts.

REFERENCES

Allodi, F., & Stiasny, S. (1990). Women as torture victims. *Canadian Journal Psychiatry, 35*, 144-148.

Amnesty International USA (1990). *Reasonable fear: Human rights and United States refugee policy.* New York: Author.

Amnesty International (1984). *Torture in the eighties.* New York. Author.

Bozzolo, R.C. (1989, October). *Psychological effects on victims of political violence.* Paper presented at the annual conference of Society for Traumatic Stress Studies, San Francisco, California.

Bunster-Burotto, X. (1986). Surviving beyond fear: Women and torture in Latin America. In J. Nash (Ed.). *Women and Change in Latin America.* (pp.297-325). Boston: Bergin & Garvey.

Chester, B. (1990). Because mercy has a human heart: Centers for victims of torture. In P. Suedfeld (Ed.). *Psychology and Torture* (pp.165-184). Washington D.C.: Hemisphere.

Chester, B. (1990). The treatment of torture under repressive regimes: Opening remarks. In J. Gruschow & K. Hannibal (Eds.). *Health services for the treatment of torture and trauma survivors* (pp.79-182). Washington D.C.: American Association for the Advancement of Science.

Christiansen, J., & Juhl, E. (Ed). (1990). Danish Medical Bulletin. Supplement No. 1.

de Mariani, M. (1987, June). *Grandmothers of the Plaza De Mayo.* Presentation at the Center For Victims of Torture. Conference. Minneapolis, Minnesota.

Diokno, M.S. (1989, June). *Torture in the Philippines.* Presentation at the Center for Victims of Torture Conference. Minneapolis. June 2-4.

Garcia-Peltoniemi, R. (1989, June). Center For Victims of Torture, *Proceedings of the Third Annual Conference on Torture Treatment.* Minneapolis, Minnesota.

Genefke, I.K., & Aalund, O. (1983). Rehabilitation of torture victims: Perspectives for research. *Mandedsskrift fur Praktist Laegegerning* 61, 31-38.

Huneeus, T., & Busto, M. (1989, October). *Women and violence in a violent society.* Presentation at the annual conference of Society for Traumatic Stress Studies. San Francisco, California.

Lenhardtson E. (1990). Some reflections about torture. In Gruschow, J. & Hannibal, K. (Eds.). *Health services for the treatment of torture and trauma survivors* (pp. 91-97). Washington D.C.:American Association for the Advancement of Science.

Lira E., Becker, D., & Castillo, M.I. (1988, October). *Psychotherapy with victims of political repression in Chile: A therapeutic and political challenge.* Presentation at the meeting of the Latin American Institute of Mental Health and Human Rights, Santiago, Chile.

Mollica, R.F. (1990). The social world destroyed: The psychiatric care of the refugee trauma survivor. In Gruschow, J., & Hannibal, K. (Eds.). *Health Services for the Treatment of Torture and Trauma Survivors.* (pp.15-34.). Washington D.C.: American Association for the Advancement of Science.

Schlapobersky, J. (1990). Torture as the perversion of a healing relationship. In J. Gruschow, & K. Hannibal (Eds.). *Health Services for the Treatment of Torture and Trauma Survivors* (pp. 51-72). Washington D.C.: American Association for the Advancement of Science.

Weschler, L. (1990). *Miracle, a universe: Settling accounts with torturers.* New York: Pantheon.

World Medical Association. (1975). *Declaration of Tokyo, Japan.* In addition, thanks to the staff of the Center for Victims of Torture, especially Leigh Bristol-Kagen, Joanne Meehan, and Linda Valerian.

Markers of Successful Aging Among Vietnamese Refugee Women

Barbara W.K. Yee

SUMMARY. This article describes several markers of successful aging for Vietnamese women. These studies suggest that feelings of control have important implications for life satisfaction and mental health of female Vietnamese refugees. Adequate satisfaction with social relationships is a key contributor to successful aging and mental health of elderly Vietnamese refugees who are female. The article concludes by discussing ways in which mental health and health care professionals can assist female elderly refugees cope with family crisis, adaptation, and acculturation issues because they are at highest risk now and into the future. Key issues were: cultural values surrounding age and gender norms, differential rates of acculturation across generations in the family, cross-cultural differences in mental health and their therapeutic implications.

The history of immigration and adaptation of many Asian groups in the United States is a fascinating topic for psychological study. The Asian elderly cohort represents living history because it is their many collective experiences which history documents. The history of each Asian ethnic group varies by time of peak immigration, migration, circumstances, motivations for coming to the United States, or American reactions toward

Barbara W.K. Yee was born in Honolulu, HI and comes from a Chinese-Hawaiian heritage. During her first year of graduate school, the plight of refugees captured her interest, especially the adaptation of middle age and elderly refugees to Western societies. Barbara W.K. Yee obtained her PhD in Developmental Psychology from the University of Denver in 1982 and is currently Assistant Professor in the Department of Graduate Studies, School of Allied Health Sciences, University of Texas Medical Branch.

Asian transplants. The following article describes psychological and social adaptation of Vietnamese elderly women in the United States, and will detail how some Vietnamese women are adapting to their experiences in this country, as defined by their perceptions of control over their lives and life satisfaction with growing older in this Western society.

The rationale for selecting Vietnamese elderly women for a study of adaptation and coping in later life is that their personal histories are likely to include a wide range of hardships prior to coming and during their lives in the United States. These elderly people have experienced many negative events that psychologists cannot ethically reproduce in the laboratory. This alternative approach would be to examine how real negative life experiences influence adaptation and coping in later life as it naturally occurred in people's lives–a so-called natural experiment. Singular negative life events that divert the path of one's life such as internment for the Japanese or migration after the fall of Saigon for the Vietnamese, coupled with enormous assimilation and acculturation requirements and experienced racism, could produce less adaptive and helpless elderly people.

Since 1975 nearly one million refugees have been resettled throughout the United States with approximately 700,000 coming from Southeast Asia. Many of these refugees faced unemployment, racial tension, social isolation, family estrangement, a new language, strange surroundings, a vastly different set of cultural norms, rules and behaviors after experiencing the trauma of forced separation from their own lands, family, and friends (see review in Holtzman & Bornemann, 1990). A growing number will develop serious adjustment problems (Beiser, 1990).

The refugees as a group face multiple adjustment problems, but the elderly have experienced more difficulty adapting to life in the United States with the passage of time. The elderly face rapid acculturation of their family members and a lesser acceptance of the elderly in American society, and are tied to more traditional ways. As a result, the elderly have less adaptive skills to allow a smooth adjustment to this culture even with the passage of time. This translates into a slow insidious development of mental health and adjustment difficulties. Some earlier work revealed that the elderly had fewer adjustment problems than their younger cohorts (Aylesworth, Ossorio & Osaki, 1980). Recent work suggests that although the elderly tended to experience fewer adjustment problems during the first five years after relocation than younger refugees, in the long run the elderly experience greater adjustment difficulties due to the changing nature of their own family members (Yee, 1990a,b; Yee and Nguyen, 1987). Rumbaut (1989) concluded that those refugees who are most at risk for psychological distress are the least educated and the least proficient in English, the most dependent upon welfare, the poorest, the most unemployed, the oldest with health problems, and those with the most traumatic migration histories–a profile that fits many elderly refugees.

Older Asian women have a difficult time dealing with their conflicting roles in American culture, especially their gender roles within the family and community. As a group, older Asian women are more traditional than the younger generations even within their own family. The pressure in American society encourages female liberation and may directly conflict with their own upbringing. This cultural clash may create ambivalent feelings concerning their gender role within a marriage and the family. The degree of difficulty depends upon the nature of the traditional gender role from the homeland, particular gender role of the individual woman, and her expectations and their expectations for her within the context of the family.

In Vietnam the norm for richer families was the extended family system. The elderly parents lived with the oldest son or the richest son. Nuclear family structures were the norm in poorer families. In contrast to other East Asian cultures, Vietnamese females had equal status with their husbands in practice, especially among younger Vietnamese. All important decisions involved both spouses. During the war years the Vietnamese women provided for the economic well being of their families while their husbands were fighting the war (Chi, 1980). Currently, younger Vietnamese women have a higher status in the eyes of many Americans (e.g., positive stereotyping of Asian females) and may even be the breadwinner of the family because they are more likely to find and accept lower occupational jobs than their husbands. The situation of older Vietnamese women is not so rosy since they are not as likely to be hired due to age biases, lack of English speaking abilities and transferable job skills. The function of many older Vietnamese women is one of grandchild caretaker and housekeeper. Even this role is diminishing with the assimilation and rapid acculturation of these grandchildren.

The majority of refugees face multiple adjustment problems immediately after migration, but a significant number of younger refugees make adequate adaptation with the passage of time (Rumbaut, 1989). By contrast, the passage of time may create more difficulties for refugee elders within their own families and dealing with society at large. Older middle age and elderly refugees, sheltered by younger family members soon after migration to this country, face serious emotional turmoil ten to fifteen years later (Yee, 1989; 1990 a,b).

Asian elderly women may be especially vulnerable to the feelings of helplessness in a strange country. Early reports in refugee camps indicated that the middle age and elderly women were more depressed than other age groups (Liu, Lamanna & Murata, 1979). This increased vulnerability coupled with the traditional role of the older woman in the family and society, as an ideal and as practiced by the individual, contributes to more difficult adjustment and eventual adaptation of these older Asian women in the United States.

Refugee elders may become more aware of their extreme isolation from the dominant society, whose cultural norms are very different from their own, and realize that they live in a society that does not esteem elderly people as compared to their homeland (Yee & Hennessey, 1982; Yee, 1990a,b). Elder refugees experience value and role conflicts with their younger relatives because these younger relatives have rapidly acculturated to American ways. Family estrangement and generational conflicts create much emotional distress for refugee elders and is their most frequently cited problem (Yee, 1990a,b).

MARKERS OF SUCCESSFUL AGING AND CONTROL

Adaptive aging could be defined in a number of different ways and appropriate questions to address this issue are "What are markers of successful aging for older women?" and "Do the markers of successful aging hold for a diverse group of elderly women such as refugee women?" These are two difficult questions and experts in gerontology are still debating the answers for the first question, so how can we expect to answer the second? I don't claim to have a definitive answer to both questions, but my research over the past 10 years can give us some clues regarding the markers of successful aging among women who are Vietnamese refugees and may allude to answers for other Pacific Islander groups.

In the following pages I will examine possible markers of successful aging among Vietnamese refugee women and examine why issues surrounding the family may be a pivotal predictor for successful aging among these refugees living in the United States. I will further describe why Vietnamese elderly women find family conflict, especially intergenerational and sex role conflicts, so emotionally charged and difficult to resolve. The following study describes the pattern of control perceptions in British and Asian elderly women (i.e., Japanese and Vietnamese) living in the United States, and examines possible variables that relate to control and adaptation in old age.

Having a sense that one controls the most important aspects of one's life is a characteristic of adaptive elders in our society. Research in this area indicates that a person's perceptions are more important than the objective level of control in helping us to predict adjustment and adaptation to aging (Langer, 1983).The question of whether this is also true of elders in other cultures or within subcultures in the United States has not been answered.

Minority elderly individuals differ from white, Anglo individuals in their culture, experiences with racism, their cultural attitudes and values related to control, their available levels of cultural and social supports in the United States (see review in Yee, 1990a,b). Any one, or combination of these variables could explain actual ethnic group differences found in a person's perceptions of control or adaptation to aging. For example, a person's particular cultural socialization may consistently produce behavioral responses which indicate that a person believes that many negative events in old age were not under his/her personal control. Or, experiences with racism or sexism may produce a person who feels powerless to achieve anything because many barriers exist for minority people or females. Another example may be that the present cultural environment may not be supportive and consistent with the immigrant elderly's culture of origin. As a result of this condition, the immigrant elderly may not feel personally able to control reinforcements such as how to increase the occurrence of positive outcomes or decrease the occurrence of negative events in his or her own life when these events are truly amenable to attempts at control. The immigrant elderly person living in a new cultural environment is required to relearn how to control reinforcements or learn what contingencies may be operating in order to understand the American social and cultural system.

I will summarize several trends found across three empirical studies conducted over the last 10 years by my colleagues and I. These three studies suggest key life domains identified by female Vietnamese refugees to be social relationships, especially family and friendships with people from their homeland. These studies suggested that adequate satisfaction with social relationships is a key contributor to successful aging and mental health of elderly Vietnamese refugee women. The article concludes by discussing ways in which mental health and health care professionals can assist elderly refugee women cope with family crisis, adaptation, and acculturation issues.

STUDIES OF ADAPTATION AGING AMONG VIETNAMESE REFUGEE WOMEN

In a series of related studies examining adaptation among multicultural middle age and elderly groups, my colleagues and I found some interesting trends concerning the effects of relocation and subsequent adaptation by Vietnamese elderly women. Each of these studies provides some clues regarding the yardstick of successful aging for this group and perhaps places where psychotherapeutic interventions may have a significant impact.

Study I. The first study examined the relationship between cognitive functioning and perceptions of control among Caucasian, Vietnamese and Japanese women who were between 51 and 91 years of age (Yee, 1977; Yee, 1984). This exploratory study examined the relationships between the elders perceptions of their aging status, positive and negative aspects of living in this country, and qualitative assessment of their adaptation to living in the United States.

This discussion will only focus upon the Vietnamese elderly respondents and will discuss the other two ethnic groups when appropriate. This sample included 30 Vietnamese respondents who were 50 years of age and older, with a mean age of 64.3 (SD = 4.9). They were a convenience sample obtained from lists of members who belonged to a number of Vietnamese Mutual Aid Societies and resettlement agencies operating in Denver, Colorado in 1975 to 1976. Respondents in Study I consisted of Vietnamese elderly women who came largely in the first wave of refugees during the Fall of Saigon in 1975 and were more educated, more Western and urbanized and of higher social class than later waves of refugee included in Studies II and III.

In response to a question about their expectations for aging in the United States, 90% of these Vietnamese women (27 respondents) were expecting positive things in old age. These positive expectations for aging in the United States goes down to 50% (15 respondents) when asked about their current realities of being an older person in this country. This group was not disappointed with their positive expectations for aging. Forty percent of the sample (12 respondents) expected positive things in old age but experienced negative aspects of growing older in this country. Only ten percent of the sample (3 respondents) had negative expectations for growing older in the United States but were pleasantly surprised and currently experiencing positive aspects of aging. No respondents had negative expectations and were currently experiencing negative aging. The respondents who expected positive things in old age and received negative experiences would be a high risk group for depression and psychotherapeutic intervention. In this first study, clues surfaced regarding the living conditions in the United States that are deemed important and related to happiness or sadness for the Vietnamese elderly women. Given that we know what these issues are, we can extrapolate and determine what might be linked with successful aging (i.e., happiness or sadness, life satisfaction).

My interviewers asked Vietnamese middle age and elderly women open-ended questions regarding positive and negative aspects of living in the United States. The Vietnamese elderly women felt that positive aspects of living in the United States were: English abilities of the younger members of their family, economic survival, having good relationships with Americans and sponsors, having good news about relatives left back in Vietnam, being able to have high a degree of contact with old friends and being able to share their past and current life experiences, being able to interact with people from their own country, having freedom and feeling no racial discrimination, when family members follow traditional family patterns, reunification of the traditional family and traditional living arrangements.

The unhappy or sad aspects of living in the United States as identified by the Vietnamese elderly women were: lack of preservation of Vietnamese culture and language, assimilation of the negative aspects of American culture, lack of economic means other than mere survival, sickness, poor health, loneliness, lack of ability to communicate with an English speaking world and resulting isolation, loss of traditional family roles such as role in caring for grandchildren, loss of status and position of the elderly in the family, changing food habits, lack of Vietnamese community, transportation problems, limitation in kind and types of activities would like to do because of financial or other barriers, being displaced in a foreign country, negative relationships with neighbors, lack of knowledge about relatives and living conditions in Vietnam, and hardships of being a refugee.

Study II. The second study used another comparison group–immigrant British women because I was curious about whether the same trends would be found among another immigrant group. The use of a British elderly sample allowed the investigator to control for immigration status, while using a group that was more culturally similar to the Caucasian American population. Again this discussion will focus upon the findings for the Vietnamese women and mention the other two groups only to provide a framework for comparison. This second study examined the relationship between key life domains and control perceptions in 60 elderly Vietnamese women living in Denver and Honolulu, with a mean age of 59.1 years of age (SD = 8.89) (Yee & Van Arsdale, 1986).

In my dissertation, I examined the relationship between control perceptions, life satisfaction, cultural values, perceived discrimination, and demographic variables among 180 British, Japanese and Vietnamese women who were between the ages of 40 and 94. This second study (Yee, 1982) revealed that the British immigrant women felt more personal control and less helplessness than either the Japanese or Vietnamese women. The Japanese immigrant women felt more control and less helpless than the Vietnamese refugee women. In order to understand these findings, I examined possible correlates of control. Age, generational and demographic differences such as income between the ethnic groups account for some of this ethnic group difference. Being younger, being born in this country and having resources such as higher income was related to feeling more control over one's life. Other variables that accounted for these ethnic group differences in personal control were cultural value orientation of independence-dependence, English language skills, and neighborhood support of their cultural habits. Believing that individuals operate as independent units, having good English skills and having an accessible and supportive social environment also helped these middle age and elderly women feel more control over their lives. I controlled for some of these demographic and cultural variables and the ethnic group differences grew smaller, yet were still statistically significant. Variations in life experiences, such as ability to cope with a different culture or trauma experienced during relocation, would account for a significant portion of this difference in a person's perception of their own control over their lives.

Life satisfaction was related to having a higher degree of personal control and a lower degree of helplessness across all three groups. The older Vietnamese women felt that they had less personal control over their lives than middle age respondents. It appears that middle age Vietnamese women were more satisfied with their life circumstances than their elderly compatriots.

Elderly Vietnamese women felt less personal control in determination of their living arrangements, the types of activities they enjoyed and their intellectual functioning than middle age women. There were no significant differences between middle age and elderly Vietnamese women in personal control over their family relationships or friendships, health or financial situation. The elderly Vietnamese women felt particularly helpless about preventing negative health consequences in comparison to the middle age refugees. These relationship are understandable given the increasing health vulnerability of these elderly women. Yet, there is much therapists and health professionals can do regarding health promotion for middle age and elderly individuals. Recent research has suggested that smoking cessation, changes in nutrition and levels of physical activity will have a significant impact on quality of life and health during the second half of life (see review in Dychtwald, 1986). Because of increased health vulnerability in the second half of life, we need to target health promotion efforts towards encouraging healthy lifestyle changes among older members of our society. The goal of acculturation in the health arena should be maintenance of healthy traditional lifestyle habits, changing unhealthy traditional habits, adopting healthy American lifestyles, while rejecting unhealthy American habits.

In my dissertation, there were ethnic differences in the amounts of control these elderly women felt over different life situations. I (Yee, 1982) found that British elderly women felt more personal control over non-social situational contexts (i.e., health, financial, living, activities, intellectual functioning) than did the Japanese or Vietnamese women. In contrast, Japanese and Vietnamese elderly women felt more personal control over their family relationships and friendships than the British women. These findings suggest that perhaps in Asian cultures, the quality of one's social relationships is more determined by one's own efforts and under more personal control than in the Western culture. Or another interpretation is that Asian elders feel and are able to exert more control over social relationships than their Caucasian counterparts. This is an interesting finding since most studies of control have not reported life domain differences between cultural groups. An interesting empirical question would be to examine whether control perceptions change in accordance with changes in social relationships and acculturation of these individuals over time.

My dissertation also revealed that older women have a more difficult adjustment than middle age women. Informal discussions with refugees suggest that older refugees are shielded from the harsh realities of being a "refugee" in the United States by their protective families and communities in the first few years after migration to this country. This situation held while the data for the first study was collected, but by the time the dissertation was collected in 1980 to 1981, hints of massive changes among the refugee community and within families surfaced. Stories of elderly refugees being abandoned by their families and stories of the rapid acculturation of younger members of refugee families came to the attention of service providers. The family and life situation of the older refugee has changed and will change in the future. They will no longer be the protected member of the family.

The situation for the middle age women was different. These middle age women had no one to protect them from the harsh realities of being a middle age person, one who should be at the pinnacle of their career, in this competitive American society. They were expected to perform like their age peers, yet didn't have many of the most basic skills that would allow them to compete, such as knowing the English language or knowing about American institutions or laws. These middle age refugees therefore had to deal with the dissonance between their cultural norms for the elderly as leaders and a source of wisdom in the community, while dealing with American society which often viewed them as a rich source of unskilled labor. Relative to adaptation and coping among the younger refugees–children and young adults–middle age refugees seemed to be less adapted and more maladjusted, but in comparison to their elders, middle age refugees were adapting better than the oldest refugees. In comparison with their mainstream age peers, middle age refugees were having a great deal of difficulty fulfilling their expectations for the middle age period.

Study III. The last study examined the mental health status of 840 adult Southeast Asian refugees who were between the ages of 18 and 93. One hundred and thirty-four were 51 or older, and self-defined as an elder or elderly, living in the Houston metropolitian area (Yee & Nguyen, 1987). The mean age of the elderly group was 61.58 years of age (SD = 7.8). The authors found that the middle age (i.e., 31 to 50) and elderly (i.e., 51 and older) refugee had less education, received more assistance, had less English speaking abilities, had more concerns and troubles than the young adult refugee. These middle age and elderly refugees were more depressed and felt that their problems were less solvable than younger cohorts.

Yee and Nguyen (1987) discussed the relationship between use of alcohol, other drugs or smoking as coping mechanisms among these adult refugees. The authors found that the higher the worries and concerns, more depression and troubles perceived by the refugee, the more substances they used to cope with these stresses. Age alone was not a good predictor of substance use, but the refugee's own assessment of their predicament and situation often determined their particular coping mechanism and adjustment during the middle years.

A closer examination of females who were 50 and older in this sample revealed that older Vietnamese women were vulnerable to alcohol and drug use or coped by stealing if they had great worries and concerns. Middle age and elderly Vietnamese women who were depressed had a greater likelihood of coping with their troubles by smoking. It appears that forgetting about their problems was more characteristic of those with less education and English speaking abilities for older Vietnamese women. Those Vietnamese women who didn't know where to get help for a variety of problems and who were less educated were more likely to talk with friends as a way of coping with their problems. The greater the English speaking ability, the less likely the older Vietnamese females were to discuss their problems with family members. It appears that those who sought professional help were more likely to be those Vietnamese women who were newly arrived in the United States.

MARKERS OF SUCCESSFUL AGING
AND THEIR THERAPEUTIC IMPLICATIONS

Based upon several empirical studies conducted by my colleagues and I, coupled with findings from other studies of mental health of refugees, a number of markers of successful aging have been identified as critical for older Vietnamese women.

Influence of cultural values and beliefs: Life cycle issues. First, expectations for the second half of life are significantly different for Vietnamese women in comparison to expectations held by many American women. For instance, the timing and number of stages of the lifecourse is significantly different for traditional Vietnamese. Instead of six major life stages (i.e., infancy, childhood, adolescence, young adulthood, middle age, and elderly) as roughly accepted by most Americans; the majority of Vietnamese hold three lifestages, childhood, adulthood, and elderhood (Hickey, 1964). The timing of these lifestages, as well as their transitions and role expectations have significant impact on successful aging of Vietnamese female elders living in this country. By American standards, becoming elderly occurs at around age 65. For most Vietnamese, however, becoming an elder occurs when one becomes a grandmother from as young as age 35 in the home country, to later than expected in this country. Synchronity between the individual's, each generation's, and society's expectations for age and sex roles must be addressed in therapy because many emotional and family problems result from these issues.

Another major issue highlighted in this body of research is cultural differences in gender roles. As discussed in Yee (1989) there are major discrepancies between gender roles as carried out in Vietnam, versus gender expectations of 40, 50 and 60+ year olds in this country. Forty and Fifty year olds living in this country, especially males, are expected to be at the pinnacle of their careers. Yet the reality for many middle age and elderly Vietnamese males, is that few attain high status positions, many more work in menial jobs if they are able to work at all. This downward mobility of Vietnamese males has major impact on Vietnamese females and their families. A common reaction to this downward mobility is heightened emotional distress that influences all family relationships. Another common reaction is an increasing demand by Vietnamese males to hold tightly to traditional values and behaviors–male and elderly superiority, and obedience to this authority by females and younger members of the family. Thus increased need to control the family by middle age and elderly Vietnamese males puts many middle age and younger females in direct conflict with their ever increasing pull towards egalitarian rights for women in America. Elderly Vietnamese women are more likely to surrender to this demand because they are more accepting of these traditionally sexist roles and behaviors.

The reality of being able to carry out these traditional gender roles are different for Vietnamese males versus females. Middle age and elderly Vietnamese females experienced upward mobility or no change. Middle age Vietnamese females have higher access to many jobs because they seek jobs that have lower skill requirements and pursue jobs where poor English skills are not a barrier to getting and keeping these jobs. In contrast, Vietnamese males are looking for comparable positions they held in the homeland, but are often disappointed because of their lack of English skills and lack of transfer of job skills allow them to only get jobs at the bottom of the ladder or they may be permanently underemployed or unemployed. As a consequence, female adult refugees find themselves to be the breadwinner or have a coequal breadwinner position with their husbands. This upward mobility in role status for Vietnamese females, in contrast to the downward mobility of Vietnamese males may create marital strife and family conflict. Signs of these stressors are increase of divorce, abuse, and family dysfunction among Vietnamese families.

Elderly Vietnamese women still carry out major family responsibilities such as cooking, housekeeping, and care of the grandchildren. Elderly Vietnamese women make significant contributions to the family and are valued for their current contributions. There are, however, significant costs for these elderly Vietnamese women. Because they are homebound with childcare and household responsibilities, these elderly women are isolated from other Vietnamese and from the larger American society. As a result, these elder women remain traditionally Vietnamese, are not familiar with American culture, and rarely have English skills.

The extremely traditional Vietnamese elderly women will find themselves at a loss when they are no longer needed to provide useful functions for the extended family. Family duties performed by middle age and elderly Vietnamese women have lessened their time and exposure to American culture that is required for successful adaptation and acculturation. This culture shock will become increasing evident some ten to twenty years after migration for these women. What makes this situation extremely difficult is that most other members of their families will have already adjusted to their new life in America many years ago. As a result, familial social supports for these elderly Vietnamese women will be less understanding of their current plight.

This valued position of elderly Vietnamese women will become increasingly tenuous with the acculturation of the younger family members.

Trends indicate that extended family living arrangements will be less frequent, elderly Vietnamese women will become less and less involved in providing critical services to their families. Trends indicate that extended family living arrangements will be less frequent, elderly Vietnamese women will become less and less involved in providing critical services to their families. This trend suggests that there are hidden costs for middle age Vietnamese women, like more liberated American women, and this translates into acquiring additional roles to the ones they already have and "DOING IT ALL." They have careers, are wives, mothers, and housekeepers. These middle age Vietnamese women are a high risk group for work and family burnout, and overall stress (Carlin, 1990). Handling these multiple roles can be overwhelming and coupled with her spouses significant downward mobility, could create an explosive situation for the family.

These middle age Vietnamese are the "Sandwich Generation" and must also intervene between the younger and grandparent generations in the extended family unit. They are caught in the middle between their children who are extremely Americanized and their elderly parents who are for the most part, very traditional. These middle age parents realize that certain American traits, such as having good English skills and some American behavioral patterns are essential to being successful in the United States. Elderly Vietnamese refugees are trying to maintain their culture, language, and traditions. These efforts are a common source of conflict within the Vietnamese extended family.

Maintenance of a central and significant role in the family is a critical marker of successful aging for Vietnamese refugee women. As my work has suggested, having a sense of control over social relationships and having input concerning matters of the family or among friends are significant areas of importance for Vietnamese elderly women. The implications for therapy is that if the refugee is having difficulty within the family or larger social network, this difficulty is likely to create serious emotional turmoil and disturbance (Carlin, 1990). Therapy with the whole family is more likely to be successful than therapy solely with the individual client. For many elderly Vietnamese, and traditional Vietnamese, problems of the individual are problems that the whole family must contend with. Therapeutic techniques designed to change the individual are likely to impact the whole family. Preparations must be made to address secondary problems that may arise from therapy.

Another critical marker of successful aging among Vietnamese women is being able to make a contribution to the economic survival of the family. This contribution may not be monetary, but may be support services such as housekeeping, cooking, and childcare responsibilities so that other family members may be free to work outside the home.

Many immigrant and refugee groups come to America expecting the Land of Gold to provide them with a wonderful lifestyle. These false high expectations exact a high price when these expectations are not realized in America and achieved within a relatively short period of time. In fact, interviews with many elderly immigrants and refugees indicate that the dreams of making it big in America and being successful oneself, transforms into hopes and dreams of success for the next generation.

Recognition of this change in life perspective and goals may significantly enhance the therapists efforts at helping the elderly refugee achieve satisfactory life satisfaction and alleviation of depression. For instance, rather than trying to help the elderly client change this perspective, the therapist might help enhance the elderly client's understanding of American culture, lifestyle and behaviors, so that they can better understand younger members of their own family. Another possible function of therapists might be to enhance the elderly persons status in the family and community by encouraging them to help maintain their original culture by actively participating in cultural festivals and traditions. This role of formally teaching younger members of their communities enhances the elders' status within the community and self-esteem because they have the need, skills, and knowledge to transmit their heritage to the next generation.

Cross-cultural issues in mental illness and therapy. Cultural differences surrounding definitions of mental health, illness (Lin, 1990) and problem solving strategies is a difficult one in therapy with elderly refugees. The first barrier is one related to being able to communicate with the elderly Vietnamese refugee women. Most of these women are monolingual Vietnamese speakers, some have additional French language skills, and a small minority have minimal English abilities (Lambert & Taylor, 1990). A significant number of elderly Vietnamese males who came to the United States from 1975 to 1976 have English abilities because many dealt with the American government in Vietnam. Spouses of these Vietnamese males, however, have very little English skills, so bridging the language barrier is a major hurdle for the non-Vietnamese speaking clinicians (Adkins, 1990). Trained paraprofessionals can be trained to provide good translations without major modifications to the client and back to the English speaking therapist and is crucial during each therapeutic session. Untrained Vietnamese translators have often clouded therapeutic assessment and relationships because cultural factors operate as barriers. For instance, the untrained translator may just decide not to ask the question or ask a different question rather than tell the therapist that the question as asked is somehow inappropriate to ask. Untrained translators may also screen clients responses back to the therapist. Gender, age, and education of the translators and interviewers have significant impact upon whether you can ask sensitive questions and whether you will get accurate answers. A good rule of thumb is that a peer who is of similar age, gender and education is likely to work best with Vietnamese refugee elders.

The issue of confidentiality and client trust is essential to any therapeutic relationship but therapists must work especially hard during the first contact with the client. Otherwise, as research had demonstrated, drop outs among Asian clients will be high (Sue, Sue, & Sue, 1975). One solution is to be able to solve a small problem and come up with a concrete set of solutions that you can propose. Traditional Southeast Asian refugee elders look upon physicians and doctorally trained professionals as authority figures who will give them answers to their problems. Relief to a specific, but smaller problem, helps build confidence in the therapist, works to established trust in the relationship, and establishes an obligation on the part of the refugee to come back. This sense of obligation can be used to benefit the client by keeping them in a therapeutic relationship until the more difficult mental health issues can be addressed.

Replacement of lost social supports is essential for life satisfaction among the elder Vietnamese refugee women. My studies indicated that social control in the areas of social relationships, family and friends is related to life satisfaction and one of the most important spheres of life for Vietnamese elderly. A crucial task of middle and old age is generativity (Erikson, 1982). This may be reinforced with establishment of Vietnamese elders in the role of cultural sages. Providing these activities for the whole Vietnamese community can also enhance establishment of new friendships among Vietnamese elders who are the most part, especially the grandmothers caring for younger relatives and isolated from other Vietnamese elders. Social teas or gathering of Vietnamese elderly on a weekly basis can be a very therapeutic experience for these individuals. Important therapeutic environments and a supportive network can be established for these clients.

CONCLUSION

Therapists must address the multiple issues of post-traumatic stress syndrome, grief, and depression; cross-cultural conflicts in values and behaviors, particularly age, gender and family roles; and intergenerational acculturation issues when confronting a Vietnamese elderly client who is female. Many refugees, particularly elders lost much after migrating to this country. They lost their homeland in which they spent the majority of their lives and a familiar comfortable culture; numerous social relationships through death, distance or contact; socioeconomic and job status; and their esteemed place in the family and community that they thought was their privilege during this last stage of the lifecycle. As Ratnavale (1983) suggests, children and the elderly refugees seem to suffer the most after migration to the new country. As my research has demonstrated the elderly have different expectations for growing older. When transplanted in this country, those expectations will probably not be fulfilled. This leaves the elderly with the job of radically changing those expectations or be forever unhappy in this great land. Our job is to help them make an adequate transition to this country. It won't be easy but therapy surrounding the issues of post-traumatic stress, grief and depression will certainly help this elderly group make a more successful adaptation to aging in the United States.

The crucial body of research on adaptation and coping of Southeast Asian refugee elders is yet to be done. In order to realistically examine adaptation and coping of elderly refugees, a longitudinal study must be conducted that examines the impact of acculturation with the passage of time and subsequent adaptation by all members of the family who belong to different generations. We need a more dynamic model for understanding the complex and changing nature of adaptation by elderly refugee women. Adaptation is a lifelong process but many elderly women give up trying to adapt to American culture. With a little assistance, these elderly Vietnamese women can make a successful and happy transition to growing old in their new home.

REFERENCES

Adkins, M.A. (1990). Role of bilingual/bicultural service providers in the delivery of mental health services. In W.H. Holtzman & T.H. Bornemann (Eds.), *Mental health of immigrants and refugees* (pp. 216-223). Proceedings of a Conference Sponsored by Hogg Foundation for Mental Health and World Federation for Mental Health.

Aylesworth, L.S., Ossario, P.G. & Osaki, L.T. (1980). Stress and mental health among Vietnamese in the United States. In R. Endo, S. Sue, & N. Wagner (Eds.), *Asian Americans: Social and Psychological Perspectives* (pp.164-180). Palo Alto: Science and Behavior Books.

Beiser, M. (1990). Mental health of refugees in resettlement countries. In W.H. Holtzman & T.H. Bornemann (Eds.), *Mental health of immigrants and refugees* (pp. 51-65). Proceedings of a Conference Sponsored by Hogg Foundation for Mental Health and World Federation for Mental Health.

Carlin, J. (1990). Refugee and immigrant populations at special risk: Women, children, and the elderly. In W.H. Holtzman & T.H. Bornemann (Eds.), *Mental health of immigrants and refugees* (pp. 224-233). Proceedings of a Conference Sponsored by Hogg Foundation for Mental Health and World Federation for Mental Health.

Chi, N.H. (1980). Vietnam: The culture of war. In E.L. Tepper (Ed.), *Southeast Asian Exodus: From Tradition to Resettlement* (pp. 15-30). Ottawa, Canada: The Canadian Asian Studies Association.

Dychtwald, K. (1986). *Wellness and health promotion for the elderly.* Rockville, MD: Aspen Publishers, Inc.

Erikson, E.H. (1982). The lifecycle completed. New York, NY: Norton.

Hickey, G.C. (1964). *Village in Vietnam.* New Haven, CT: Yale University Press.

Holtzman, W.H. & Bornemann, T.H.(Eds.) (1990). *Mental health of immigrants and refugees.* Proceedings of a Conference Sponsored by Hogg Foundation for Mental Health and World Federation for Mental Health.

Langer, E.J. (1983). *The psychology of control.* Beverly Hills: Sage Publications.

Lambert, W.E., & Taylor, D.M. (1990). Language and culture in the lives of immigrants and refugees. In W.H. Holtzman & T.H. Bornemann (Eds.), *Mental health of immigrants and refugees* (pp. 103-128). Proceedings of a Conference Sponsored by Hogg Foundation for Mental Health and World Federation for Mental Health.

Lin, K.M. (1990). Assessment and diagnostic issues in the psychiatric care of refugee patients. In W.H. Holtzman & T.H. Bornemann (Eds.), *Mental health of immigrants and refugees* (pp. 198-206), Proceedings of a Conference Sponsored by Hogg Foundation for Mental Health and World Federation for Mental Health.

Liu, W.T., Lamanna, M. & Murata, A. (1979). *Transition to nowhere:Vietnamese refugees in America.* Nashville: Charter House Publishers Inc.

Ratnavale, D.N. (1983). The mental health needs of refugees and other victims of disasters. *The American Journal of Social Psychiatry, 3,* 39-46.

Rumbaut, R.G. (1989). Portraits, patterns and predictors of refugee adaptation process. In D.W. Haines, *Refugees as Immigrants: Cambodians, Laotians and Vietnamese in America* (pp. 138-182). Totowa, N.J.: Rowman & Littlefield.

Sue, S., Sue, D.W., & Sue, D.W. (1975). Asian American as a minority group. *American Psychologist, 30,* 906-910.

Yee, B.W.K. (1977, August). *Psychology and its relationship to ethnic minorities: The Asian-American elderly life span developmental approach to minorities.* Paper presented at the meeting of the American Psychological Association, San Francisco, CA.

Yee, B.W.K. (1982). Control in British and Asian Elderly Women. (Doctoral Dissertation, University of Denver), *Dissertation Abstracts International, 43*, 699.

Yee, B.W.K. (1984). Multidimensional perceptions of control in Caucasian, Japanese, and Vietnamese elderly women. *Journal of Minority Aging, 9*, 76-84.

Yee, B.W.K. (1989). Loss of one's homeland and culture during the middle years. In R.A. Kalish (Ed.), *Coping with the losses of middle age* (pp. 281-300). Newbury Park, CA: Sage Publications.

Yee, B.W.K. (1990a). *Variations in aging: Older minorities,* (2nd ed.) Curriculum Module, Texas Consortium of Geriatric Education Centers, Univ. of Texas Medical Branch, U.S. DHHS Grant #5-D31-AH66005-05, Bureau of Health Professions.

Yee, B.W.K. (1990b). Gender and family issues in minority groups, *Generations, 14*(3), 39-42.

Yee, B.W.K., & Hennessey, S.T. (1982). Pacific/Asian families and mental health. In F.U. Munoz & R. Endo (Eds.), *Perspectives on minority group mental health* (pp. 53-70). Washington D.C.: University Press of America.

Yee, B.W.K., & Nguyen, D.T. (1987). Correlates of drug use and abuse among Indochinese refugees: Mental health implications. *Journal of Psychoactive Drugs, 19*, 77-83.

Yee, B.W.K., & Van Arsdale, P. (1986). Adaptation and coping of Vietnamese elderly women: Review, research, and speculation. *High Plains Applied Anthropologist, 6*, 11-17.

SECTION V:
DIAGNOSTIC STUDIES
ACROSS CULTURES

Treatment for Psychosomatic Blindness Among Cambodian Refugee Women

Gretchen B. Van Boemel
Patricia D. Rozée

Gretchen B. Van Boemel is Director of Clinical Electrophysiology at the University of Southern California's Doheny Eye Institute, and is a graduate student studying health psychology at the University of California-Irvine in the Social Ecology Department. Patricia D. Rozée (formerly Rozée-Koker), PhD, is Associate Professor of Psychology and Women's Studies at California State University-Long Beach with research interests in women and violence and cross-cultural psychology.

The authors wish to thank Konthea Kang and Santa Smith for their invaluable assistance as consultants on Cambodian culture and traditions and as group facilitators. They also thank Florentius Chan for consultations on therapy with Cambodian clients and Wanna Jung, Celia Knopf and Kolvady Men for their skills in Khmer translation. They also thank Ann Dawson and Lynn Fowler for their editorial comments and suggestions. In addition, they wish to thank Doris DeHardt for her thoughtful comments on the manuscript and Charlene Wynne for her assistance in data entry and analysis.

This research was carried out with faculty grant support from California State University, Long Beach.

SUMMARY. A number of older Cambodian women came to the attention of the authors because of their overrepresentation among a larger group of people who exhibited functional or psychosomatic blindness: visual loss with no physiologic basis. Myriad problems are faced by the psychosomatically blind Cambodian refugee, including war-based trauma, improper diagnosis resulting in denial of claims of disability, and feelings of severe depression and isolation. It was our intention to design and test an intervention program for the 150 psychosomatically blind Cambodian women whom we have seen over a four year period. Working with fifteen of these clients, we wished to test the relative effectiveness of two different treatments in reducing psychological distress and improving well-being and visual acuity: (1) *Skills in living group:* treatment consisted of group sessions designed to teach minimal skills such as using the telephone and public transportation; and (2) *Therapy group:* treatment consisted of group therapy conducted by a Cambodian therapist. Both treatment modalities were designed to be culturally relevant, implemented by Cambodians and in the Khmer language. Extensive pre and post-treatment interviews were conducted to assess level of visual acuity, psychological and physiological functioning and experiential background. Comparison of pre and post measures showed significantly better perceived well-being and improved visual acuity in the treatment groups as compared to the control group. Such findings suggest that treatment may be beneficial in reducing psychological distress and improving vision.

Entering the large courtyard of a very old apartment building, I see many young children playing and several old men sitting on a stoop, passing the time. The building is in disrepair, but the little bit of soil that is available contains a pristine communal vegetable garden that contrasts greatly with the torn screens and peeling paint of the building that surrounds it. As I approach one of the doors, all eyes are on me, for I am the only Caucasian in the area. Many pairs of shoes, some large, some small are arranged outside of the apartment, telling me that many people live in this one-bedroom apartment. I knock on the door, which is answer-

An earlier version of this paper was presented at the Association for Women in Psychology Annual Meeting, Tempe, AZ, 1989.

Requests for reprints may be sent to the senior author: Gretchen B. Van Boemel, Doheny Eye Institute, 1355 San Pablo Street, Los Angeles, CA 90033.

ed by a man, probably a son of the person I will interview. High around the perimeter of the room are black and white photographs. These photographs are of relatives who have died, and act as sentinels for the remaining family, watching over the activities of the living. On a shelf is an altar decorated with red candles and remnants of burned incense; pictures of Buddha adorn the wall above the altar. In a corner of the room is my client, the person I came to see. She sits quietly unmoving, head bowed; then, sensing my presence she lifts her head, places her palms together in front of her face, and bows slightly, greeting me in the traditional Khmer manner. I return the gesture. Her son asks me to sit and brings me something to drink. We begin the interview. She slowly and deliberately recounts the horrors of the past, her fears of the present, and her feelings of isolation that led her to her psychosomatic blindness. In her isolation, she does not know that she is not the only one to be afflicted, but rather, is one of many similar women in the Southern California area.

Over the past sixteen years there has been a dramatic increase in the number of Southeast Asians entering the United States. Escaping from battered homelands, these refugees bring with them numerous physical and emotional problems. Many suffer from post-traumatic stress disorder (Boehnlein, Kinzie, Rath, & Fleck, 1985; Kinzie, Fredrickson, Ben, Fleck, & Karl, 1984), and have medical histories that include malaria, tuberculosis and malnutrition (Aronson, 1987; Muecke, 1983a). These problems can be, at least in part, attributed to the horrific conditions under which they lived for many years (Aronson, 1987; Muecke, 1983a). Although each of the refugee groups has seen and experienced atrocities during the war in Southeast Asia, the refugees from Cambodia have seen more than most Americans can imagine (Mollica, Wyshak, & Lavelle, 1987). For the sake of economy, readers are referred to "The psychological effects of war trauma and abuse on older Cambodian refugee women" by P. Rozée and G. Van Boemel in *Women and Therapy, 8,* 23-50 (1989) for a recounting of the history of Cambodia during the period from 1975 to 1979. It must be mentioned however, that during the period from 1975 to 1979 when Pol Pot ruled Cambodia, an estimated one to three million Cambodians died from either execution, starvation, or illness, resulting in the virtual extermination of Cambodian culture as it was known. Individuals who survived the executions were incorporated into existing peasant villages and forced to work 18 to 20 hours per day and the laborers were fed only one-half cup of watery rice per day (Szymusiak, 1986).

Most of the Cambodians who finally came to the United States were poor and infirm, with little education and few skills, and suffered from extreme emotional and physical trauma. Typical symptoms affecting Cambodian refugees are feelings of depression, and suicidal tendencies. Many report vague complaints of headaches, dizziness, shortness of breath and malaise, that are not based on organic pathology, thereby suggesting a psychosomatic component. Although many are severely or chronically ill, help seeking behavior for illness or psychological problems is often influenced by cultural factors (Van Boemel, Salamida, & Kann, 1991).

Traditionally, in rural parts of Cambodia, health problems were dealt with by the family. Body parts were implicated in both physical and mental health problems, and generally both were dealt with similarly (Aronson, 1987; Muecke, 1983b). In many cases, treatment consisted of dermal therapy which was used to balance the hot and cold winds within the body. If treatment administered by the family did not work, a folk doctor was summoned to dispense herbal medicines. If those treatments failed, a monk was contacted to perform exorcisms of demons that were blamed for the person's problems (Muecke, 1983b). If all treatments proved ineffective and if the problem were severe and believed to stem from a nonphysical source, the individual was sent to a mental health facility. However, prior to the fall of Cambodia in 1975, there existed in Cambodia only one mental hospital, where only the extremely debilitated were housed. Few people were familiar with this institution and its residents numbered under 100 (personal communication, P. Pan, February, 1988).

The American therapist must keep in mind that the refugee living in the United States may continue to try to follow these traditional practices, and may seek help through a family member. If that proves ineffective, the individual may seek help for both physical and psychological problems through a general practice physician. The Cambodian client may offer both explicit physical and vague somatic complaints, reflecting both biomedical and psychological problems. Because most physicians have little training in psychology and concentrate on diagnosing physical ailments, the client's somatic complaints may go unnoticed or may be considered part of the physical illness (Miranda, Perez-Stable, Munoz, Hargreaves & Henke, 1991). Nguyen (1982) reported that physicians often ordered numerous laboratory tests for refugees who reported vague complaints, before referring the individuals to mental health facilities. The infirm Cambodian is left feeling ill, with insufficient treatment, inadequate diagnosis, lack of referral to a mental health facility, and without the resources to pay for additional diagnostic procedures, which are seen as necessary for proper diagnosis. Furthermore, although many Cambodians living in the United States may suffer from severe depression and suicidal tendencies, their lack of familiarity with mental health clinics and with the self-referral process results in the under utilization of much needed mental health services by this group of people. This is compounded by the primary care physician's lack of understanding of Cambodian customs and lack of appreciation of the atrocities these people have endured, which results in less than adequate medical care and counseling. Grave consequences may result from this lack of understanding, as was the case with a number of older Cambodian women who came to the attention of the authors, because of a similar and very debilitating problem (Rozée & Van Boemel, 1989).

PSYCHOSOMATIC BLINDNESS

In our earlier work, we had the opportunity to interview 30 Cambodian refugee women who presented with an extreme form of psychosomatic illness: functional blindness (Rozée & Van Boemel, 1989; Van Boemel & Rozée-Koker, 1986). Each of these women had been referred to Gretchen B. Van Boemel by the Social Security Administration Disability Evaluation Division for specialized electrodiagnostic tests[1] of the visual system following an eye examination by an ophthalmologist, who had reported normal findings. Each of these women reported severe loss of vision, had normal results on electrodiagnostic visual tests, and upon questioning, described witnessing or experiencing atrocities, such as watching loved ones being killed, immediately prior to the onset of their vision loss. We hypothesized that the traumatic experiences were implicated in the etiology of the vision loss. We conducted extensive interviews with the 30 women, who had been seen only in eye clinics or by general practice physicians prior to our interview. Questioning revealed that all had lived through the overthrow of their country, had experienced forced labor and starvation under Pol Pot, and had fled to Thailand, where they resettled in unsanitary, inhumane, and disease-infested refugee camps. Psychiatric evaluations had not been conducted on any of these women at any time, although 90% reported severe crying spells daily, while the remaining 10% reported crying spells at least several times a week. Consistent with findings of other researchers (Kinzie & Fleck, 1987; Mollica et al., 1987), 90% of our respondents had from one to ten family members killed during the Pol Pot regime, 90% reported feelings of depression (Boehnlein et al., 1985; Kinzie et al., 1984; Kinzie & Fleck, 1987; Mollica et al., 1987; Muecke, 1983a; Nicassio, 1983, 1985; Nguyen, 1982), 62% reported characteristic symptoms of post-traumatic stress disorder (PTSD), especially nightmares and intrusive thoughts (Kinzie et al., 1984; Kinzie & Fleck, 1987; Mollica et al., 1987), and 92% reported symptoms associated with somatization, especially dizziness, headaches and malaise (Beiser & Fleming, 1986; Mollica et al., 1987).

The findings from our first study supported our original hypothesis, that functional vision loss seen in these refugees was based on their trauma experiences. Respondents with more extensive vision loss reported longer duration of combined internment in Cambodia and Thailand (Rozée & Van Boemel, 1989). Additionally, since the respondents had been referred to the eye clinic by the Social Security Administration Disability Evaluation Division for confirmation or refutation of alleged vision loss, the normal electrodiagnostic findings resulted in denial of blind disability benefits. Informal follow-up examination revealed that, despite having been denied disability benefits based on blindness, the women continued to complain of severe loss of vision, thus ruling against a diagnosis of malingering (Van Boemel and Rozée-Koker, 1989).

Unfortunately, functional loss of vision is often misdiagnosed or completely overlooked. In most cases, an individual with psychosomatic vision loss will seek treatment from an ophthalmologist. The ophthalmologist, who may be the only physician to see the individual, may not recognize the blindness as a psychosomatic problem, but rather, may conclude that the individual is either uncooperative or does not comprehend the task of vision screening, especially if they do not speak the same language.

Compounding the problems brought about by language and cultural differences is the very real possibility that, after seeing several Cambodians who complain of severe vision loss, have normal eye examinations, and who are applying for blind disability benefits, some ophthalmologists may conclude that the refugees are trying to swindle the government (Keltner, May, Johnson, & Post, 1985). Not only are disability benefits not recommended, but a diagnosis of malingering is made which implies that the refugee is cheating to obtain funds, which precludes a psychiatric referral. An additional tragedy occurs when the ophthalmologist begins to assume that every Cambodian seeking blind disability benefits is malingering, regardless of physical findings. We have seen many Cambodians who have been diagnosed inappropriately as malingering, but several had physical eye problems. One such individual was found to have an hereditary defect of the muscles that control the eyes and the lids, which made it impossible for him to open or move his eyes. He had to bend his head back in order to see through the tiny slit between his almost completely closed eye lids. He had two toddlers with similar problems. He and his children were presumed to be malingering, to obtain disability benefits, by the ophthalmologist who performed the original evaluation. In another case, a Cambodian stated that he could see very well with glasses, but that he had recently lost his. He also was given a diagnosis of malingering, when, in fact, all he needed was a new prescription for glasses.

Ophthalmologists are not the only ones who do not readily identify or diagnose psychosomatic blindness: therapists may have difficulties as well. Clients who present with psychosomatic vision loss usually complain of blurred or fuzzy vision; rarely do they state that they cannot see anything at all (Rada, Meyer, & Kellner, 1978). We have found that therapists working with Cambodian clients often report that their clients have vision problems. Yet, because the client is able to ambulate (as is true with many individuals who have very poor but some functioning vision), the therapists assume that the poor vision is a side effect of psychotropic medication or a result of vitamin A deficiency (personal communication, P. Chan, August, 1988). Even when the psychosomatically blind Cambodian finally reaches a mental health facility, the magnitude of her complaints are not recognized and it is impossible to determine whether her undetected vision loss was been improved with therapy.

In light of myriad problems faced by psychosomatically blind Cambodian refugee women, we believe that intervention is mandatory. Accordingly, we wanted to investigate possible treatment modalities that would reduce the symptoms of psychosomatic blindness, reduce feelings of isolation and increase the sense of well-being in these individuals. We hypothesized that the protracted vision loss of these women was exacerbated, at least in part, by their sense of isolation–both physical and emotional. In our original study, we found that the sampled population felt isolated and feared leaving their homes (Rozée & Van Boemel, 1989). The data suggested that the respondents had few contacts with the world outside of their homes and had little contact with friends or neighbors.

The study described herein, was designed to put into practice and evaluate an intervention program that takes into account the background and cultural beliefs of the Cambodian refugee–a program that would improve vision, lessen feelings of isolation and increase feelings of well-being. A two-treatment, one control group, pre-test/post-test design was used to answer the question, "Which type of treatment is more effective for psychosomatically blind Cambodian women?"

One treatment group was based on "talk" therapies that are currently being utilized for this population. Several researchers have suggested that traditional talking therapies in which the client is asked to recount a detailed history of past traumas is an important aspect of the therapeutic process (Haldane, 1987; Mollica et al., 1987). Others, however, suggest that such a systematic recounting simply intensifies the trauma rather than providing catharsis (Kinzie et al., 1984; Nguyen, 1982). The latter researchers suggest that the client should try to forget the past. Our experience suggests that many Cambodian women want to tell of their traumatic past. It is our feeling that, if the assessment is done with respect and sensitivity, the woman is not only willing, but is eager to tell her story. "Since the trauma is constantly replaying itself in the mind of the client, the outward signs of distress at telling the story are most likely the result and not the cause of her distress" (Rozée & Van Boemel, 1989).

The second treatment seeks to correct deficiencies that Cambodians have identified as causing problems in their day-to-day lives, such as English language skills, telephone usage, and understanding traffic signals (Rozée & Van Boemel, 1989). Respondents in our first study were asked to indicate what they believed was the primary or secondary cause of their remaining isolated at home. Seventy-one percent spontaneously reported poor vision as either a primary or secondary reason for staying at home, 30% reported dizziness and/or malaise, and 30% of the respondents identified lack of familiarity with the outside environment, including such things as fear of traffic (10%), fear of getting lost (10%), and fear of having to speak English (10%). It is postulated that lack of such living skills may be a factor contributing to vision loss among psychosomatically blind Cambodians. Nicassio, Solomon, Guest, and McCullough (1986) previously reported a strong correlation between low English proficiency and high levels of depression among Southeast Asian refugees, suggesting that lack of familiarity with the host culture may result in psychological distress.

Both treatment modalities in the current study were implemented by Khmer speaking, Cambodian social workers. The present study attempted to evaluate whether symptoms of psychosomatic blindness can be reduced (based on improved reported visual acuity), by means of therapeutic intervention. Second, we wanted to test whether traditional group therapy or training in daily living skills (telephone usage, etc.) would be more effective in improving visual acuity, reducing feelings of isolation, and improving feelings of well-being in the sample population. We hypothesized that either intervention would result in improvement compared to the "no treatment" control group, since all participants would be required to leave the home and to interact with others, thereby creating a social network of sorts (Nguyen, 1982).

METHOD

Subjects

A total of 15 psychosomatically blind women from Long Beach, California participated in the study. Women were chosen for the study since there are many more surviving Cambodian women than men and a far greater number of Cambodian women have been identified as displaying symptoms of psychosomatic blindness. Participants were located by means of referral to the study by either the Doheny Eye Institute or by an ophthalmologist practicing in Long Beach. All respondents had undergone a complete eye examination by an ophthalmologist, with normal findings, (suggesting that the participant should report normal, 20/20 vision on the eye chart) but complained of vision worse than 20/200 (legal blindness) at the time of ophthalmologic examination. Seven of the fifteen women had also undergone visual evoked response (VER) testing at the Doheny Eye Institute (which determined physiologic level of visual acuity as indicated by normal brain activity to visual stimuli). Two of the seven women had participated in our original study.

A total of 150 women were originally identified who were psychosomatically blind. Of these, 100 had moved away since their ophthalmologic examination, and fifteen others were undergoing psychiatric treatment, so were excluded from the study. The remaining 35 women were contacted by telephone through an interpreter who worked with the authors, and asked if they would mind talking with us in person; it was explained to them that we were starting a group for women like themselves, who had problems with their eyes and who experienced feelings of great sadness. If they agreed, the women were visited in their homes by the first author and an interpreter.

Convincing the women to participate proved to be quite a challenge. In many cases, we had to persuade the eldest male family member of the merits of the study; if he were convinced, the woman was more likely to participate. On the other hand, if the eldest family member did not think it was a good idea, the woman did not participate. Many of the women alluded that they were too sick or too afraid to leave their homes, and illness was often mentioned, when the participant was asked to sign the "human subject" consent form. Although the women were assured that only an "X" was required, should they be unable to actually sign a name, this reassurance did not increase level of participation. Of the 35 individuals contacted, ten consented to participate in the treatment groups. Random assignment was used to place the ten women into one of two treatment groups. Women who were not interested in participating in the treatment groups were asked if they would be willing to be interviewed at that time and ten weeks later (which would coincide with completion of the intervention). Five women agreed to serve as a self-selected no-treatment control group.

Instrument

The entrance interview questionnaire was comprised of several scales that had been validated previously with other Southeast Asian groups. The questionnaire consisted of a psychosomatic checklist, and sections regarding medical and ocular history, experiences in Southeast Asia (Cambodia) and in refugees camps (Thailand), adjustment in the United States, and a well-being inventory. All questionnaire items were translated from English to Khmer by one translator, and then translated from Khmer back to English by a second translator, to ensure consistency in translation.

The exit interview consisted of portions of the entrance questionnaire, including the psychosomatic checklist, the sections relating to adjustment in the United States, and the well-being inventory. In addition, the exit questionnaire contained items to assess the effectiveness of the treatment. As a control measure, family members were also interviewed at the time of the exit interview to elicit their impression of the functioning level of the study participant.

PROCEDURE

Interview

All interviews were conducted in Khmer and responses were translated back to English on the printed questionnaire. After consent to participate was obtained, each woman was interviewed. At the conclusion of the first interview, or at the first treatment session, each participant had her vision tested with a standard screening device designed for use with the illiterate. Interviews lasted from one to three hours. The exit interviews were also conducted in Khmer, generally during the final group session; the remainder were conducted in the participants' homes. Each participant's family was also interviewed during the exit phase to ascertain if they had noticed a change in the woman since her enrollment in the treatment group.

Intervention

The ten participants were randomly assigned to one of the two intervention programs. Each group met for one hour each week for ten consecutive weeks. The sessions were conducted at the Community Psychology Clinic at California State University, Long Beach. The women were transported to and from the clinic by English-speaking female students.

"Skills Group"

The skills group was led by a female Cambodian social worker whose primary job is teaching refugees about living in the United States. The purpose of these sessions was to familiarize the women with items common in day-to-day life in the United States, to teach them basic communication in English, how to use the telephone, handle U.S. currency, public transportation, traffic signals and directions, and some North American customs. During the very first session, the women learned how to dial the emergency "911" telephone system and ask for assistance; for every woman, this was the first time that she had ever dialed a telephone. Also, the women practiced reciting their names, addresses and national origin in English. During the final sessions, the women were taken on the bus to familiarize them with public transportation.

"Therapy Group"

The "therapy group" treatment was led by a second female Cambodian social worker. The sessions were designed so that every woman was encouraged to speak freely about how she was feeling at the present time and to recall her traumas of the past. During the first session they shared their life stories, talked of their lives in Cambodia under Pol Pot, and learned of the similarities and differences in their personal and trauma backgrounds. During the ensuing weeks the women learned to share with and trust one another. That this level of openness was achieved can best be illustrated by one woman's willingness to discuss the fact that she was in a battering relationship. When she stated that she was fearful of being at home, every other member of the group offered her a place to stay. At the final session, the therapy group participants learned how to dial the emergency "911" telephone number and request assistance. We felt ethically obligated to share this information with the members of this group.

At the end of the ten sessions, the participants were referred to other facilities, such as the Asian Pacific Mental Health Center, for additional therapy, skills in living training, and so on. They were also provided a list of the telephone numbers of all the other women in their group and encouraged to keep in touch with this new support network.

RESULTS AND DISCUSSION

Demographic Characteristics of the Sample

The women ranged in age from 47 to 63 years (mean 57.8 years, SD 5.5 years). Eight of the 15 women were widowed, six were married and one was divorced; all of the women lived with at least one and up to ten other people (mean 5.2 people, SD 2.4). All of the women had emigrated to the United States, via Thai refugee camps, after the fall of Pol Pot's Cambodia to Vietnamese forces in 1979. They had lived in the United States anywhere from three to eight years (mean 6.4 years, SD .5 years); nine women had lived in the United States for seven or eight years. None of the women have been able to manage a house or work outside of the home since resettling in the United States, although, all of them had been able to perform these tasks prior to the Khmer Rouge takeover. They reported gruesome trauma histories and complained of multiple health problems. Ten of the women had received no formal education while living in Cambodia, and four had completed several years of grade school; only one of the women had completed a sixth grade education.

Efficacy of Treatment Modalities

The purpose of the study was to evaluate the efficacy of treatment modalities for improving the lives of psychosomatically blind, older female, Cambodian refugees. The authors assessed several key variables for determining level of improvement, which included: visual acuity, level of happiness, level of sadness and feelings of isolation. We wanted to test whether traditional group therapy or a skills in living intervention would be more effective. First, we hypothesized that those who underwent group therapy treatment would feel happier and less isolated than those who did not participate. Second, we hypothesized that those who underwent skills in living treatment would participate to a greater extent in United States culture by means of speaking more English and talking more frequently on the telephone. Third, we hypothesized that either intervention would improve visual acuity as compared to the no treatment control group.[2] Percentage change for these variables across the groups is listed in Table 1.

Pre-treatment levels of happiness, sadness, and frequency of crying were compared with post-treatment levels. As indicated in Table 1, both treatment modalities resulted in increased feelings of happiness, decreased feelings of sadness, and reduction in frequency of crying. Virtually no change was noted in the control group.

Pre-treatment visual acuity was compared with post-treatment visual acuity in fourteen of the fifteen women.[3] Upon completion of the interventions, visual acuity for both treatment groups generally was better than that of the control group. There was a substantial improvement (improvement of three or more lines on the Snellen acuity chart) in eight out of nine respondents from the intervention groups. There was substantial improvement in only one woman from the control group; during the period between her initial and final interviews, she had sought counseling on her own.

We hypothesized further that those participants in the skills group would utilize their newly acquired skills of English language and telephone usage more than would those in either the therapy or control groups. This was not the case. Forty percent of those in both the skills and the therapy groups reported increased English usage, but 40% of those in the therapy group also reported increased telephone usage, while

TABLE 1

Compares the percentage of improvement for each intervention group and the control group.

Dependent Variables	Pre-Post % Improvement		
	Talk Therapy	Skills Group	Control
Vision	80%	80%	20%
Happiness	100	80	0
Sadness	80	40	0
Crying	80	60	20
Nightmares	40	80	0
Fear of Traffic	60	20	0
Fear of Using Money	40	20	0
Telephone Usage	40	20	0
English Usage	40	40	0

$N = 15.$

only 20% of those in the skills group reported such changes. No change in either English or telephone use was noted by those in the control group.

The lack of change in both English and telephone use in the "skills" group may be due to the nature of the actual skills that were taught. Participants spent most of the time practicing how to dial the emergency telephone number (i.e., "911"), and learned English phrases that went along with such help seeking (e.g., "There's a fire, please help. I live at this address . . . I speak Cambodian."). Unless there were numerous emergencies in the home, one would expect little change in English or telephone usage.

No appreciable change was noted by family members of either control or treatment group participants on any of the above mentioned variables. This may be due to the internal nature of the change noted by the participants.

Trauma History

The experiences that this sample population endured while in Cambodia were gruesome but were quite similar to those of other Cambodian samples in therapeutic settings. Seventy-three percent reported having lost from one to nine close family members, and 27% reported having witnessed the death(s). Fifty-three percent reported that at least one family member was left in Cambodia during the escape, or in Thailand during resettlement to the United States. Sixty-seven percent witnessed the destruction of their town or village, and 40% reported that someone had tried to kill them while in Cambodia, under Pol Pot's rule. Fifty-three percent of the women reported that male soldiers or guards tried to harm them physically, while they were in either Cambodia or Thailand.

Despite her outward symptoms, the Cambodian refugee who lived through Pol Pot's reign experienced unimaginable traumas; this is particularly true of women. A thorough trauma and medical history, combined with onset of health complaints, may provide the therapist with useful information about the extent of the traumas and the severity of the symptoms associated with those traumas. Our data indicate that at least 53% experienced attempted rape or assault. When the women were asked if they had been harmed, some women answered affirmatively, while others turned their heads away from the interviewer and interpreter and quickly answered "no." This contrasted greatly with the openness with which most women answered even the most painful questions. Those who answered "yes" are not likely to represent the actual number of assault victims, since it is culturally unacceptable for a woman to be physically assaulted or raped,[4] and those who answered "no" may not be accurately describing their trauma histories. In Cambodian culture once a woman has been "soiled," she can never be pure again. According to folk wisdom, women are represented by cotton; once cotton has fallen in the soil, it can never be washed completely clean. Men, on the other hand, are represented by diamonds; if they fall in the soil, they can be cleansed easily and will shine again (Mollica, 1986). Men have actual purification rituals that monks will perform for them, so that they may regain their purity. Such rituals are not available to the woman who has been raped (Mollica, 1986). The sense of remaining impure for the remainder of one's life could have devastating consequences that may need to be addressed in therapy. The therapist and client may need to explore means by which the woman can feel as pure as possible given cultural constraints. Cleansing rituals may be appropriate if both the client and therapist feel comfortable with such practices. It is unlikely that she will feel completely cleansed without traditional rituals, however, therapeutic sessions with the individual may eliminate some intensity of those feelings.

Trust Within the Therapeutic Setting

Although building trust is essential in all therapeutic relationships, issues of trust have even greater importance for the Cambodian refugee (Kinzie and Fleck, 1987). During the reign of Pol Pot, neighbors spied on neighbors and children were informants against their parents. It is not surprising that the Cambodian client may be reluctant to trust others who she does not know well. Several elements can enhance feelings of trust. Trust can be encouraged by the demeanor of the therapist. We have found that speaking to the Cambodian women in a soft spoken, respectful manner can be useful. Employing a same sexed interpreter is essential. Using Khmer phrases, removing shoes when entering her home and bowing when greeting her may be helpful as well. This lets the client know that the therapist is aware of and respects her culture, and as such is probably aware of her traumatic experiences. Additionally, never confine a client in a room, where she is the only one with the therapist; this can resemble interrogation. Group therapy may be the solution to the problems of apparent "interrogation." Group therapy has been hypothesized as providing or reconstructing a social network for the client (Nguyen, 1982).

A group therapy setting also may increase the client's sense of power within the therapeutic relationship. The therapist has power in any therapeutic relationship, however this may be exaggerated by cultural factors.

In Cambodia, the practitioner of the healing arts was viewed as a priest, and, as such, had powers necessary to negotiate with the gods, and remove the evil curses that caused sicknesses. The sick individual was not included in any decision making in regards to the illness (Muecke, 1983b). This belief increases the power differential between the client and the therapist within the therapeutic situation.

Language and educational differences may increase the power imbalance within the therapeutic relationship as well. The client will likely have had little formal education and may speak only rudimentary Khmer. The therapist, who is well educated, may be viewed by the client as an expert (as well as a priest), and therefore more knowledgeable about the client's needs than the client is herself. The therapist must acknowledge this presumed difference and continually reassure the client(s) that the therapist is a facilitator for the client's growth; the client is to set her own goals. At first, goal setting may be very difficult for the Cambodian client. This can best be understood by the following example. A group of Cambodian women attending survival ESL[5] classes were to practice making daily life decisions. For the first several weeks the women were unaware of how to make a decision. It was not until they had watched a Cambodian instructor make several decisions, that they began to understand the process of decision making (personal communication, M.A. Salamida, April, 1991). Initial goal setting may be best facilitated by a Cambodian role model–someone who has gone through the therapeutic process and has learned how to set goals within that setting. Eventually, the group will be able to set its own goals. This form of control over the therapeutic process may lead to feelings of empowerment, which should be very helpful for the individual.

Feelings of Isolation

Nguyen (1982) has suggested that "network" therapy, in which refugees have the opportunity to meet with one another and establish new social support networks, is essential in reducing feelings of isolation. Accordingly, group therapy sessions should provide the means for the reconstruction of social networks that were disrupted due to the deaths and relocation of vital members of the network. Based on this information, we hypothesized that those in the therapy sessions would experience diminished feelings of isolation. A multiple regression model was used to predict which of the two types of treatment was more effective in reducing feelings of isolation, when controlling for pre-treatment isolation (see

Table 2a). The data tend to support Nguyen's contention that group therapy can help mend the client's social network by reducing her feelings of isolation.

Subjective Well-Being

In our attempt to better understand the level to which these women's lives could be subjectively improved, we addressed the issue of subjective well-being for this sample. Subjective well-being was a combined score from a multi-item scale, which was operationalized as how the respondent felt about her family and social relationships, her ability to perform her expected tasks, her spiritual life, her ability to participate in American society, and her adjustment to living in the United States. Past research on other geriatric populations suggests that several domains influence subjective well-being, including: poor health, low income, lack of social support, current marital status, and problems with food and shelter. Pearson correlation coefficients were produced using the domains of health, visual acuity, somatic complaints, feelings of isolation, problems with living in the United States, marital status, and adequacy of food and shelter, at time one. The results from the Pearson correlations suggest that poor health, reduced vision, numerous somatic complaints, feelings of isolation, or many problems with living in the United States, negatively correlate with feelings of subjective positive well-being. Only the domains of adequacy of food and shelter and of marital status were not correlated with well-being (see Table 2b).

The data suggest that increased health problems, numerous somatic complaints, and visual problems reduce feelings of subjective positive well-being. This is similar to data collected on other geriatric populations (Larson, 1977). Two additional factors may contribute to the psychosomatically blind female refugees' well-being–feelings of isolation and problems related to living in a "foreign" country, i.e., the United States. Those with fewer feelings of isolation reported a greater sense of positive well-being. This reinforces the idea that social support networks are necessary and should be enhanced when possible. Those with fewer "acculturation" problems (those women more familiar with the currency, language, etc.) reported more positive feelings of well-being. This further supports our hypothesis that improved living skills may decrease psychological complaints and may be an important component to include in therapy and when assessing subjective well-being in this population.

TABLE 2a
Multiple Regression Analysis: Predictors of increased numbers of social contacts.

Predictor	Increased number of social contacts		
	B	SE B	beta
Pre-treatment social contacts	.47619	.37704	.28854
"Skills" group	-.79048	1.55273	-.13346
"Therapy" group	2.91429*	1.56186	.49204

F (3, 12) = 2.86* R^2 = .43835, Adjusted R^2 = .28517

B = Partial regression coefficients
SE B = Estimated standard error of partial regression coefficients
Beta = B_k x (Standard deviation$_x$/Standard deviation$_y$)
F = Mean square regression/mean square residual
R^2 = 1 - Residual sum of squares/total sum of squares
Adjusted R^2 = 1 - Residual sum of squares/(N-#Ind var. - 1)/Total sum of squares/(N - 1)
from SPSS/PC+ V2.0 Base Manual

Health Complaints

In our study, respondents complained of many health and emotional problems. Eighty-seven percent reported frequent problems in sleeping, 93% reported frequent nightmares, 93% reported frequent feelings of nervousness, 73% reported that they did nothing all day long, and 53% reported suicidal ideation. Moreover, 87% reported frequent feelings of dizziness, 93% reported frequent headaches, 87% reported frequent feelings of a racing heart, and 93% reported frequent feelings of being unhealthy.

Health issues must be discussed in the therapeutic setting; poor health keeps the client house bound and can be a cause of great distress. Our original work (Rozée & Van Boemel, 1989), showed that 30% of the respondents indicated that their health problems kept them from leaving their homes. Preliminary results from other work by the first author, show that one of the most common causes of reported feelings of sadness among Cambodian refugees was poor health (Van Boemel, Salamida, & Kann, 1991). Since health problems may keep the Cambodian refugee house bound, increase her feelings of sadness, or decrease her sense of well-being, such issues need to be addressed in the therapeutic setting. As mentioned earlier, differentiation between physical and somatic complaints can be difficult. To insure that the client does not have an underlying illness, it may be advisable to include a medical history during initial

TABLE 2b
Correlation of predictor variables with subjective well-being.

Health complaints	-.5909[*]	Problems with living in the U.S	-.4888[*]
Vision complaints	-.6259[**]	Marital status	.0973
Somatic complaints	-.9143[****]	Adequate food and shelter	-.4266
Feelings of isolation	-.6773[**]		

[*] $p < .10$
[**] $p < .05$
[***] $p < .01$
[****] $p < .001$

consultation. The medical history may be less threatening and provide an initial frame of reference from which to start. Questions regarding past and present illness should be discussed, as well as treatment regimens for current illness. Inspection of the client's medication may be beneficial; make sure that the client is taking the medication properly and has received appropriate follow-up care. Due to health care beliefs and practices, self-medication may be common (Muecke, 1983a). The client may take the prescribed medication until the original symptom diminishes, or may take more or less medicine than was prescribed (Muecke, 1983a). The client should be reinstructed on how to take the medication. Since many Cambodian refugees are pre-literate, or are unable to see well, as in the case of clients with psychosomatic blindness, instructions should be given in a manner that does not require reading skills. If the client is taking numerous medications simultaneously some of her symptoms may be a direct result of adverse drug interactions (personal communication, B. Deckard, 1980). Consulting with a pharmacologist in such instances may be advisable.

Once health complaints have been identified and etiologies determined, estimate when the somatic complaints are greatest. Do certain events exacerbate the symptoms? What remedies relieve those symptoms? Help the client identify activities that relieve symptoms and have her increase those activities. Encourage her to use traditional herbal and dermal therapies if she feels that they are effective. Conversely, help her decide which situations to avoid. This process may help in the reduction of somatic health problems, and, as such, may be an important first step in the over-all remission of symptoms.

Accessing Mental Health Facilities

The isolated Cambodian refugee may be in dire need of psychological intervention, but may be unaware of those services or have few opportunities to access such services. Lack of access may be due to the absence of culturally sensitive services, the trauma histories themselves or the stigma of mental illness (Muecke, 1983b). Culturally sensitive mental health facilities may not be available that provide Khmer-speaking practitioners and exhibit awareness and respect for Cambodian culture and traditions. The trauma itself may affect access in that the clients most in need of mental health services may be unable or too fearful to leave the home environment. Cambodian refugees who do seek help, may do so through a general practice physician, due to the cultural stigma of mental illness. Referral patterns may need to be established between the therapist and the general practice physician seeing Cambodians. The therapist may be in a position to help the physician decipher numerous vague physical symptoms, likewise the physician may be able to suggest to the family that the ailment is caused by great sadness. The therapist would provide treatment for the sadness or the family problem.

Referral patterns such as the one just mentioned may be adequate, but access to those in need, may be better accomplished via a more traditional route: the religious leader of the community. It may be that the distressed individual (or her family) has already sought treatment through a Buddhist monk, since monks were providers of such services in Cambodia. The monk can perform traditional exorcisms, but the treatment may not fully accomplish the desired results. The monk may be in need of an individual to whom he can refer his members. The individual in need may be unwilling or unable to leave the home and may not trust the outside world enough to make the trip to the clinic. To reach the severely isolated Cambodian, home visits may be necessary. In that setting, a trusting relationship can be established, so that the client will finally venture outside of the home in order to continue treatment. In the current study, we found several women who wanted to participate, but who were too fearful to leave the home environment. Such an intervention strategy as the one just mentioned might be very useful for the extremely fearful individual.

Systems Change

Many of the problems faced by the Cambodian client stem from past trauma histories, however this may not be true for all problems. In many instances, the problems faced by the Cambodian client stem from institutionalized racism or lack of understanding, by those within the majority culture, of Cambodian culture and beliefs. We have seen several instances of institutionalized racism which we have been able to help correct as a result of our research efforts. When we first began this research, any Cambodian woman who was seeking blind disability benefits, who had a normal VER,[6] was denied those benefits, and possibly given a diagnosis of malingering. Since our initial research, (Van Boemel & Rozée, 1986) we have had the opportunity to work with physicians and analysts from the Social Security Administration Disability Evaluation Department within Southern California and now local disability departments obtain full psychiatric examinations on all individuals with suspected psychosomatic vision loss. (A person is suspected of having psychosomatic vision loss, by the Social Security Administration, if the person has a normal eye examination and a normal VER.) This is a tremendous breakthrough and results in the appropriate evaluation of numerous individuals who would have been denied otherwise.

In the case of the physicians who have inappropriately labeled ill Cambodians as malingerers, we have interceded. As a result several changes have occurred. First, one physician who believed that every Cambodian client was malingering, and who conducted Disability evaluations for Social Security, no longer sees Cambodian referrals from Social Security. Second, we now see many more diagnoses of "possible psychosomatic visual loss" from referring ophthalmologists as compared to the past when most diagnoses consisted of maligning terms such as "rule out malingering." These examples support the philosophy promoted by Kinzie and Fleck (1987) that all health and mental health care professionals should assist the refugee client in as many ways as possible. In the event that we are aware of injustices, we must come to the client's defense.

In addition, we have informed therapists who are working with Cambodian clients of our findings on psychosomatic blindness. They have identified several clients with similar complaints, and now have groups specifically for the psychosomatically blind. Previously, those symptoms went unnoticed.

Qualitative Results

In order to truly understand the plight of the psychosomatically blind Cambodian refugee woman and the effectiveness of even moderate amounts of treatment, we feel that it is important to read of the experiences of individual women. These two women's lives exemplify the lives of psychosomatically blind Cambodian women.

Case History

L.P. is a 53-year-old widow whose husband and five children were killed by the Khmer Rouge. She had lived in a small town outside of Battambong, and fled the village as it was being destroyed by Khmer Rouge soldiers; she was one of few survivors. Her life under Pol Pot was gruesome. She labored long hours and was often required to dig graves for the burial of children. She watched many people beaten and killed at the hands of the Khmer Rouge soldiers and as her husband had been a Lon Nol soldier, she feared for her life every day, since the Khmer Rouge frequently killed the spouses of former government officials. She escaped to Thailand after the fall of the Khmer Rouge in 1979; she lived in Thailand until 1984, when she emigrated to the United States. She claims that moving to the United States brought about no improvement in her life. She is very angry about her life in the U.S. and states that her life would have been very prosperous had Pol Pot not taken over. Prior to his death, her husband had purchased rights to a gem mine, which would have resulted in financial security throughout her remaining years. She lives in a very small one bedroom apartment with her only remaining relative, a nephew, his wife and their daughter. Prior to the intervention program she cried frequently, sat in one position all day long, was able to do nothing, and rarely left the house. She complained of frequent nightmares, during which Khmer Rouge soldiers forced her to drink poisoned medicine, and she reported continuous feelings of sadness and despair, and frequently felt suicidal. Her vision on our first visit was considered to be "hand motions," which means that she was able to see hands move in front of her face, but could not discern individual fingers. During the intervention she improved dramatically and would wait on the sidewalk to be picked up by the research assistants. She reported feeling happier after the intervention and stated that she cried less often. Her vision improved to where she could count fingers about six inches away from her face. She continues to improve;

she chants regularly, often going to Temple, and her vision has improved to where she can count fingers at about 15 feet from her face.

Case History

C.I. is a 60-year-old widow and mother of nine who was married to a Lon Nol soldier who was killed by Khmer Rouge forces in Cambodia prior to 1975. Prior to the Khmer Rouge takeover, C.I. sold food in a marketplace in Battambong, a city in the northern portion of Cambodia. After the Khmer Rouge took over Phnom Penh, she and all of her family were forced to evacuate their homes, leaving behind all of their possessions. She was relocated to a small village outside of Battambong, but a short time later, Khmer Rouge soldiers transported her to the base of a small mountain where they left her. During the trek back to her "new" village, she walked over the bodies of slain Cambodian citizens. During a nightly meeting a short time after the takeover, she recalled seeing a man nearly beaten to death; everyone in the village was forced to witness such events, so that they might understand the power of the Khmer Rouge soldiers and their leader. After torturing the man, the soldiers threw him into a pit of fire to burn to death. C.I. said that she could still hear his screams and stated that those sights were the last things she saw clearly. Since that time her vision has become increasingly worse.

Following the fall of Pol Pot to the Vietnamese in 1979, C.I. and several of her children fled to the Thai border, where they remained for two years. She reported being hurt and beaten during that time by Thai soldiers and has been fearful of them ever since. She arrived in the United States in 1981, with several of her children; three others were killed during Pol Pot's reign. Aside from the children with whom she lives, she leads an isolated life, reliving her nightmares, disabled by blindness. When we first visited her, she was able only to count fingers two feet away from her face. She sat in a fetal position throughout the day, cried frequently and was unable to care for herself. After the intervention program she began to perform small tasks and said that she felt less sad. Her vision improved to where she could count fingers 12 feet away, and stated that when she felt better, she could see better. We visited her again in the Fall of 1990. To our surprise and delight, she was in the kitchen cooking dinner. We had a full conversation in English. She told us that she had been taking English classes for almost one year, and took the bus to school two times every week. When not cooking for her family, she liked to stroll around her neighborhood.

CONCLUSION

The data suggest that both types of treatments were effective in reducing the respondents' feelings of sadness, and in increasing their feelings of happiness, as well as in improving their vision, with some increased utilization of English and telephone skills; although, the participants' family members did not report an appreciable improvement when asked about the status of the individuals. This may be due to the subjective, internal nature of the change reported by the respondent. However, the experiences of individual women, as demonstrated in the case histories suggest that the treatment has long lasting effects. When observing percentage change across variables, it appears that the talk therapy may have been more effective than the skills group in producing the desired outcomes. However, since both treatment groups resulted in improvement of visual acuity, increased feelings of happiness, and decreased feelings of sadness, "treatment" per se may be the necessary ingredient for improvement.

Despite the problems of sample size and comparability, we are particularly encouraged by the improvement in subjective vision reported by those participating in the groups. Treatment of psychosomatic blindness is generally unsuccessful or variable (Rada, Meyer, & Kellner, 1978), so evidence of any improvement, particularly in such a short time frame, is promising. Unfortunately, vision loss can recur if the individual experiences situations similar to those that caused the initial onset of loss (Rada et al., 1978). The results imply that with more comprehensive intervention additional recovery and improvement in living may be possible.

On a more personal note, both authors observed great improvement in the outward behaviors of the women during the ten-week intervention. The first day the women arrived at the clinic, they were very sad, and many appeared to be or have been crying; they spoke very little and walked very slowly. By the end of the ten weeks, the women laughed and joked with one another, walked briskly and rarely cried.

Finally, we believe that a treatment strategy that combines group therapy, living skills training, and traditional Cambodian health practices may be the most beneficial. Group therapy has been shown to be beneficial in reducing symptoms of psychological distress. Additionally, group therapy can decrease feelings of isolation of this and other samples by enhancing social networks: reduction in feelings of isolation increases feelings of positive well-being. Feelings of psychological distress can be further reduced and feelings of positive well-being can be further enhanced with the inclusion of living skills training in the group therapy setting. Muecke

(1983a) has suggested that lack of client compliance to medical regimens may have its roots in the client's lack of familiarity with such items as the telephone or appointment schedules. A client may fail to call the doctor in a medical emergency, thus jeopardizing her health and increasing her feelings of distress (Van Boemel et al., 1991), due to her lack of knowledge of how to use the telephone or out of fear of having to speak English. Lack of English language skills among Cambodian refugees is extensive. Van Boemel et al. (1991) showed that as many as 79% of all the Cambodian refugees they interviewed had little or no English language skills. This has serious consequences for any Cambodian refugee, since lack of English language skills has been associated with greater feelings of depression in Southeast Asian refugees (Nicassio et al., 1986).

Living skills may increase the Cambodian client's ability to obtain proper health care. She will be able to use the telephone to make an appointment and will be able to take the bus to the designated location. Increased access to health care facilities may result in reduced health complaints and increased feelings of positive well-being. Finally, empowerment may come from feelings of being in control of a situation. The refugee client who can use the telephone to call for help may feel more in control of her environment than she would without those skills. Additionally, those with fewer acculturation problems may report fewer instances of psychological distress, with eventual feelings of increased positive well-being.

From our work we noticed that those in the skills group frequently wanted to discuss their personal problems and trauma stories. Likewise, those in the therapy sessions wanted to learn the skills being taught to the other group. Both groups seemed to want sessions combining both strategies. Thus, a treatment combining both strategies may increase participation in the group and reduce symptoms of psychological distress more effectively than either strategy would alone.

Inclusion of traditional therapies, such as herbs or exorcisms, may be beneficial. Mock cleansing or purification rituals may be helpful also. Such treatments are essential parts of the client's culture, and may be as effective as any Western treatments.

This combined treatment strategy provides psychological intervention, social network enhancement, and skills training needed to thrive in the United States. At the same time, traditional Cambodian values and beliefs are respected and upheld. The more the client feels empowered, in control of her life, and supported by her therapist, the greater her potential for recovery. Likewise, a show of love, concern, and respect for the client by the therapist may be as helpful as any treatment strategy.

It was interesting to note that when I returned to the battered court-yard, to complete the exit interview, the same eyes watched as I approached the door. But this time I was expected. I was greeted by the same young man, and my client was there waiting for me. She bowed to me and I returned the gesture, then, more warmly, she held out her arms in the universally understood request for a hug.

NOTES

1. The test performed was a Visual Evoked Response (VER), which indicates whether the eye and brain center are functioning normally and estimates the level of the individual's visual acuity.

2. Since the control group was self-selected, we felt it necessary to establish comparability between the treatment groups and the self-selected control group. There were no significant pre-treatment differences between those who participated in the groups and those in the self-selected control group on measures of visual acuity, complaints of somatic illness, English language use, feelings of isolation, or problems with living in the United States. There was one exception, that of well-being ($t(13) = -3.09, p < .01$); those who participated in the treatment groups had a more positive sense of well-being than did those in the self-selected control group. However, since the key analysis in this research was based on the amount of *change* from pre- to post-intervention, the noted difference would be controlled for in subsequent analyses.

3. All participants had their vision checked after they had undergone the first interview. One woman, who had complained of severe loneliness and depression, was found at this time to have relatively normal vision, despite the fact that at one time she had been given a diagnosis of psychosomatic blindness. In light of her feelings of severe isolation we felt it necessary to allow her to participate. Her vision scores were eliminated from the analysis; other findings were included.

4. Mollica (1986) estimated that 95% of the Cambodian women he had seen in therapy had been sexually assaulted, however it took clients an average of three years in therapy before broaching the subject.

5. English as a second language.

6. Visual Evoked Response.

REFERENCES

Aronson, L. (1987). Traditional Cambodian health beliefs and practices. *Rhode Island Medical Journal, 70,* 73-78.

Beiser, M. & Fleming, J. (1986). Measuring psychiatric disorders among Southeast Asian refugees. *Psychological Medicine, 16,* 627-639.

Boehnlein, J. Kinzie, J. Rath, B., & Fleck, J. (1985). One-year follow-up study of posttraumatic stress disorder among survivors of Cambodian concentration camps. *American Journal of Psychiatry, 142*, 956-959.

Haldane, D. (1987, June 6). Cambodians: Leaving 'Killing Fields' behind. *Los Angeles Times*, pp. 1, 35.

Keltner, J., May, W., Johnson, C., & Post, R. (1985). The California syndrome: Functional visual complaints with potential economic impact. *Ophthalmology, 92*, 427-435.

Kinzie, D., Fredrickson, R., Ben, R., Fleck, J., & Karls, W. (1984). Posttraumatic stress disorder among survivors of Cambodian concentration camps. *American Journal of Psychiatry, 141*, 645-650.

Kinzie, D., & Fleck, J. (1987). Psychotherapy with severely traumatized refugees. *American Journal of Psychotherapy, 41*, 82-93.

Larson, R. (1977). Thirty years of research on the subjective well-being of older Americans. *Journal of Gerontology, 33*, 109-125.

Miranda, J., Perez-Stable, E., Munoz, R., Hargreaves, W., & Henke, C. (1991). Somatization, psychiatric disorder, and stress in utilization of ambulatory medical services. *Health Psychology, 10*, 46-51.

Mollica, R. (1986, August). *Cambodian refugee women at risk*. Paper presented at the American Psychological Association Annual Meeting, Washington, D. C.

Mollica, R., Wyshak G., & Lavelle, J. (1987). The psychological impact of war trauma and torture on Southeast Asian refugees. *American Journal of Psychiatry, 144*, 1567-1571.

Muecke, M. A. (1983a). Caring for Southeast Asian refugee patients in the USA. *American Journal of Public Health, 73*, 431-438.

Muecke, M. A. (1983b). In search of healers–Southeast Asian refugees in the American health care system. *Cross-Cultural Medicine, 139*, 835-840.

Nicassio, P. (1983). Psychosocial correlates of alienation: Study of a sample of Indochinese refugees. *Journal of Cross-Cultural Psychology, 14*, 337-351.

Nicassio, P. (1985). The psychosocial adjustment of the Southeast Asian refugee: An overview of empirical findings and theoretical models. *Journal of Cross-Cultural Psychology, 16*, 153-173.

Nicassio, P., Solomon, G., Guest, S., & McCullough, J. (1986). Emigration stress and language proficiency as correlates of depression in a sample of Southeast Asian refugees. *International Journal of Social Psychiatry, 32*, 22-28.

Nguyen, S. (1982). Psychiatric and psychosomatic problems among Southeast Asian refugees. *Psychiatric Journal of Ottawa 7*, 163-172.

Rada, R., Meyer, G., & Kellner, R. (1978). Visual conversion reaction in children and adults. *Journal of Nervous and Mental Disorders, 166*, 135-141.

Rozée, P. & Van Boemel, G. (1989). The psychological effects of war trauma and abuse on older Cambodian refugee women. *Women and Therapy, 8*, 23-50.

Szymusiak, M. (1986). *The stones cry out: A Cambodian childhood, 1975-1980*. New York: Hill and Wang.

Van Boemel, G., & Rozée-Koker, P. (1986, August). *Environmental stress-in-*

duced blindness in Cambodian female refugees. Paper presented at the American Psychological Association Annual Meeting, Washington, D.C.

Van Boemel, G. & Rozée-Koker, (1989, September). *Psychosomatic blindness in older Cambodian females.* Paper presented at the University of Southern California Department of Ophthalmology and Doheny Eye Institute Annual Meeting, Los Angeles, CA.

Van Boemel, G. Salamida, M.A., & Kann, D. (1991). *Outreach and education: Reducing black market enrollment.* (Contract number 14-S-10006-9-01). Baltimore, MD: Social Security Administration.

Post-Traumatic Stress Disorder Among Salvadoran Women: Empirical Evidence and Description of Treatment

Deborah J. Bowen
Lisa Carscadden
Kate Beighle
India Fleming

SUMMARY. Previous research has documented post-traumatic stress disorder among Salvadoran refugees in this country, but information on refugees living in El Salvador is not available. This study investigated patterns of psychological distress and documented the existence of PTSD in Salvadoran refugee women in El Salvador. A team of U.S. mental health workers travelled to a refugee camp in El Salvador to interview women about their traumatic experiences and current symptoms of distress. This study provides strong evidence that many refugee women in El Salvador have developed

Deborah J. Bowen, PhD, Assistant Member, Fred Hutchinson Cancer Research Center and Research Assistant Professor, Department of Psychology, University of Washington, is a Health Psychologist who conducts research in health promotion and health behavior change.

Lisa Carscadden, MA, has a Bachelor's degree in Social Work and an MA in teaching English as a second language. She has worked with refugee programs as a teacher, an advocate, and a grassroots activist. She is currently teaching at the University of Washington.

Kate Beighle is a massage therapist and a Registered Movement Therapist in Seattle. She has been working for social change in the U.S. and Latin America in a variety of different movements and is pursuing a Master's degree in Social Work.

India Fleming, PhD, is a Fellow in the Family Practice Department at the University of California, Davis Medical. She is a Clinical and Research Psychologist whose interests are in stress and coping.

267

PTSD and that many others show significant signs of distress. Data from this study also provided insight into clinical issues for Salvadoran women experiencing PTSD. In response to requests from Salvadoran mental health providers, a treatment program was developed to help Salvadoran women reduce their distress. Goals of the treatment included associating distress with the trauma as a normal reaction to a very abnormal event, reducing feelings of loss of control, reducing "survivor guilt," and lessening anxiety and high arousal level. These goals were accomplished using cognitive-behavioral and community-oriented strategies.

THE RESEARCH PROJECT

One of the most dramatic consequences of severe victimization is post-traumatic stress disorder (PTSD). PTSD is characterized by a specific set of symptoms that follow a psychologically distressing event outside the range of usual human experience (American Psychiatric Association, 1987). PTSD has been studied in populations such as Vietnam war veterans, concentration camp survivors, and disaster victims (e.g., Gleser, Green & Winget, 1981; Kinzie, Fredrickson, Ben, Flick & Karls, 1984; Laufer, Brett & Gallops, 1984; Lindy, 1988; Silver & Iacono, 1986). Members of these diverse groups share the experience of severe trauma, such as serious threat to one's life, witnessing harm of one's family, and the sudden destruction of home or community. A group currently experiencing this type of trauma and victimization is the population of El Salvador.

Symptoms of PTSD include recurrent and intrusive recollections, dreams, or intense experience of feelings associated with the event, persistent numbing of responsiveness and avoidance of stimuli associated with the trauma, and increased arousal including sleep difficulties and exaggerated startle response. If untreated, many victims of traumatic events may experience many years of depression, anxiety, difficulty controlling their behavior and "survivors guilt." When large groups of people or entire communities are subjected to a trauma, such as a war or a disaster, these symptoms can cause prolonged individual distress and disruption of marital and family relationships (Roberts et al., 1982).

Since 1980 the Salvadoran population and countryside have experienced one of the most extensive bombing campaigns in history, funded by over $1.5 million daily in U.S. tax dollars (Environmental Project on Central America, 1989). The war against the Salvadoran population has been characterized as a "dirty" and "psychological" war, because of the attacks against civilians and non-military institutions, the destruction of minds, and the use of both psychological and physical repression (Martin-Baro, 1988). Continuous government repression has resulted in over 6,000 people "disappeared," over 75,000 people killed in the last decade, and countless rapes, tortures, and other abuses of human rights (America's Watch, 1990; Physicians for Human Rights, 1990). Women have been particularly vulnerable to the effects of the trauma because of the impact of war on family and community life, both central to women's gender roles in Central America. Alternatively, if given the opportunity and skills, women could play an important role in necessary healing because of their investment in family and community life. Mental health workers returning from El Salvador have anecdotally described symptoms among refugees characteristic of PTSD. Prior research has documented PTSD among Salvadoran refugees in this country (Aron, 1986; 1988). However, refugees in the U.S. have undergone a major cultural transition that may influence their symptoms. The purpose of this study was to investigate patterns of psychological distress and to document the evidence for the existence of PTSD among Salvadoran women refugees who have remained within the borders of El Salvador.

METHOD

Interviewers. Three U.S. women travelled to a refugee camp in El Salvador to conduct this field study. These women travelled as part of the Women's Skills and Resource Exchange, a Seattle-based women's collective focused on exchanging skills, resources, and information between North and Central Americans who are working to improve the lives of Central American women and children.

Subjects. Subjects in the present study were drawn from a Catholic church refugee camp 10 miles outside of San Salvador. The 31 adult female participants in this study were among the 250 women, 20 men, and over 500 children living at the camp. Most of the adults at the camp came from illiterate subsistence farming communities from all over El Salvador. It proved impossible to randomly sample women from the camp population. The subjects in this study were individuals who volunteered to be interviewed. Each interview was conducted by a team consisting of a trained female U.S. interviewer and a Salvadoran lay mental health worker who resided at the camp. All interviews were conducted in Spanish.

Interview Content. To elicit information about their experiences of trauma, participants were asked to tell the story of how they came to be at the camp. This section took between 40-80 minutes and was recorded in outline form. Next, participants were asked a series of questions designed to identify symptoms of PTSD as described by the diagnostic criteria in DSM-III-R. Each symptom category was initiated by a prompt, then followed by unstructured probes to obtain details of the particular symptom (e.g., duration, nature, etc.). Specifically, symptoms were assessed from the following categories: re-experience of the trauma; persistent avoidance of stimuli associated with the trauma; and numbing of affect. The symptom-reporting portion of the interview took approximately 30-40 minutes. Finally, to assess prior history of mental illness, a brief history of psychopathology and associated behaviors (alcoholism, etc.) was taken.

RESULTS

All interviews were coded by trained coders as to the presence or absence of each symptom category. Three questions were explored in the analyses of the interview data: (1) had the subjects experienced significant traumas; (2) what was the pattern of symptoms experienced by these refugees; and (3) was there evidence that PTSD occurs in this population?

All subjects reported experiencing traumatic events sufficient to induce PTSD. These events included witnessing the murders of their families and friends, and living for months or years in caves to avoid being killed. Most participants (87%) reported 3 or more traumatic experiences. Table 1 presents the types and frequencies of traumas reported by participants. Most frequently experienced traumatic events were witnessing damage to one's home, witnessing others' assaults, and hiding from government soldiers. Women also reported personal assaults, rapes, and in about 20% of cases, torture. Most of these events occurring alone have been found traumatic enough to induce PTSD.

These refugees reported symptom patterns similar to those found among other groups with PTSD. Table 2 summarizes the incidence of PTSD symptoms in this sample. Frequently reported symptoms included experiencing intrusive thoughts of the events, having recurrent distressing dreams of the events, avoiding reminders of the event, and experiencing a restricted range of emotions or numb affect. All of these symptoms were reported by more than 50% of the respondents. Using conservative criteria that required evidence of re-experience of the trauma, avoidance of trauma, and numbing of affect (as well as a positive rating on the limited number of items assessing increased arousal), 41 percent (13 out of 31 individuals) reported the range and severity of symptoms required to meet DSM-III-R diagnostic criteria for PTSD.

Table 1. Categories and Frequencies of Trauma Experienced by Participants

Type of Trauma	Percent (n=31)
Assault	55%
Rape	32%
Torture	19%
Home destroyed	94%
Witness family member's assault	61%
Witness friend/community member's assault	100%
Living undercover	81%
Death of family members	42%

DISCUSSION

This study provides strong evidence that refugee women in El Salvador are experiencing PTSD and that many others show significant signs of distress. Although it is unclear as to how representative of all Salvadoran people or all refugees this sample is, the high incidence of distress in the sample suggests that there may be serious distress in large numbers of Salvadoran women. It is estimated that over half a million Salvadorans have fled their homes; many more have witnessed trauma associated with the war (MacEoin & Riley, 1982). This suggests, then, that there may be a high incidence of PTSD among the general population of El Salvador, with particularly traumatic effects on women. Further support for PTSD in similar populations can be found in the work of Aron (1986) who found a high incidence of PTSD in Salvadoran refugees in California.

Patterns of symptoms show both similarity to and divergence from patterns reported elsewhere (Roberts et al., 1982; Silver & Iacono, 1986). The surprising finding that 100% of participants experienced intrusive thoughts and recurrent dreams of traumatic events may be due to constant environmental reminders of the trauma, to cultural differences affecting the reporting of these experiences, or to the cultural meaning of dreams. Similarly, the infrequent reporting of feelings of detachment from others

Table 2. Reported Symptoms of Post-Traumatic Stress Disorder

Diagnostic Category	Percent
Symptom	
A. Experience Traumatic Event	100%
B. Re-experience of Event	
Intrusive thoughts of events	100%
Dreams of events	100%
Feeling as if events recurring	87%
C. Avoidance of Stimuli and Numbing of Responsiveness	
Avoids reminders of events	84%
Decreased interest in pleasurable activities	58%
Feeling detached from others	16%
Restricted experience/expression of emotion	77%
D. Persistent Symptoms of Arousal	
Difficulty falling or staying asleep	68%
Difficulty thinking or working	55%

may be a function of the participants' culturally determined close ties with others or of living with others who shared similar experiences. This continuous connection with others is also congruent with women's gender roles.

THE TREATMENT PROGRAM

As research psychologists, we have the responsibility to document health problems in victimized populations. As clinicians we have responsibility to provide expertise to those serving the health needs of these populations. Because of these dual roles a multidisciplinary team was formed to develop a treatment program for victims of trauma in El Salvador. The program was initially based on programs developed for use with nonrefugee populations. The psychologists and community organizers rapidly determined that adaptation would be needed for the existing programs.

Several considerations influenced the subsequent development of the program. First, most of these treatment programs were designed for U.S. male Vietnam combat veterans (e.g., Fairbank & Nichols, 1987; Keane, Zimering & Caddell, 1985; Lindy, 1986), and so their direct applicability was inappropriate. The focus of the program was Central American women; data from the previous study and knowledge of the culture were used to modify some of the components of existing approaches or to design new ones as needed. Second, the situation in El Salvador is that of a war-torn country and its people. Individual talk-style therapies were beyond the means and realities of peasant women who struggle to maintain daily life for them and for their families and communities. Third, the combination of gender and cultural roles for women in El Salvador presented exciting possibilities for treatment components designed to make use of these role distinctions. With these considerations in mind, the program was developed by a team of four psychologists, two health care specialists, and several other women familiar with Central American life and culture. The general goals of treatment were to reduce the levels of experienced stress and distressing symptoms and to help women find ways to continue with their daily lives despite the losses they had experienced. The treatment program had five specific goals, each associated with one or more techniques that could be easily taught and handed from woman to woman.

Program Goals

The first goal of the program was to clearly associate the experienced symptoms to the traumatic event. Many people with PTSD do not clearly understand that their symptoms are, in fact, a fairly normal reaction to a very abnormal event. This basic educational goal has been incorporated into many individual and group treatments of PTSD (e.g., Keane, Fairbank, Caddell, Zimering & Bender, 1985; Lindy, 1988). Helping people understand that their symptoms were caused by traumatic events was seen as an important step in the treatment of PTSD. This understanding was assisted by encouraging women to talk to each other about their shared experiences, their lives before the trauma, and their current feelings. Developing close mutually supportive relationships with others was encouraged as very beneficial to the recovery process (Foy, Donahoe, Carroll, Gallers & Reno, 1987; Solomon, 1986). Strategies for building social support on a family and a community level were included as an initial component of the program.

A second goal was to help people overcome the feelings of helplessness and loss of control over their lives that are commonly experienced by people with PTSD (Horowitz & Kaltreider, 1979; Janoff-Bulman & Frieze, 1983; Silver & Wortman, 1980). Encouraging people to make their own decisions and to have control over even small events in their lives was seen as important in the recovery process (Taylor, 1983; Thompson, 1985). For example, to the extent possible, women were encouraged to set their own schedules for events like meals, socializing with others, and group activities, instead of having them structured centrally. Groups of people who have experienced similar traumatic events were encouraged to take responsibility for helping one another. The ability to help someone else was used as an effective way to reduce feelings of helplessness. Social support-building strategies were used to build mutually supportive structures to give women more perceived control and to help identify women who were particularly damaged by trauma and who needed more intensive help.

Reducing the "survivor guilt" was another goal included in the treatment for PTSD. Even though this guilt usually seems irrational given the circumstances surrounding the trauma, it is a common symptom of PTSD and must be addressed in treatment (Horowitz, 1986; Lindy, 1988). Helping others in the context of social support strategies was seen as beneficial because it could help lessen the guilt experienced by people who have survived events which killed others. Art therapy and play therapy were presented as techniques for reliving the traumatic events in a safe and healing way. This reliving process assisted in identifying and reducing "survivor guilt." Also, the reliving experience was used to reduce feelings of helplessness and loss of control. Both art and play therapy were used to discover hidden negative thoughts and feelings about the traumatic events that led to PTSD.

A fourth treatment goal was to lessen the anxiety and arousal that are a common experience in PTSD. In part, understanding the relationship between the symptoms and the event, and regaining a sense of control over life reduced the anxiety and arousal. However, other activities that help people relax are also useful techniques in reducing anxiety and other negative feelings that often accompany PTSD (Kipper, 1977). Movement and massage therapy, two techniques that were used to allow people to become more aware of their bodily sensations and to reduce negative emotions, were included in the program.

Finally, PTSD often involves a discontinuity from one's life before the event and a difficulty with planning one's future (Janoff-Bulman & Frieze, 1983; Taylor, 1983). Because people have often lost family members, friends, and their communities, this discontinuity can be hard to overcome. Helping people with PTSD realize that although their life has changed dramatically they are still the same person was a final goal of the treatment program (Beck & Emory, 1985, pp.288-313; Janoff-Bulman, 1985). Encouraging people to participate in activities they enjoyed before the traumatic event and to form new communities was included to help address this issue.

COMMUNITY ORGANIZING STRATEGIES

Based on these goals, several strategies were identified and developed into a treatment manual. The first step in organizing systems of support was to identify any existing networks that could serve as sources of support. These networks included:

- *The family.* The family was an important bounded network that can be used to promote support. If family members were living together or within close proximity, as many members of the unit as possible were involved.
- *The workplace.* Many people spent many hours per day at some work. The workplace was sometimes formal; a factory, shop union, farm, or craftsplace can be used as an existing network. Women tended to work in more informal structures (e.g., around the camp-fire to make food in a communal setting) places or jobs where the women worked or congregated were identified.
- *The playgrounds and schools.* Children were found at the play-ground, school, or field. Where children gathered consistently, there were good opportunities for promoting support among children and their caretakers.
- *Churches.* In a community of people that values religious beliefs and activities, churches were often a focal gathering point. In this church-based camp most women attended one of at least three church-es. This frequent, important part of most women's lives were used to promote support.
- *Informal gatherings.* Often certain places in a community of people became central gathering points. For example, women gathered to wash clothes at the stream and talk about their families and com-munity events. Men went to have a drink at the local bar after work. These places were used to promote support in the particular commu-nities or parts of communities that gathered there.

Once the existing networks were located, the next step was to identify people in each of these networks to provide information on needs and problems within the network. The easiest way to do this was to ask network members for good resources for the network. As the list of possibilities grew, information was checked with the next network member. Usually a few leaders of the network were identified. These people were knowledgeable about their network, willing to talk with the facilitator, and popular with the network members. They worked closely with the facilitator to accomplish the treatment goals.

If identified leaders seemed agreeable, group activities were proposed to the leaders. For example, people needed to know that there are a variety of reactions to trauma. The group sessions helped to reduce feelings of shame or guilt about their own problems. Most people had some problems dealing with major trauma and so they can empathize with others who were also having problems. Often people had not shared their traumatic stories because of fear of reprisal. The community leaders encouraged people to talk in the network.

In the groups women were encouraged to fill in for the loss and grief experienced by everyone who had gone through trauma. Trauma almost always involved loss–loss of friends, family, property, functioning. People helped one another with these common losses by taking the place of a loved one or friend, or by sharing property, or by helping someone who has lost a limb or sight. People were organized to look for ways that they needed help and that others in their community needed help, in order to exchange support.

Women who had been through a common trauma were encouraged to become united for a common goal. The goals were many: building a church or school, harvesting crops, or setting up a kitchen. Any goal was appropriate that unified a group of people. This unification contributed to a spirit of working together for mutual good.

Finally, women who were experiencing difficulties because of trauma benefitted from other healing techniques (art, play, movement, or massage therapy). Particularly for people who were very dysfunctional and noncommunicative, these techniques provided nonverbal methods for dealing with some of the problems caused by the traumatic events. Specific detailed instructions for each therapy technique were included in the manual using both text and pictures.

Art Therapy

Art therapy is the expression of thoughts and emotions through the creation of an art product. It is useful for revealing unconscious thoughts and feelings not easily identified by simply asking. Art therapy is useful for the expression of immediate emotions, processing grief, and mourning. The non-verbal aspect gave the women a chance to express interpersonal and unconscious material difficult for them to say to a facilitator or too painful to put into words. Art therapy was used in almost any setting. It was not necessary that those guiding the activities be able to interpret what was created, although the interpretation is often useful. Art therapy was used once or many times, as the group or individual decided.

Women used simple art media in their creations. The use of everyday familiar materials helped women to be creative when designing their art projects and allowed everyone, not just experienced artists, to be involved. Common materials of art therapy were felt-tipped markers, crayons, scissors, glue, and paper. Women also used materials that were readily available in their environment, such as old cloth and food or plant products.

Massage Therapy

The primary reason for using massage is to relax (Downing, 1972). Behavioral approaches to treating PTSD emphasize training in relaxation which is compatible with the stress response (e.g., Keane et al., 1985). Another benefit of massage lies in its unique way of communicating without words. In itself this is not unusual; by touching and hugging, for example, one can find acceptance. Since physical and mental sensations are so closely connected, relaxation of the body can facilitate emotional relaxation. When an individual experiences a physical or emotional trauma the event is recorded in the mind in the form of a conscious or unconscious memory. Many times the body "records" a memory of the same event.

Women who have been traumatized by events in their lives were able to identify these memories and move beyond them. Many emotions, such as anger and sadness, surfaced when the women learned massage. They needed support during the massage. Women were encouraged to breathe deeply to induce relaxation and to help release physical and emotional tension. Specific steps for simple massage techniques were used and taught to women who had experienced trauma.

Play Therapy

Play therapy is a way of recreating events and feelings by using objects which are common tools for play. This method usually involved two people: the observer/helper and the client, often a child. In El Salvador it was used with groups of children at play. The women and children led the way: setting the scene, naming the objects, letting the helper know what is going on through words and actions. Materials for play therapy were varied. Puppets, paints or crayons and drawing paper, stick or paper figures, sand or dirt surroundings, cardboard boxes or miniature houses made of wood scraps were used. Most of the things that children found during play were used in play therapy.

Movement Therapy

Movement therapy is based on the theory that unexpressed emotions and stress are held in the body as muscular tension (Kelemen, 1979). By learning how and where in our bodies tension and stress are held, new techniques can be developed to release the tension and relax.

Women were provided with the opportunity to discover for themselves how they responded to a situation and where they held tension/stress in their bodies. In traumatic situations, many women disassociated to avoid and cope with overwhelming experiences including emotional trauma, physical pain and injury. Because disassociation was protective, work proceeded slowly with traumatized individuals who were still suffering the effects of their trauma.

CONCLUSIONS

Some of the symptoms of PTSD protect people from feeling too much pain. The treatment approach was designed to proceed slowly, letting the affected individual set the pace. The positive impact of a self-paced approach–particularly for a community rather than an individual intervention–will likely help increase feelings of control over one's emotions and environment. Some people will need only a little encouragement, and others will take years to heal. We have not had an opportunity to assess the efficacy of this program, but we hope that it will help the refugees in this community.

These data and clinical experiences also have relevance to other political refugees living around the world. International estimates of refugees living in other countries number 15 million, with an additional 15 million "displaced persons" living inside their native country (Vernez, 1991). National and international policies must be directed at assisting populations and individuals to rebuild communities and lives torn by trauma. Developing programs for primary prevention of distress is equally important (Williams & Berry, 1991). These programs range from mental health interventions to prevent acculturation distress through more open and inclusive immigration policies to international peace-making and negotiation to prevent people from becoming refugees.

REFERENCES

American Psychiatric Association (1987). Diagnostic and statistical manual of mental disorders-III-R. Washington D.C.: American Psychiatric Association.

America's Watch. (1990). *Green Paper #4*. San Francisco, CA: Author.

Aron, A. (1988). Refugees without sanctuary: Salvadorans in the United States. In A. Aron *Flight, exile, and return: Mental health and the refugee* (pp. 23-53). San Francisco, CA: Committee for Health Rights in Central America.

Aron, A. (1986, August). *Psychological problems of Salvadoran refugees in California*. Paper presented at the annual convention of the American Psychological Association, Washington, D.C.

Beck, A.T. & Emory, G. (1985). *Anxiety disorders: A cognitive perspective*. New York: Basic Books.

Downing, G. (1972). *The Massage Book*. City: Random House.

Environmental Project on Central America (1989). *Update*. San Francisco, CA.

Fairbank, J.A. & Nichols, R.A. (1987). Theoretical and empirical issues in the treatment of post-traumatic stress disorder in Vietnam veterans. *Journal of Consulting and Clinical Psychology, 43*, 44-55.

Foy, P.W., Donahoe, C.P., Carroll, E.M., Gallers, J., & Reno, R. (1987). Post-traumatic stress disorder. In L. Michelson & L.M. Ascher (Eds.) *Anxiety and stress disorders* (pp. 361-378). New York: Guildford Press.

Gleser, G.C., Green, B.L., & Winget, C.N. (1981). *Prolonged effects of disaster: A study of Buffalo Creek*. New York: Academic Press.

Horowitz, M.J. (1986). *Stress response syndromes (2nd ed.)*. Northvale, NJ: Jason Aarson.

Horowitz, M.J. & Kaltreider, N. (1979). Brief therapy of stress response syndromes. *Psychiatric Clinics of North America, 2*, 365-378.

Janoff-Bulman, R. (1985). The aftermath of victimization: Rebuilding shattered assumptions. In C.R. Figley (Ed.), *Trauma and its wake: The study and treatment of post-traumatic stress disorder* (pp. 15-35). New York: Brunner Mazel.

Janoff-Bulman, R. & Frieze, J. (1983). A theoretical perspective for understanding reactions to victimization. *Journal of Social Issues, 39*, 1-17.

Keane, T.M., Fairbank, J.A., Caddell, J.M., Zimering, R.T., & Bender, M.E. (1985). A behavioral approach to assessing and treating post-traumatic stress disorder in Vietnam veterans. In C.R. Filey (Ed.), *Trauma and its wake II: Traumatic stress, theory, research and intervention* (pp. 257-294). New York: Brunner Mazel.

Keane, T.M., Zimering, R.T. & Caddell, J.M. (1985). A behavioral formulation of post-traumatic stress disorder in Vietnam veterans. *Behavior Therapist, 8*, 9-12.

Keleman, S. (1979). *Somatic reality*. Berkeley, CA: Center Press.

Kinzie, J.D., Fredrickson, R.H., Ben, R., Flick, J., & Karls, W. (1984). Post-traumatic stress disorder among survivors of Cambodian concentration camps. *American Journal of Psychiatry, 14*, 645-650.

Kipper, P.A. (1977). Behavior therapy for fears brought on by war experiences. *Journal of Consulting and Clinical Psychology, 45*, 261-221.

Laufer, R.S., Brett, E., & Gallops, M.D. (1984). Post-traumatic stress disorder reconsidered: PTSD among Vietnam veterans. In B.A. Van Derkolk (Ed.), *Post-traumatic stress disorder: Psychological and biological sequelae* (pp. 59-80). Washington D.C.: American Psychiatric Press.

Lindy, J.D. (1986). An outline for the psychoanalytic psychotherapy of post-traumatic stress disorder. In C.R. Figley (Ed.), *Trauma and its wake II: Traumatic stress, theory, research and intervention* (pp. 195-212). New York: Brunner Mazel.

Lindy, J.D. (1988). *Vietnam: A casebook.* New York: Brunner Mazel.

MacEoin, G. & Riley, N. (1982). *No promised land: American refugee policy and the rule of law.* Boston: Oxfam America, p. 41.

Martin-Baro, I. (1988). From dirty war to psychological war: The case of El Salvador. In A. Aron, *Flight, exile, and return: mental health and the refugee* (pp. 2-22). San Francisco, CA: Committee for Health Rights in Central America.

Physicians for Human Rights. (1990, February). *El Salvador: Health care under siege–Violations of medical neutrality during the civil conflict.*

Roberts, W.R., Penk, W.E., Gearing, M.L., Robinowitz, R., Dolan, M.P., & Patterson, E.T. (1982). Interpersonal problems of Vietnam combat veterans with symptoms of post-traumatic stress disorder. *Journal of Abnormal Psychology, 91*, 444-450.

Silver, R.L. & Wortman, C.B. (1980). Coping with undesirable life events. In J. Gerber and M.E.P. Seligman (Eds.), *Human helplessness theory and applications* (pp. 279-340). New York: Academic Press.

Silver, S.M. & Iacono, C. (1986). Symptom groups and family patterns of Vietnam veterans with post traumatic stress disorders. In C.R. Figley (Ed.), *Trauma and its wake II: Traumatic stress theory, research and intervention* (pp. 78-96). New York: Brunner/Mazel.

Solomon, S. (1986). Mobilizing social support networks in times of disaster. In C.R. Figley (Ed.), *Trauma and its wake II: Traumatic stress theory, research and intervention* (pp. 232-263). New York: Brunner Mazel.

Taylor, S.E. (1983). Adjustment to threatening events: A theory of cognitive adaptation. *American Psychologist, 38*, 1161-1173.

Thompson, S.C. (1985). Finding positive meaning in a stressful event and coping. *Basic and Applied Social Psychology, 6*, 279-295.

Vernez, G. (1991). Current Global Refugee Situation and International Public Policy. *American Psychologist*, 627-631.

Williams, C.L. & Berry, J.W. (1991). Primary prevention of acculturative stress among refugees: Application of psychological theory and practice. *American Psychologist*, 632-641.

Post-Traumatic Stress Disorder in Vietnamese Women

Judith Shepherd

SUMMARY. This article describes the extraordinary events Vietnamese women immigrants and refugees experienced prior to their resettlement in the United States. Oral history data illustrate the need for sensitization to issues of Post-Traumatic Stress Disorder and the historical-cultural background of this special population.

Oral history narratives from five Vietnamese women suggest differences in the way men and women define wartime trauma, and that women's biological makeup may precipitate some stress reactions unique to women. These narratives are examined in terms of Post-Traumatic Stress Disorder (PTSD), a diagnosis that has been applied primarily to male veterans in treating their physical and psychological problems resulting from war, not to Vietnamese women who lived under war conditions.

Post-Traumatic Stress Disorder is a normal reaction to an abnormal amount of stress and includes the symptoms of depression, emotional numbness, and the avoidance of people, places, and things that remind the individual of the original traumatic event. Many Vietnamese women who have immigrated to the U.S. have not been diagnosed for PTSD until recently because PTSD has been regarded, with few exceptions (Rothblum & Cole, 1986), as a male problem. As women comprise half of Vietnam's population, and lived through and participated in the war, their systematic exclusion from consideration by mental health professionals for the same

Judith Shepherd received a DSW from the University of California, Berkeley in 1980. She has taught at UC Berkeley and San Francisco State University, and is currently employed by San Francisco General Hospital, where she does mental health assessments and runs PTSD support groups for refugees from Southeast Asia as well as Central and South America.

war-related disabilities suffered by American veterans seems unwarranted and unjustified.

Health and mental health providers may more readily appreciate the recent application of the PTSD diagnosis to Vietnamese women if they understand why the diagnosis has taken so long to be made.

DEVELOPMENT OF THE PTSD DIAGNOSIS

Post-Traumatic Stress Disorder was first observed in soldiers who saw combat in World War I, and then again after World War II and the Korean war. Some of the first symptoms of stress were depression and agitation resulting from surviving the death of friends or comrades. Researchers also observed that survivors of concentration camps who had witnessed the death of family members were often overcome with feelings of unworthiness and depression long after they were freed from the camps (Lauffer, Gallops & Frey-Wonters, 1984). This symptom became known as "survivor guilt," one of many defined in 1980 as part of the PTSD reaction to unduly stressful situations.

The United States, during its involvement in Vietnam, dropped more than three times the tonnage of explosives used during all of World War II. A former high-ranking Vietcong official commented that the relentless American bombing created an atmosphere of terror that was renewed daily, and that ended only when the Americans withdrew. He said the first time he experienced a B-52 raid he thought he had been caught in the Apocalypse. As he pressed himself into the bunker floor he remembers losing control of his body functions while his mind screamed incomprehensible orders to get out (Tang, 1985).

Unfortunately, during the 1970s the traumatic experiences of Vietnamese women went unacknowledged or unappreciated by the professionals who were treating American veterans for war-related disabilities. American women veterans of the Vietnam war fared only slightly better. American nurses returned to the U.S. at the same time as many male veterans, and at least some of them went to VA hospitals seeking help for their problems. As VA hospitals in the late 1960s and 1970s were not yet conscious of the need to reach out to this population, however, they had no services for female veterans.

The association between women and PTSD had not yet been drawn. The *Diagnostic and Statistical Manual of Mental Disorders* of the American Psychiatric Association (known as DSM II), then in effect, had no diagnostic category to recognize and treat people who exhibited the new stress reactions Vietnam veterans were bringing home. Veterans might enter a VA hospital for alleviation of symptoms of survivor guilt, intrusive thoughts, or sleep disorders. Since there was no unified PTSD diagnostic category to cover all the varied symptoms a veteran might exhibit, he or she might be diagnosed according to criteria for manic-depressive illness, schizophrenia, or some other category cited in DSM II. Veterans exhibiting what we would now categorize as PTSD symptoms were frequently diagnosed and treated according to criteria that did not really fit their symptoms. In many instances, their complaints went ignored.

Neither male nor female veterans were accorded any major systematic relief from Vietnam War-related stress reactions until the mental health profession revised its diagnostic and treatment manual in 1980 to include PTSD. Once DSM III had been issued and the PTSD diagnostic and treatment category defined, the ability to diagnose and care for male Vietnam veterans improved markedly.

DSM III noted that some stressors clearly produced PTSD more often than others. It has been found, for example, that the disorder is more severe and longer lasting when the stressor is human. Thus, torture usually has longer-lasting and more severe effects than trauma resulting from an accident or a natural disaster. A person with PTSD might constantly seek to avoid stimuli associated with a traumatic event, and make major efforts to avoid thoughts or feelings that might serve as reminders. He or she might feel an emotional numbness or lack of responsiveness that did not exist before the trauma. Emotional detachment or estrangement from people, or inability to experience intimacy, tenderness, and sexuality, would not be uncommon. A PTSD sufferer may be unable to fall asleep, or may wake up intermittently. Some sufferers may experience exaggerated startle responses under some conditions, as when the backfire of a car is mistaken for artillery fire. Women veterans and Vietnamese immigrants and refugees began to appear at veterans' hospitals and mental health centers seeking help for problems like flashbacks, nightmares, insomnia, and depression. It was becoming clear that PTSD was also a women's issue; but since the number of female Vietnam veterans was small relative to the number of male veterans, they had to struggle to make their needs heard.

Ironically, it was the women's movement rather than an understanding of war-related trauma that did the most to extend the PTSD diagnosis to women. Extensive research on rape was published during the late '70s and early '80s. Many of the studies showed that rape victims experienced the PTSD symptoms described in DSM III. Now there were two categories of women to whom the previously all male paradigm of PTSD could be applied: female veterans of Vietnam and rape victims.

The extension of the PTSD model to Vietnamese women, however, has been slow in forthcoming, despite the large number of Vietnamese immigrants and refugees who have entered the United States. Although the PTSD literature throughout the 1970s and 1980s began to reflect the two other groups of women, there was no parallel growth in the literature on the coping mechanisms of Vietnamese women. A few articles were published describing the harrowing experiences of the boat people trying to flee Vietnam, in particular involving rape (Burton, 1983), but these were the exception rather than the rule. Studies on secondary migration (Desbarats, 1987) and welfare programs like AFDC and family assistance patterns have been more the norm.

What we know about trauma and the relation of PTSD to Vietnamese and American women war veterans is still measured largely by what we know about male veterans. The following narratives support the notion that Vietnamese women may have serious mental health problems left unattended. At the same time, it has also become apparent that although the PTSD paradigm is a useful mental health diagnosis and treatment tool, it gives us only one part of the picture for understanding the effect of war trauma on women.

In order to help women overcome Post-Traumatic Stress Disorder, we need to know more about their past than the trauma. We also need to know about their coping mechanisms and other strengths in order to design effective treatment interventions. Oral history data can give professionals a deeper understanding of the historical/cultural context of the women's lives, as well as a fuller understanding of their positive as well as negative reactions to trauma.

The following excerpts from five oral histories give a sense of the context and tremendous complexity of women's lives during the Vietnam war. The interviews were open-ended, and thus not collected with the intent of eliciting data on PTSD. Nonetheless, much of the material relates to the traumas women experienced and the positive ways they responded. These excerpts show how the PTSD literature can be expanded to include a notion of how culture, gender, and coping skills factor into our understanding of women's mastery of trauma during wartime.

CHAU PHAM

Dr. Chau Pham was one of the small minority of women in South Vietnam to attend medical school during the 1950s. Her training was French in more than language, exemplifying the influence of the French occupa-

tion in South Vietnam in matters academic and professional. Women like Chau Pham, and her husband, a physicist, were particularly suspect under the Communist regime in 1975 because of their elite background and the relative comfort they enjoyed during the American presence in Vietnam.

Chau Pham relives the trauma of escape from Vietnam in the following excerpt. Like many women, success did not occur on the first try. The description of conditions aboard the boat that took her family to Malaysia gives us a clear picture of the trauma women had to endure.

I was trying for these three years to find the right connection, but every night for those three years we went through the same thing. It was kind of a strange life. They were always watching us. During the day we acted normal. But I was always trying to find someone to take us out of Vietnam.

At night, it was as if we were crazy. We would fight and argue all the time. My husband wanted to go with one guy, I wanted to go with another. One time, when we were feeling particularly crazy, we didn't know how to choose who to take us, so we asked a fortune teller to help us. Since this fortune teller told my husband he would organize the boat, and that the trip would be successful, we decided to go with him. But I didn't like this guy. So we were fighting every night about the same thing. We didn't want people to know we were fighting, so we would shut the doors and fight whispering. . . .

So, at 5:00 a.m., we left the house. Right away we saw the police at the corner. We didn't have a car anymore. Finally, we came to the meeting place by "push-push"–a bus-like vehicle. We were more than 20 people. The bus took us from Saigon to a little town near the shore, near the beach. All of us were people trying to escape. I think they bribed the police. At every checkpoint the owner went down and said, OK, so. . . . But we had to go very slowly, and it took one day to go from Saigon to this town. I think it was less than 100 miles away. They planned on the bus arriving at the beach around 9:00 p.m. It was dark when we got to the meeting point, really dark. Then they brought us into a very, very small boat. You could not move; there were too many people in this small boat. This "taxi" would wait near where the river meets the sea, where we would be transferred to another boat. We were very crowded: about 200 people, for a boat of around 17 meters long.

The pilot brought the boat to a sandbank, where we got stuck. We waited for the police to come and catch us. They put us in jail, all 200 people on the whole boat, including women and children. They put us in jail one week before the [lunar] new year. We hoped we could get out. Happily, some people took pity on us. When they transferred us from the boat to the jail my nephew threw some money on the ground, with a slip of paper with the name of my sister. One of the girls who was very honest sent a letter to my sister, and my sister asked this Chinese man to try to take us out from the jail. We had to spend some more gold to get out of jail. One week later, we were out of jail. But the men stayed for a month.

I think we had to experience jail to understand what jail is like. You are *nothing*. We were in a very small room with bars. We could not just sit down, and we could not lay down, because so many people were caught. My son was a very picky eater. I remember it was the first time he was so hungry. He told me, "I didn't know eating just soy sauce was so good," because he was so hungry. Every day we could go out of the cell, just four families at a time.

After that we tried again, with the same 12 people. But one guy, a young relative, got scared on the bus. It was the same schedule as before, but this time we were late in getting to the meeting place because my mother was crying and my mother-in-law and my sister told me to pray at the ancestor altar before we left. When we left the house there was no transportation, no bus. At the meeting place everybody was gone. Only the owner was still waiting for us, because he was a good friend. He asked why we were so late, the bus had gone already.

My gosh, we were so scared! Then suddenly a motorcycle bus, the very noisy kind, came along. The man driving said, "get on, come here, come here." We didn't know if he was a policeman or not. He just stared at us. He said, "Come on, come on, I'll take you." There were four or five of us in this small thing–me, my husband, the owner, the Chinese guy, had a Vespa. My husband and my nephew were with him. So, this motorscooter brought us to catch up with the bus. Outside of Saigon there is another checkpoint, and you can get into the bus, at last. We were so scared.

Because of all these problems, the young relative said, "I think this trip will be an unlucky one too." So at first we tried to go back. But we hesitated. I decided I will not go back home. He returned, alone. We came to the meeting point. From the small taxi to the boat, we were 288; you must remember the number, because 288, for a boat like–it was bamboo, a very small one! And my daughter was very weak. We had nothing. I just brought two cans of condensed milk, and a half of kilo of dry rice. On the boat I met the son of a friend of mine. This young guy was very, very clever. He said he would try to steal a container from the owner to get some water for us. Because getting water was a big problem. So he stole a container holding 20 liters, and told me, stay in the dirtiest place of the boat, so nobody will want to take your place. So I went to the dirtiest part, the place where everything falls on you. I sat there, and put the container behind my back. I sat down, with my two children, my husband, my nephew.

There were 288 of us in this boat. On the first day we drank a lot. They cooked some rice for us. They put some sugar in with rice the first day. By the second day the water became scarce, and we had some trouble. On the third day, people started to act crazy because they didn't have enough water. One guy became crazy. He was the first one. Since it was the third day people were becoming thirsty and acting abnormally. The owner and the crew had food and drink, but we were not allowed to have any. On this day they started to distribute their water, but it wasn't enough for the friend of my husband, who was also a professor at the University of Science. He was dead because of lack of water. His wife and sisters also died. There were six dead on the third day. The distribution of water was *after* the deaths, not before. But the first was on the third day.

In another family, the first to die was the eldest son, who was 11 years old. But now I was very weak because I was hungry, and thirsty, too. We had water, but we didn't dare to drink a lot. We just waited until night, and took just a little bit and drank it. I remember my husband calling me, "Chau, you have to look at this boy because I think there is something wrong. He is sick." But I was so weak. I looked at him, I said, "Oh, he's dead; my God, he's dead." I didn't know the son died first. When my husband called me, his friend, the professor, was having convulsions. People thought he had some kind of flu or something. But I said no, he's dying. They asked me to treat him. I had nothing, because I didn't want to bring medicine.

After 15 minutes of convulsions he died. The father died in the afternoon, and the son died in the evening. The wife started to become disoriented. She had a high fever. We had nothing to give her but some aspirin. The one who controlled the boat . . . told us to throw the body away. So we had to throw the body overboard. The wife was becoming disoriented, and my husband said, "She has a high fever and you have to treat her, to keep her alive." She had two more children, I think a 6- and 7-year old. A boy and a girl. That was a very unlucky for her, because she was becoming weak and comatose. At this time, the owner started to give water to the wife. An orange and some water. She was comatose, but still half-conscious. She kept telling us: "I have hidden some gold somewhere. Please try to find it and give to my children." So everyone hunted for it. "And please tell to the owner that I have a sister in Australia." As she became unconscious my husband kept asking me if we had some water. Every 15 minutes he gave her a little bit of water, just to keep her alive. He thought that he could keep her alive.

The next day, the fourth day, we met a ship. We had someone on board who spoke good English, a woman who was a teacher at the university. We were somewhere near Malaysia. And we saw people at their platform, but they didn't want to take us; they refused. But they said, "OK, we'll give you some water and some food." By now I think we had four dead. One just jumped from the boat, then two, son and father, three, and one more woman. People were so thirsty that when they gave us the bag of water, one teenager, 16 or 18 years old, put the bag in his mouth. He was killed right away. I think it was the pressure. Right away he fell and died, just like that! And we were trying, fighting, to have the water. I remember I was yelling at some guys: "It is my container, I want my container." I was crazy! This guy died. The woman professor who came to the platform to make the people take us, was so weak that she fell unconscious. They brought her back to the boat. They said, "Go, go away." She forgot the lady comatose in the boat. She must have told them that we had someone dying, so please save her. But they asked her to go away. These were Oriental guys on the platform. And there were one or two Americans.

We were so hungry, and really, it was so hot in the boat. We were nearly 300, and my husband tried to keep us alive. He took the milk can and hung it from a long pole, and he put some water, sea water, into it to shower us just to keep us not very dehydrated, because it was so hot. I think he was the only one who could move. We were so weak we could not move. There was nothing to eat. But he didn't eat, and I told him, if you don't eat, you will die like your friend.

About the wife of my husband's professor friend who had died. When we left the platform we met a storm, right after. We thought it would last four to eight hours. Just a half-day after we left the shore, our motor broke. The motor was crazy, it kept starting and stopping. The people on the boat told us we were near the Malaysian shore. So about eight hours after the storm the lady died. I will always remember what happened before she died. It is why I was so scared for my children. The night before she died, when she was comatose, she kept yelling, yelling and crying. She kept calling her children to come with her. But her children were scared! She called, come with me, but the children stayed away from her. In the boat there was no light. The whole bunch of people sat down here. And the girl, the 6-year old girl, was becoming disturbed, disoriented, because of her mother. She was trying to find her father and mother, and she kept asking us, "Where is my father? Where is my mother?"

During the night we were so scared, so depressed. Nobody told her. We only said "Shut up!" We just let her cry. The mother was comatose, and yelling and crying. The children were crying. I think it was the most terrible night I ever experienced in my life. My children remember this night. Early in the morning, they asked us to throw her body away very quickly. They said, if we went to the shore with a dead body, they would not allow us to come. So we threw it away. . . .

For the first time of my life I was so ashamed. Because I was dirty. During the boat you had no bath. The boat had two levels. I got so upset because a lady at the upper level made pee and feces on us. I had it all over my body. It was all over me. I was so dirty. I had no clothes. I came to the camp and the camp was overcrowded. The camp had no clothes. Suddenly an old woman saw me and asked, "Do you need clothes? I have some old clothes. If you don't have any, I'll give them to you." Me, who my father always bought things for. I always had what I wanted. This period of time, we didn't have fresh food, but the Red Cross gave us rice, oil, and some little bit of dried fish. We needed fresh vegetables but could not get them. My son just had hepatitis, and was vomiting. It was just terrible. . . .

I always had nightmares when I was in Vietnam. During the night I only slept very lightly. I would listen to the dogs. There were dogs around us in our neighborhood. If the dogs barked, it meant the police. And you couldn't be sure when the police would come to your house, or to someone else's house, and take you away. . . .

TAM NGUYEN

Tam Nguyen recently immigrated to the United States with her children (in 1988). The separation from and death of her husband in Vietnam created major hardships for her family. Her vivid recollection of the havoc rendered by the Tet Offensive of 1968 involves the search for safety for herself and her two small children, and illustrates the plight of many Vietnamese women caught in cities.

My husband's brother studied at the National Military Academy in Dalat. His friend wanted to go to Saigon to visit his family. He took a bus from Dalat to Saigon. On the way home he did not wear his school clothes just in case the bus was stopped by the VC, so he wouldn't be recognized as a student from the National Military Academy. His bus was stopped by the VC on the way to Saigon. The VC called two men out of the bus. His friend was one of the two. The VC noticed a ring on his friend's finger, so they knew he was studying at that school. They cut him into pieces. I did not see it but I heard it from the passengers who were in the bus at that time.

One year after my husband had been led away to re-education camp, I lost contact with him. I tried to contact a few friends who had relatives in the North, where my husband lived. But none had any clue. One day, I received a note from the local township, asking me to come to see them. At first, I thought my family might be forced to leave for the new economic zone because of my husband's background, or maybe my husband died already. I had not had any contact with him for a year. I did not trust the VC anymore. I was told by the VC that my husband had died. He left home in 1975; then he was transferred to the North in 1976. We did not have any contact in 1977. But I did not know he had died until they told me in 1978. When I received that bad news, I was unconscious. I kept thinking about my five children at home. I was informed by a friend who was kept in the same camp with me that my husband died in 1977. That was why I had not had any contact with him since that year.

I was a seamstress at that time. I sew clothes at home. Later, because the materials were so expensive, I did not have enough customers to make a living, so I changed my job to that of a vendor. I sold rice noodle soup in front of my house. My family's income was fair enough to live on. My growing children had to help me, too.

After 1978, the VC allowed us to visit prisoners in the re-education camps. Everybody could visit their relatives. Gifts from many countries were allowed to be sent in. So the import materials started coming back. I had my customers again, so I started sewing clothes as I did before. I had a friend whose husband was kept in the retention camp in the North at the same place with my husband. After she got back from visiting him she told me that my husband died because of dysentery. He did not have any medication for his illness and there was no nutrition for him to get better. He did not have enough food to eat. Before he died he weighed about 75 kg, and when he died he was 38 kg. At that time, if anybody got sick they would die easily, because there were no medicines or nutritions.

On the day of my husband's funeral, no one was allowed to attend. There were only four men who carried my husband's body, escorted by six VC to check to see no one escaped. They put my husband's body in a plastic bag and tied his body with strings. The four prisoners had to carry him on their shoulders and bury him. The other prisoners who could not come to share their grief and sorrows were left standing inside the fence, watching them.

The prisoners did not have anything to eat except manioc. They had to continue working even though they were really sick. When my husband was alive, he had to go to work with two friends carrying him on both sides. At that time, it was rare to find a piece of sugar to make a drink for him. One day, the VC didn't see my husband. They came back to the camp and found my husband lying dead on his bed. Some prisoners could barely walk. They were exhausted and their strength was giving out. They crawled around the halls even though they were not sick. Some women had to sell their jewelry and houses to support their husbands, even though their husbands were kept in the retention camp without having any sentences.

MIHN PHU

After the reunification of Vietnam in 1975, schoolteachers and other professionals were closely monitored for any movement or behavior that demonstrated a lack of compliance with new government policy. Mihn Phu risked her job as a high school teacher to attempt to leave Vietnam by boat. Here, she begins by chronicling how careful she had to be at school so as not to jeopardize a successful escape. When one attempt didn't succeed, Mihn had to live with chronic fear while planning successive attempts. Since many arrests took place at night in people's homes, there were periods when people simply didn't return home from work in order to be safe. One night, Mihn attempted an escape by boat with 12 students.

When they caught me, there were 13 of us in a group. We became 13 prisoners. Three were little kids. The oldest was 13, and his brother and younger sister. The youngest was only three years old at that time. One family had five sisters and brothers. The mother had three kids with our group. The father took two others. The father took two kids to the boat, and the mother and the three kids were with us, trying to meet them. But we never met up with the father and kids. We never made it to the big boat. We were arrested at night. I didn't bring anything with me, only a small ring; no money. I put two pants and shirts on together. That's all I had. In the morning they tried to send us to a village. Only two young kids were in charge of us then. There were 13 of us, but one little boy from our group escaped. We kept thinking: shall we push those kids, the guards, into the sea? We thought we would try. But nobody dared to do anything. And everybody discussed it. Shall we push them into the sea so we can escape? But they had a gun. There were two men in our group who were soldiers. They knew how to use the weapons. We thought we could push the kids into the sea, and take that chance and go to the big ship to meet the people. But nobody dared do anything.

I don't think those two children in charge knew how to operate the gun, which was a machine-gun. I think the two men who were soldiers in our group could have just overpowered them. But the two kids, who were only 17 and 19–under 20–were somebody's kids. And we were thinking, it's too cruel to kill them. We could not do it. We had to stay in the prison 89 days. They did give us some rice to cook, but there is no place to cook, nothing to cook with. We try to do it ourselves. During the daytime, women like me and other women and kids were forced to do cleaning and gardening. The men went to the rice fields. Some men took rats to eat. They also ate snakes. . . .

THI LOAN

Thi Loan was born into a farming family from central Vietnam. Because times were hard she was adopted by another family when she was seven. Not only does her story raise questions regarding pregnant women and new mothers' responses to battle, but it also exposes little-heard firsthand accounts of atrocites perpetrated by Vietnamese against Vietnamese. Thi Loan gives us a little background on the events leading up to the traumatic explosion of Tet (New Year's), 1968.

I got married when I was 26 years old. My husband was from the North. Two weeks after our marriage we moved to Nha-Trang. My husband was 11 years older than me. He was in the construction business. He had lived in Hue for three years before he met me. At first, I didn't think about him because he was too old for me, and because my parents did not want me to leave them.

When we left for Nha-Trang, we had saved some money and started a small business. The business was small at the beginning then got improved and expanded gradually.

Then in 1968, after the Mau Than New Year's event, it happened. Ten days after giving birth to my second baby, I found that the placenta wasn't taken out completely. The nurse had to take it out again. I was very weak after that. Then, about 12 a.m., my husband and I heard a lot of firecracker noises. We didn't think it was gunfire or grenades. Until 12:30 a.m., my husband was able to open the door and see a lot of fires. It was a big fight. The government dropped rockets. Then we saw people run back and forth until 4:30 a.m. People were looking for cover at my front door. My neighbors and I brought some food to them. In the morning, the gunfires stopped. The planes did not drop any more rockets, and the Communists withdrew. Nha-Trang, Binh-Dinh went back to normal.

On the second day of New Year, suddenly a security group came to our house and searched us. They said that we held Communists in the house. My husband said no, but they still searched anyway. They found nothing but still took my husband away. He was released after 24 hours.

After a few months, I went to Hue to visit my family because I was told by my friends that Hue was seriously damaged after the Tet fight. My friends had been killed, their properties destroyed, my adopted parents' house burned down. I don't know if you believe it or not, but at that time I didn't think it was real. . . .

I had a friend who came to Hue from Saigon to visit and celebrate the New Year with his wife. He was stuck in Gia-Hoi, which the VC had occupied. He begged them to let him go because his wife was living in a different area, where the government was still in control. He kept begging the VC to let him go. Finally the VC got so angry, they pulled him out and shot him. Many people were killed by the VC without any reasons.

My brother at that time was a warrant officer. His wife, my sister-in-law, took her child to a suburb of Hue to visit our parents. But the VC apprehended her and said she was a spy. They wanted to terrify her by forcing her to stand on the edge of a crater, to get her to confess to her true role. She started crying and kept swearing that she was not involved with the government. Because she was pregnant and carrying her baby in her arms, she kept begging the VC to release her. One of the VC took pity on my sister's situation, and he asked her comrades to release her. Early next morning my sister carried her baby and ran through the forest, to get away.

A lot of people who worked for the government were arrested by the VC in 1968. The VC held them in a secret place. Later, the government was able to expel the VC from Hue. They found a big hole in which more than a hundred people were buried. My sister was one of the people who had been forced to dig the grave. All of them were buried alive, because their bodies were tied up together. I think the VC killed many people and there was more than one such a cave in Hue. At that time, my family and relatives had suffered a lot of damage.

LE THI TU

The trauma Le Thi Tu experienced began shortly after she got married, when her husband was wounded by a grenade. Her life as a mother and wife illustrates how many women whose husbands became disabled coped with the war.

Before the Communists took over the country I lived with my husband's family, and then we moved out. He got injured by a grenade after three years of marriage. His gall bladder and liver were destroyed by the grenade explosion. After the injuries, he stayed on the bed all day. I had to change his clothes when he stool in his pants. I had to put a nylon bag when he needed to urinate. He was a paralyzed person. These infective wounds caused him to be sick all the time. I had to suffer everything because I knew he was discomforted by these wounds and easy to get angry. I had to feed him, and gave him a bath every day. My children were too young to do housework.

After 1975, we had two children. Our life wasn't happy at all. Living under Communists was terrible. My husband stayed in the wheelchair but still got bothered all the time. I worked very hard to support him because his body was paralyzed along one side. In April 1984 I carried him and escaped by boat with my two children. The boat arrived in Malaysia and my husband died two months later.

He was all right for two months after we got to Malaysia, but then his previous wounds opened up again and he died. I had to stay in Malaysia three months after that and then six months in the Philippines before we came to the United States.

After 1975, I worked extremely hard to support my husband and two children. We had saved some money to escape. We never thought that we would succeed, and then my husband died just after we finally made it. I am so sad. I never faced such a terrible situation as this. I had to bear all kinds of misfortunes. I never believed that he would die.

In Vietnam, my children couldn't go to school because the Communists knew my family had tried to escape twice. Because of that, they did not allow my children to go to school. My children just knew a little.

When my husband was alive he was forced to go to the re-education camp. He had to be re-educated in his wheelchair! They released him after a while because no one could look after him. He had stool in his pants, so they returned him back home. Then he had to be re-educated at home. The VC came back and forth to our house all the time. It caused problems for my business. They forced me to pay taxes to the township. My husband told them that I did not make enough money. I had just enough for his medication and to buy food for the family. We sometimes had to borrow money from his mother. They did not listen. They told my husband to stay in the wheelchair from morning until the evening and forced him to tell the truth. He had to say whatever they wanted him to say. Once he was forced to stay in the wheelchair for two days. His skin started bleeding because of an infection he got. The blood spread all over the wheelchair, but they didn't care. After 1975, when he was in the hospital, the nurses took very good care of him. He was hospitalized for two years. . . .

When we left Vietnam I had to carry him. Luckily, I was asked to pay only two taels of gold in advance for my entire family. Then after that I had to pay four more. We left the house at 3:00 in the morning. We saved one bench for my husband to lie down on. We arrived at Ca Mau at 4:00 a.m., and later we took a ferry to see the boat owner. We then stayed with the boat owner for three days. Then the ferry again brought us to a boat. The boat carried 35 people. They did not allow me to bring a wheelchair to the boat; we had to throw it away. We used two pieces of styrofoam for him to sit on. When our boat was drifting out to the territorial waters, we were stopped by the VC Security Navy. They asked us to move to their boat, and then they searched our boat. They took all medicine, jewelry, and clothes, then they told us to move back to our boat and left right away. We kept going even though the VC thought that we had nothing left to live on at sea.

We also ran into a Thai pirates' boat. They jumped into our boat and searched everywhere, but they couldn't find anything to take, so they left. I had to put some engine oil on my face to make it look dirty and ugly.

Our boat was floating in the sea for three days and four nights. My husband's wounds started bleeding again. Finally we arrived on an uncultivated island in Malaysia. A Malaysian ship came to us and started making the registration. The procedures were completed in one day. The doctors were asked to help us and tears were in their eyes when they saw my husband's wounds.

CONCLUSION

The success of any psychosocial intervention on behalf of Vietnamese immigrant and refugee women is largely dependent upon the quality of biographical information a mental health professional is able to collect. As the above excerpts from Vietnamese women illustrate, the richness and depth one gains from life history interviews is considerably more than that gained by brief psychosocial questionnaires and checklists. By taking the time to establish necessary rapport with a refugee or immigrant woman, and by collecting extensive data on that individual's life prior to coming to the U.S., we assure the client that we have gained as full a picture as possible of all the variables that need to be factored into her diagnosis and intervention.

Specifically, detailed life histories make it possible to consider the impact of PTSD on refugee women. Without such data mental health professionals may fail to meet the diagnostic treatment needs of this special population.

REFERENCES

American Psychiatric Association (1987). *Diagnostic and Statistical Manual of Mental Disorders* (DSM III). 3rd Ed., Rev. Washington, DC.

Burton, E. (1983). *Surviving the Flight of Horror: The Story of Refugee Women.* Washington DC: Indochina Project, Center for International Policy.

Desbarats, J. (1987). *Economic Consequences of Indochinese Chain Migration.* Berkeley: California Policy Seminar, University of California.

Lauffer, S.L., Gallops, M.S., & Frey-Wonters, E. (1984). War stress and trauma: The Vietnam experience. *Journal of Health and Social Behavior, 25,* 65-85.

Rothblum, E., & Cole, E. (1986). *Another Silenced Trauma.* New York: Harrington Park Press, Inc.

Tang, T. N. (1985). *Vietcong Memoir.* New York: Harcourt, Brace, Jovanovich.

Healing Their Wounds:
Guatemalan Refugee Women
as Political Activists

Deborah Light

SUMMARY. Guatemalan refugee women living in the camps of southern Mexico for the past decade have become a remarkable example of self-empowerment despite the severe psychological trauma of the experiences which led to their exile. The successful organizing of these women (the majority of whom are of Mayan ethnic identity) into a productive force for social advancement raises interesting questions about the roles of physical, social, and cultural environment in post-traumatic recovery. This article seeks to explore these issues by looking at the activism of Guatemalan refugee women and examining it the context of their refugee experience.

INTRODUCTION

In the fall of 1991, my research partner, Fern Dorresteyn, and I arrived in southern Mexico to do a two-month study of Guatemalan refugee women living in U.N. supported camps. It was our intention to focus on their economic contribution to subsistance. However, our inquiry was quickly redirected, by the refugee women themselves, to their political activities. Their process of becoming politicized through the refugee experience has been long and slow, stretching out over nearly a decade before exploding into the vibrant productive movement it is now. The women's network

Deborah Light recently received her BA in Anthropology from SUNY-Plattsburgh. Prior to her field work among Guatemalan refugee women in Chiapas, Mexico, she was one of a group of three researchers collecting oral histories from Central American refugee women in Plattsburgh. She plans to begin graduate study in Anthropology in the fall of 1992.

297

they established is both an indication of the healing and empowering aspects of community support and an agent for the continued emotional healing of the women of a deeply scarred population.

THE MOVEMENT

In the spring of 1990, after nearly a decade had passed in refuge, eight women from the refugee camps of Chiapas, Mexico, began talking, planning a first meeting of a refugee women's organization. Women, they agreed, had no voice; they were not taken into account in the decisions, large or small, that affected their daily lives. But where were the words to express these feelings and who were the women who would speak them? The first organized meeting, May 20, 1990, in the town of Palenque (Chiapas, Mexico) would answer these questions and open the floodgates for an entire population of women who would find the words.

This first meeting was attended by 47 women from three Mexican states where the Guatemalan refugee camps are scattered. For the first time, refugee women shared with each other the suffering and frustration which had characterized their lives since long before the flight from their country. They shared stories and analyzed the common threads: "women are not worth anything," "the woman is only to stay in the house and can't do anything else," "we can't decide, can't think," "we have to be under men's hands." They described their new found organization as one in which "the participation of all of us would be important" (Interview, Oct. 25, 1991).

Of equal significance, arising almost simultaneously to the theme of women's subordination, was the concern over the loss of traditional culture. The abandoning of their homelands had, in itself, separated them from the practice of many cultural traditions which revolved around the their connection with the land. Now many women were no longer speaking their native languages to their children or wearing their traditional dress. They acknowledged the difficulties in maintaining even these cultural traditions in refuge, where all the institutions on which they are dependent are Spanish speaking, and it is nearly impossible to obtain the materials for traditional dress. Yet they feared increasing alienation from their ethnic identity would threaten their cultural survival. It was decided that their organization would be given the name "Mama Maquin," after a Mayan *ancianita*–beloved elder–killed in a massacre of 100, defending her land and that of her companeros in the northern highlands of Guatemala. The concerns that arose from that initial meeting of only 47 women would reflect the voiced concerns of over a thousand within six months.

In the fall of 1990, organizers of Mama Maquin set out to do a survey of refugee women, to study their situation, hear their opinions and identify areas of greatest need. This survey was supported by UNHCR (U.N. High Commission on Refugees) and CIAM (Centro de investigation y Accion para la Mujer) and carried out by refugee women; 865 women in 80 camps were interviewed. The women worked in groups of six, struggling to bridge the gap created by the existence of distinct ethnic groups within the refugee population, each with its own language and with the majority of individuals being monolingual. This was an enormous undertaking, especially as many of the women conducting the survey were themselves barely literate. Manuela, a member of the surveying team explains:

> We held a workshop, training ourselves for five days. About half of the 40 who participated can read and write, but the ones who know how to read and write managed to help those who didn't. And we saw how we could pull the others along. And those who spoke Spanish also translated for those who didn't.

One of the most significant results of the survey was the identification of illiteracy as the single most important problem of refugee women. The next task of Mama Maquin was the development of peer literacy programs begun in March, 1991. More than 700 women in 27 camps participated in these programs in the first six months. This work, along with the continued organizing among women of the 132 camps in southern Mexico, constitutes the main focus of Mama Maquin. The outlook among organizers and members is positive, with an eye to the future is fixed firmly on their return to Guatemala and the continuation of the struggle for women's rights and a democratic society in their home country.

BACKGROUND

To appreciate the significance of the empowering activitism taking place among Guatemalan refugee women it is necessary to first understand something of the situation in Guatemala which led to their forced migration. In the late 1970's, in response to complex social and political pressures, an insurgency movement arose among the largely indigenous population of the western highlands of Guatemala. The reaction of the Guatemalan government was to launch a brutal counterinsurgency campaign. At its height, between 1980 through 1983, this campaign claimed the lives of more than 50,000 peasants, internally displaced nearly one million (half the rural population) and created an estimated 150,000 to 250,000 external refugees (Smith, 1990). Those fleeing the countryside arrived on foot in southern Mexico without possessions: homeless, starving, and traumatized by terror and loss.

The reign of terror and atrocities perpetrated by the army on the rural highland population continued throughout the 80's. By the 90's the tactics and pattern of repression had changed to fit more closely, in outward appearance, the promise of the civilian government to curb human rights abuses. Nevertheless, the Guatemalan Human Rights Commission Bulletin (June, 1991) states that 473 extrajudicial executions and 71 detainments/disappearances were reported during the first six months of 1991. By September of '91 the number of deaths and disappearances had risen to over 650.

The large scale massacres seem to have ended but the slow, steady assault on human life continues as witnessed by the bodies of seven Guatemalan peasants recently discovered in one of the Mexico-Guatemala border rivers in southeastern Chiapas (Interview, Nov. 1, 1991). These occurrences do not go unnoticed by Guatemalan refugees in Mexico, most of whom are settled in camps in this same border area.

Repression in Guatemala, not unlike other countries, has taken a special shape in regard to women. In a study of post-traumatic stress disorder (Aron, Corne, Furstland & Zelwer, 1991), acts of violence by army soldiers against women in Guatemala during this period are seen to be clearly centered on gender, as well as ethnicity. Sexual abuse of Indian women by soldiers is an institutionalized form of control, sanctioned by the government. It is understood clearly by both the perpetrator and the victim that there will be no repercussions for the former, no protection for the latter. Thus the special repression of women includes: acts of sexual violence, pervasive threat of sexual violence, and the clear message that there is no escape from either one.

State terrorism of women through sexual abuse is widespread as evidenced by the testimony of villagers in the province of Quiche that "the army's pattern of raping young women has made it difficult in some communities to find women between the ages of 11 and 15 who have not been sexually abused by the army" (Aron et al., 1991, p.38). Neither is the special abuse of women confined to rape. Sexual torture and/or the forced witnessing of sexual torture of other women (including one's daughter or mother) are not uncommon experiences (Burgos-Debray, 1984), nor is the witnessing of brutal executions such as the case in which

18 female prisoners were made to watch as another prisoner was singled out, had her blouse torn open and her breasts hacked off with a machete (Aron et al., 1991). Since military presence was pervasive throughout the most of western highlands by the early 80's, it can be justifiably assumed that a high percentage of refugee women who have fled from rural Guatemalan communities to the camps of southern Mexico have experienced such abuse. It can also be assumed that all Guatemalan refugee women bear the psychological scars of this gender-specific abuse policy, as well as the physical and psychological scars of specific acts.

Finally, in understanding the psychological trauma experienced by Guatemalan peasant women, it must be pointed out that these special abuses of women do not constitute the whole of their trauma but rather compound the general traumas of war in which life and livelihood are under constant attack and loss of children, spouses and parents, and/or the witnessing of brutality to same are commonplace. Mental health professionals categorize this type of psychological trauma as "severe to catastrophic" (Aron et al., 1991).

For refugee women the trauma of sexual abuse and state terrorism is combined with the trauma of forced relocation in another country. A compounding factor among Guatemalan refugee women in Mexico is the transitory nature of their experience in exile–refugee camps in the state of Chiapas have been subject to frequent moves over the past 10 years, due to ongoing pressure from the local population over competition for limited natural resources, mainly arable land. The lack of a permanent location in which to rebuild family and community stability and normalize everyday life must serve to undermine, to some degree, the progress individuals might otherwise make in psychological trauma recovery.

Nevertheless, at some point in their refugee experience, the will to act became a reality for some of the women, who then became the catalyst for self-empowerment for hundreds of others. This widespread readiness among Guatemalan refugee women to move ahead in their lives is a significant step in the process of post-traumatic recovery. But how and why did the original eight women begin to imagine such an organization? What prompted their visions and actions? What is motivating and supporting hundreds of women in Guatemalan refugee communities to move beyond the confines of society and even the constructs of traditional culture?

It is clear, through their own words, that outside influence played a part. In an interview, Maria Francisco, one of the eight founders of Mama Maquin, told us how she began working on women's issues:

I remember in Cieneguitas [camp], a doctora arrived and suggested that we organize because of the problem of the camps. The women did not take their children to be vaccinated and did not go to the doctor when they were pregnant because of the shame or who knows why. So that was why the woman doctor suggested this to us. Women would be ashamed to go to a male doctor but maybe among women this could be solved. So this woman doctor called us all together and in the beginning all the women didn't want to form a group. I said, I was the first to say, that I was willing to give support to her, to this idea, and commit a year to it.

This eventually grew to a group of 16 women working on issues of women and children's health. A year later, in the same camp, a group of women including Maria Francisco applied to a U.S. women's organization for a grain mill and received it. They set up on their own woman-run operation to grind corn. This single operation served to free women's time enormously, relieving them of the many hours of daily labor required to grind corn by hand to make their staple food–tortillas.

THE REFUGEE ENVIRONMENT

While the influence and support of women outside the refugee community was a fundamental part of these first organizing activities, outside influences attempting to set agendas for refugee women rarely succeed if the women themselves do not see the value of the proposed activity (Interview, Nov. 5, 1991; Interview, Nov. 14, 1991). For all the outside support that was eventually forthcoming, the impetus has clearly come from the refugee women themselves. It is necessary, then, to look at the environment within which the refugees live. For this purpose, three features of environment will be given special attention: the refugee community; refugee society; and the traditional culture.

Community: Diversity, Unity and Support

Community is the backbone of refugee life for Guatemalans in the camps of southern Mexico. It is the complex social network which allows the refugees to function as a group to secure basic needs which benefit the whole. It is also the social structure which defines the identity of the group, thereby reinforcing the identity of individuals within that group.

Community life for Guatemalan refugees is characterized by three factors: ethnicity, diversity, and a kind of national identity. The Guatemalan refugee population includes eight ethno-linguistic groups (7 indigenous Mayan groups and a small percent of Spanish-speaking ladino peasants). Refugees often fled as whole villages creating some continuity of community in which immediate and extended families live in close proximity, and ethnic identity is reinforced. On the other hand, each refugee camp includes a number of different ethnic groups as people flowing over the border concentrated in areas where basic resources were available. Eventually, a kind of indigenous national identity developed among refugees of different and traditionally separated if not isolated ethnic groups, an identity based on common experiences of oppression, terrorism, and loss in Guatemala.

For refugee women then, community can be seen to be supportive in several significant ways: through extended family support; through the positive reinforcement of ethnic identities which had previously targeted them for brutal repression; and through the development of a united Guatemalan Indian identity from which new strength and hope to confront their abusers has arisen.

Refugee Society: Changing the Boundaries

The social roles of women and men among indigenous Guatemalan groups are traditionally sex segregated with little or no overlap. Although the status of women in traditional society was subordinate to that of men, women nonetheless had a certain amount of prestige and autonomy (particularly as artisans). They also had security in the stability (no matter how harsh the reality) of traditional life. This stability, especially significant to their central role as mothers and homemakers, helped maintain the status quo between the sexes.

After the serious disruption of traditional life by the army's counterinsurgency campaign, and the forced migration to Mexico, some semblence of normalcy was achieved in the resettlement communities, and traditional social roles of men and women were resumed.

However, while the roles of men, in the public sphere, were expanded through the circumstance of refugee life, the roles of women, in the private sphere, were reduced to the most basic components, that of mother and homemaker. What distinguishing activities women had, such as weaving and other artisan skills, were largely impossible to maintain in the new environment away from the resources of their home communities.

The combined mother/homemaker role, it should be noted, accounts for the greatest part of the daily work necessary for the survival of all community members. Men, the majority of whom are day laborers, have no work for much of the year, and when they do it is generally an eight-hour workday. Women, by contrast, work every day of the year, an average of 14 to 16 hours a day (Mama Maquin, 1991, p.8).

Women, who were bearing most of the burden of the frequent moves which have characterized the refugee experience in Chiapas, had no voice in the public sphere where decisions about camp life were made. In the relative stability of traditional life, a voice in the public affairs of the community was not critical to their well-being, as such status-gaining and autonomous activities as were available to women were undisturbed. But here in refuge real autonomy no longer existed. While the men could replace lost autonomy with the internal administrative authority designated to them by the external relief agencies on which they were dependent, the women ceased to have even the limited control they had held over their lives in their traditional communities.

Additionally, stability as a motivator for maintaining the status quo of power between women and men was largely lost in the refugee setting where communities are impermanent, resources are unreliable, and neither women nor men have real control over basic conditions. Women, therefore, not only experienced reduced roles but were also facing increased difficulty in fulfilling the only role left to them, that of homemaker, due to the conditions of refugee life.

It seems that the balance of power between men and women as it existed in the structure of traditional society eventually became unsustainable in the structure of refugee society, as women, as a group, lost the motivation to support it. This prolonged period in which women had little or no control over situations which greatly disrupted their lives and those of their children helped set the stage for organizing among women.

Refugee women are moving beyond social constraints to begin building a new social order. In the same way they are moving, to some extent, beyond cultural constructs to redefine the social institutions of family and community, while maintaining their ethnic identity. They are maintaining the cultural construct of what it means to be Indian but redefining what it means to be Indian women and Indian men. The positive effects of women's increased participation in community health, education, and technology is creating a shift in the balance of power between men and women toward greater equality and helping to bring about increased stability within the community. As this end has begun to be realized, refugee men are beginning to support the empowerment of refugee women.

Traditional Culture: Oppressive or Progressive?

In discussing the role of traditional culture in refugee women's self-empowerment it should be understood that Guatemalan refugee women fighting for equality within their communities see this struggle as equal, and inextricably bound, to their struggle for equality as Indians and/or peasants within the nation state of Guatemala. While the majority of Guatemalan refugee women are Mayan Indians there is also, as previously stated, a small number of Ladino women in the refugee population. Since the Guatemalan refugee women's own organization, Mama Maquin, strongly reflects the indigenous majority, an examination of the role of traditional culture in refugee women's activism will focus mainly on Mayan culture and then on the parallel role of Ladino peasant culture.

Mayan Indian culture (the traditional world view and value system of their ancestors) is extremely important to indigenous Guatemalan refugee women. At the same time they reject the limitations of the culturally prescribed gender roles which have defined their place in the social community. Clearly, indigenous Guatemalan refugee women identify traditional culture as progressive rather than oppressive despite their rejection of women's traditional role in society. Understanding this apparent contradiction can help illuminate the role of traditional culture in Guatemalan refugee women's activism.

One reason Guatemalan refugee women seek to maintain traditional Mayan culture is the importance of unity; cultural tradition and identity is the unifying factor among Guatemalan refugee women that helps provide them with a medium for discourse and the strength for action to create change. As Mayan Indians they have struggled against colonial and neo-colonial oppressors for hundreds of years, successfully resisting efforts at cultural genocide directed against them. They have survived, as a people, by faithfully guarding the secrets of their ancestors–carefully observing the rituals which guide community life and keep them connected to each other and to the land, on which they depend. Pride in their Mayan identity and the strength derived from a historical sense of self has also sustained them through the past 500 years of racist brutality which continues today.

A second reason for the maintenance of traditional culture relates to the content of that culture. Although Guatemalan refugee women are redefining gender roles in the community, the philosophy of traditional Mayan culture–the values of cooperation, the primacy of community over the individual, and a strong connection to the natural world–continues to be seen by Indian women as life-giving and life-sustaining.

Underlying their ability to both embrace traditional culture and reject traditional gender roles is the nature of culture itself. As a product of the human community, the culture of every society is dynamic and fluid–able to be changed and shaped. If a social order no longer adequately reflects a groups needs and values, a new social order can emerge to take its place, without necessarily destroying the existing cultural base. Since the cultural base is positively reinforcing to indigenous Guatemalan refugee women, it was neither necessary nor desirable to disassociate themselves from their cultural identity in order to seek more egalitarian gender relations.

Although they do not share the cultural heritage of the indigenous women, Ladino women within the refugee community have identified their struggle with that of their Mayan sisters. Ladino peasants lived in Guatemala under much the same conditions as Indian peasants in terms of their everyday hardships, their labor and the oppression suffered at the hands of the ruling class. Ladino peasant culture shares many features with indigenous cultures as both groups have a fundamental connection to the land as well as an intertwined history of 500 years. Ladino refugees view the popular struggle of their peasant culture within the dominant society in much the same way as Guatemalan Indians view their struggle for indigenous rights. Likewise, while Ladino peasant refugee women are rejecting culturally prescribed gender roles, their traditional cultural identity is a source of positive support for women's empowerment, similar to the supportive role traditional culture plays in the empowering activities of Mayan refugee women.

CONCLUSION

In 1992, Guatemalan refugees in Mexico are faced with the choice of repatriating to Guatemala or settling permanently in Mexico without further U.N. or Mexican Government refugee assistance. In view of the significant differences between camp conditions and future prospects for self-sufficiency in the three states of Chiapas, Campeche, and Quintana Roo, there is no absolute consensus among the refugee population on this issue. In an interview with the director of UNHCR in Chiapas in November, 1991, we were told that while refugees in Campeche and Quintana Roo were split almost evenly on the issue, the majority of refugees in Chiapas, where land and other basic resource pressures are greatest, have already stated they will return.

In a group meeting with organizers of "Mama Maquin" in October 1991, we were told that while some members are planning to remain in Mexico, the goals of the current organization reflect the plans of the majority: to return to Guatemala, to continue organizing for women's rights, and to help create real democracy for all Guatemalans.

For those members of "Mama Maquin" who choose to remain in Mexico, it is clear that strong connections with their sisters in Guatemala will be maintained and that the goal of organizing for women's rights will continue to be a united effort between them. As a pamphlet published by "Mama Maquin" states, their objectives include supporting "the work, demands and organizing of Latin American women and women throughout the world for equality, democracy and peace."

State terrorism and institutionalized sexual abuse, such as was experienced by Guatemalan refugee women, are gender-specific and ethnic-specific ways of demoralizing and disabling a targeted population, affecting not only the individual but also the collective groups with which one identifies–in this case, women and Indians. Therefore, the most effective therapy for the individual is that which includes and strengthens their gender and ethnic identities, empowering the individual and enabling her to overcome the dysfunctional effects of such emotional trauma.

The events of the past two years, and the decision by many to return to their homeland despite knowledge that violent repression persists, clearly shows that Guatemalan refugee women have succeeded, if not in erasing past trauma, at least in coming to terms with it. The mutual support among women in the refugee community setting, along with international support, have allowed Guatemalan refugee women to overcome negative associations with their gender and ethnicity, supporting a strong and positive self-identification. Ultimately these impacts are credited with creating increased participation of women in community and organizing activities, increased opportunities for women in refugee society, and the strength to face their suffering, confront their oppressors, and take control of their lives.

For us, as women, witnessing such empowering events among Guatemalan refugee women has been an overwhelmingly inspiring experience. It has also been a valuable opportunity to connect with feminists of another culture, indeed, another world from our own. As researchers, this experience reminds us of what might be considered simple and obvious but is all too often overlooked: that the strongest element in healing and empowerment lies within ourselves–our positive self-identity and connection with others. As women seeking to support each other cross-culturally, we must look for ways to connect that acknowledge and support our diversity.

REFERENCES

Aron, Adrianne, Corne, Shawn, Fursland, Anthea, & Zelwer, Barbara (1991). The Gender Specific Terror of El Salvador and Guatemala, Post Traumatic Stress Disorder in Central American Refugee Women. *Women's Studies International Forum*, 14, 37-47.

Burgos-Debray, Elizabeth (Ed.) (1983). *I, Rigaberto Menchu*. New York: Verso.

Mama Maquin Guatemalan Refugee Women's organization (1991). *Situacion de las Mujeres Guatemaltecas Refugiadas en Chiapas*. Chiapas, Mexico: UNHCR and Mama Maquin.

Smith, Carol A. (1990). The Militarization of Civil Society in Guatemala. *Latin American Perspectives*, 17, 8-41.